OPERATION PARADISE

Effective environmental healing with orgone energy

By Georg Ritschl

With text contributions by
Don Croft
Dr Paul Batiibwe
Kelly McKennon (Laozu)
Ryan Mc Ginty

© 2007 Georg Ritschl

All Rights Reserved

Second Edition
Published Dec 2007 by CREATESPACE.COM

Content identical to First Edition Nov 2007 by LULU.COM

You can contact the author and stay informed of the latest developments via the Orgonise Africa website

www.orgoniseafrica.com

and by mail

PO Box 72397
Parkview
Johannesburg
2122
Republic of South Africa

Foreword

Georg Ritschl has composed a useful and beautiful book about the general applications of orgonite and related technology, after I published what might be called a book of essays, THE LIFE ETHERIC WITH CAROL CROFT.

Georg feels that people can use a practical, illustrated compendium and I agree with him.

Perhaps one might see that there is a map of this global paradigm we have all been entering and initiating, at least, and it is an awfully interesting one, if one can drop one's prejudices, fears, and ideological restraints. We in the West have all been programmed to believe that reality is essentially chaotic and pointless, so it is refreshing to learn that there is purpose and order in the world, for good and ill. This is an era of potential peace, unity, and prosperity; also an age in which the unseen is being revealed to everyone who cares to observe. The genuine scholars and scientists will come along, later, to validate for everyone else what we, in the gifting movement, are discovering and producing and they will be very welcome.

In early 2004, two years after he had done an enormous amount of gifting and distributed a lot of orgonite cloudbusters in several countries of Southern Africa, and right after he and I had gotten busy in Uganda with our tireless and resourceful Baganda associates, Georg led many more orgonite safaris to disable the scores of weather-warfare transmitter arrays along the Indian Ocean coast, from Mozambique to the Cape, effectively ending a severe drought and greening much of the Kalahari and other arid regions. He had previously built and helped to set up about 20 orgonite cloudbusters in strategic spots in Botswana's Kalahari region.

This is not an organised movement. Dr Wilhelm Reich, whom many of us feel exemplified the emerging science paradigm, reckoned that organisation is death, and it should be avoided as much as possible. We have taken this to heart in this vital movement. In my opinion, there is no more need to organise what we all do than there is to form an organisation around the use of matches, aspirin, or wheels.

This book is, partly, a photographic record of an impressive sampling of the gifting work in Africa and beyond, since the media people, whom I like to call "The What To Think Network", have studiously avoided any mention of this miraculous trend. Georg and I agree that there is a relatively safe middle path that threads between complete obscurity and widespread notoriety. Carol and I originally put out my journal reports in June 2001, following our discovery of what orgonite cloudbusters can do, because we were operating in a little too much obscurity under the circumstances. The hatred that had been fatally vented by the "world order" towards Dr Reich seemed to be getting transferred to us, after our success with the first orgonite cloudbuster in March of that year. It had been a long time since anyone had put Dr Reich's earthshaking discoveries to practical use on that scale, after all.

The reason Carol and I went to Africa is that we felt that the liberation of the people of that continent from at least a century of extreme oppression (the rapid decline of old, stable cultures; easy prey for enslaving missionaries, merchants, soldiers, miners, then bureaucrats) is a requisite step towards the liberation of humanity, in general.

We were thrilled to discover that the African people mostly have an innate understanding of orgonite's potential and applications.

Georg is doing more than anyone to ensure that this grassroots movement will continue to spread on the "Dark Continent" and he has made some personal sacrifices along the way, including some jail time in Zimbabwe. Axel G. of Austria shared that cramped, dark cell with Georg and several Zimbabweans, and he is also undaunted by that potentially deadly experience. Nobody else in this unorganised global network has been tested that way. In my estimation, that sort of demonstrated commitment counts for more than anything else.

It is good to remember that this movement is still new. Everyone who comes to it brings a fresh insight and, potentially, more and crucial information and observations to share. Making and distributing orgonite devices is arguably the most empowering, grand-scale healing activity one can participate in, because the confirmations it produces are consistently grand and inspiring. If you do not know what I am talking about, I am afraid you are only going to understand it by actually doing the work, so we invite you to do so, then, "Welcome to the unorganisation"!

Don Croft

About this book

Many people all over the world are aware that things "have not been in order" for quite a while. Wars, diseases, pollution, apparent climate change and an extremely unbalanced distribution of resources, education and wealth seem to threaten the very existence of humankind.

At the same time, there is an undeniable push by the assumed state powers to gain more and more control over the lives of individuals, with new restrictions on the freedom of speech, movement and economic activity being announced almost daily, not to mention the energy crisis that is pictured as inevitable.

The common denominator of all these messages we are being bombarded with on a daily basis is FEAR!

Over the last few years, a network of independent individuals, inspired by the example of maverick inventor and activist Don Croft, have silently started to reverse the underlying condition of negativity that produces the symptoms of decay and degeneration on our planet.

At the centre of the activities of this group is the concept of orgone or life energy, based on the astonishing and groundbreaking research of Dr Wilhelm Reich, one of the greatest thinkers of the 20th century, who was scorned and eventually (we think) killed by the scientific and political-military establishment.

According to Dr Reich, the unhindered flow of orgone is the basis for healthy life processes on a cosmic, planetary and organismic level.

Blocking the flow of this energy leads to degenerative diseases like cancer, AIDS, etc in an organism, criminality, corruption, violence and decay in society and biodegradation, with the end result of a barren desert on the planetary level.

This network goes beyond the achievements of Dr Wilhelm Reich, in that it integrates his findings with the new experience of spirituality and intuition that has become possible only in recent years.

In that sense, it is linked to all tendencies striving towards a new, holistic understanding of Life and the universe, a new emerging paradigm that will unite physics and metaphysics.

It is not based on theories, but hands-on experience and live confirmations.

Even though a few individuals have made greater contributions to this network than others, nobody claims to be a guru or leader of this loose affiliation of people who often do not even know of each other. There is no formal structure and we feel there should not be, as all formalised movements that ever posed a threat to the existing order of things on this planet in the past, have been successfully infiltrated, undermined and ultimately destroyed by the forces resisting freedom and change.

In this book, I am trying to give an

introduction to the basic ideas driving the growth and activism of this network. I also give some practical hints how you can join this effort by making your own environmental orgone healing tools and demonstrate how to use them to heal your part of the planet.
The very attainable goal of all this is

Paradise on Earth

Acknowledgements

The orgone work that this book talks about, with our expeditions all over Africa, would not have been possible without the support of the following people to whom I express my gratitude:

Don Croft, Andy Brown, Steve Baron, Jerome Boyer, John Wannerot, Joseph Rossie, Karin and Stefan Bamberg, Mary Anders, Morgan Kielty, Norman Williams, Piet Venter, Karin Horn, Palma Piccioni, Peter Kerscher, Philip Mc Adams, Rainer Lindhorst, Rosemarie and Ulrich Dressler, Benjamin Schordt, Stuart Jackson, Ted Shustermann, Wade Nelson, Christopher Murphy, Eric Carlsen, Jürgen Meisel, Michael Krzyzak, Torsten Spittka, Anthony Walmsley, Axel G., Klaus Peter Wilke, John Leach, Steven Smith and many others, who through material contributions, have enabled us to make our expeditions happen and experience the wonderful transformation and change brought about by them.

Special thanks also to all those who have accompanied me on my trips, especially Trevor Toerin, Arjen Arnold, Sam Mudau, Kevin Montenari †, Dr Chipangula, Mark Gouws, Robert Vonk, Kelly McKennon (Laozu), Axel, Don Croft and Drs Kayiwa and Batiibwe.

My thanks also go to those who have supported us spiritually over the years of this incredible journey of discovery, especially the ethericwarriors.com group and the members of the chatblast group on www.-cb-forum.com as well as our friend Karin Horn.

Thanks also to Ryan Mc Ginty, Dr Batiibwe, Kelly McKennon and Don Croft for contributing articles to this book.

Last but not least my special thanks to Judy Lubulwa and Pam Thornley for looking through the manuscript for faults and inconsistencies, and their combined input towards making this book more readable and hopefully enjoyable.

Special thanks also to Credo Vusamazulu Mutwa for inspiring in me a deep love and appreciation of Africa and its traditional culture.

Above all, I thank my wife Friederike for being with me through all these years, and my kids for enduring many dusty and bumpy detours on our trips.

Of course this list is incomplete, and the contribution of those whom I have inadvertently omitted are not appreciated any less.

Georg Ritschl
September 2007

CONTENTS

I. HISTORY AND THEORY — 1

What is orgone? — 1
On the shoulders of a giant: Wilhelm Reich — 3
From Accumulator to Generator – In comes Don Croft — 6

Manifested DOR: The world in which we live — 8
DOR on a social level: Conspiracy theory or alternative history? — 9
The occult foundations of the New World Order — 12
The Money Scam – Hypnosis in Action — 15
Chemtrails, HAARP, mind control — 19

Orgone and related fields of research — 26
Alternative healing — 26
Free energy — 27
The undeniable reality of the paranormal — 30

The arsenal of the peaceful orgone guerrilla — 32
What it's all made of: Orgonite — 32
The Don Croft Cloudbuster — 32
The Holy Hand Grenade — 33
The Tower Buster — 33
The Earth Pipe — 34
The Etheric Stick Hand Grenade — 35
The Orgone Zapper — 35
Interactive Tools: SP-Crystals and Power Wands — 40

II. THE QUESTION OF PROOF: DOES THIS REALLY WORK? — 42

Which science do you mean? (A reflection on principles) — 42
Observations and confirmations — 43

Buster's Diary: The Orgonise Africa Expeditions — 51
How it all started — 51
Zimbabwe, September 2002 — 52
Vendaland, December 2002 — 54
Free State, December 200 — 56
Ndebele Tour, July 2003 — 59
Encounter with a remarkable man — 61
Obstacle course to the Makgaben, July 2003 — 67
Uganda, travelling with the Don, November 2003 — 70
Disabling the Kruger Barrier, December 2003 — 92
Disabling the coastal barrier — 102
Free State busted again – confirmations galore — 104
From paradise to Masonic Street and back — 109

Three days in Cape Town	115
Mama Mbeki's zapper and cloud buster	124
Mozambique – another African country de-HAARP-ed	127
Operation Desert Rain, Namibia	134
The Big Hole: Filling a gap in Kimberley	160
Obstacle run to the Western Cape,	167
Mr Tata's Isandlwana	178
The Sky above Germany	183
Counterattack in the Kalahari	195
Matatiele – instant satisfaction as usual,	203
Making rain – Does this look like a drought?	212
Ocean Gifting – Part I	214
Vortex hunting with Laozu	219
All that Rain!	229
Clipped wings – the prisoners of orgone	233
Zanzibar - spice Island with a new flavour	252
Matatiele revisited and a mountain paradise	257
Cape Town – Sylphs in the sky and a nuke plant revisited	262
The Vast Interior	264
The mighty Zambesi – gifted	279
Outlook and future plans	302

And is it worth the effort? — 303

III. YOU CAN DO IT TOO! — 304

Creating paradise: The simple art of gifting — 304

People have different talents and preferences	304
Sort out your own life first	304
Gifting FAQ	305

DIY – Make your own orgonite — 309

Making orgonite is easy!	309
The easiest to start with: making TBs	310
The next step: making HHGs	314
Finally: Build your own CB	317
SP-Crystals and Mobius coils	322

IV. FURTHER READING — 325

Books	325
Websites (URLs were accurate at time of writing)	326
Text References	328

I. HISTORY AND THEORY

WHAT IS ORGONE?

Orgone is the name given by Dr Wilhelm Reich – who spent the latter part of his life researching this phenomenon – to the all-pervading omnipresent Life Energy.

Dr Wilhelm Reich

Wilhelm Reich, who had started out in Austria and Germany as a medical doctor and psychiatrist, was closely associated with Sigmund Freud. He contributed greatly to the understanding of the link between human sexuality and psychology and never ceased to open up new frontiers of knowledge and understanding during his life.

Starting from his observations as a psychiatrist and venturing into the fields of biology, astronomy and physics, Reich was in the process of creating a new and holistic life science, when his life and work were cruelly interrupted by misguided institutions of the very "land of the free" he had fled to, in order to escape the wrath of the book-burning Nazis in Central Europe.

Yet Reich was not the first or the last one to observe the working of what he observed to be a "living energy" or "anti-entropic force".

Before the victory of the mechanistic world view a few hundred years ago (Newton and Co., you remember?), the concept of a "sea of energy" out of which all material forms manifest, was universally known.

This can easily be shown in the Hindu (prana), Buddhist and Taoist (Chi, Ki as in Rei-Ki) traditions of the Far East, but continues down to the Greeks (ether) and Romans.

The same concept is intuitively or explicitly known to all traditional healers of shamanic traditions the world over.

In post-Newtonian Europe, now (purposely?) forgotten personalities, such as the Bohemian steel magnate Baron Karl v. Reichenbach, or the famous Austrian Anton Mesmer (that's why we still speak of a "mesmerising personality") or Viktor Schauberger, contributed valuable research and experiences, and were well noted in their time.

In recent years we see not only a re-emergence of life energy based healing techniques such as Reiki, (Rei-Ki = Holy Life Energy), but also a convergence of the findings of the most advanced quantum physics with this old "mystical world view".

Modern physics, in its drive to mechanistically dissect matter ever further in order to finally arrive at the ultimate elementary particle, has finally reached a point where it is forced to question its own paradigm.

Quantum physicists now question the stability of matter itself and seem to arrive at a concept where elementary particles are seen as mere perturbations "on the surface of an endless sea of energy", which some scientists have agreed to call "Zero point energy" or "Torsion Fields" (Kozyrev et al.).

Don't you all hear a few wise Yogis laugh through the millennia over so much foolishness and late dawning of truth? They knew it all along!

I personally believe that the emerging new paradigm is characterised by a fusion of mystic knowledge and quantum physics. Do not expect to read that in the school and university textbooks yet, but you can smell it in the air.

To sum it up: We are talking about a new world view that will finally enable us to integrate the paranormal and other observations that are not readily explained with the increasingly obsolete models of mid-20th century physics. This new paradigm will resolve the contradictions between Einstein's relativity theory and quantum physics.

Entropy is the principle of reduction of complexity, thereby liberating the stored energy. This takes place when we burn fossil fuels, split the atom or basically undertake any technological process that humankind has recently come up with.

Almost like the idea of destroying something in order to utilise it, or rather a minimal aspect of it!

Viktor Schauberger talked of the opposing principles of explosion versus implosion, in order to demonstrate this basic difference.

We can find that the scientific paradigm of mainstream 20th century thinking understands only processes that are based on entropy. The ultimate idea of entropy is death, because at some point in the future, all differences in energy levels (potentials) must necessarily be depleted.

The concept of orgone as a creative energy postulates a principle that is opposed to entropy; a creative organising force. This force can be equated with life. Strangely, although our well-equipped and funded corporate and state scientists can describe many intricate processes in living organisms, the miracle of life itself must and does remain an enigma to them.

We find the idea of two opposing tendencies in the universe in the old eastern teachings of Yin and Yang, but also in the Eros and Thanatos of Sigmund Freud (an early mentor of Wilhelm Reich).

Learning to harness the creative power of Orgone will lead to an understanding of what is now called "free energy", a concept ridiculed by entropic science because it contradicts the "2nd Law of

Thermodynamics" (read second Law of Entropy). Interestingly, all this does not really contradict the most advanced scientific concepts. In my mind, it's rather the popular version of science that seems to be at odds.

Quantum physics has long postulated the reality of "parallel universes", the generation of matter out of "nothing" (of course it's not nothing but energy), and the equation of energy and consciousness.

In fact the age old concept of creation, the world being nothing but God's mind dreaming of itself and reflecting its own beauty, finds an ever-growing following amongst the theoretical physicists, the high priests of today's strange and elusive culture.

On the shoulders of a giant: Wilhelm Reich

While this book is not a book about Wilhelm Reich, the fact that we are frequently using the term "orgone energy", which he invented, makes it necessary to at least try to introduce him and his groundbreaking work, at least in a very sketchy fashion.

If you are interested in Dr Wilhelm Reich's life and work, I can heartily recommend the excellent biography by David Boadella,[1] apart of course from reading his own books.

Dr Wilhelm Reich was born in 1897 in Austria. After the First World War he studied medicine in Vienna and soon gravitated towards the new and then revolutionary psychoanalysis of Sigmund Freud. He became a close collaborator with Freud and a member of Freud's inner circle that attended regular meetings in Freud's house to discuss the latest theories. At that time, in the early 1920s, he was one of the pre-eminent members of the young psychoanalytical association. Soon though, the development of his thought had to lead to a growing alienation between himself and Freud and the more orthodox psychoanalysts.

While Freud, like Wilhelm Reich, was looking for the origin of neurotic behaviour and psychosis in early childhood trauma and the suppression of sexuality, this remained mostly abstract in Freudian therapy. For Reich, it became more and more evident from his clinical work with patients that this blocked memory of traumatic stress had its somatic expression in permanent "habitual" muscular tension that was strangling the life energy of the neurotic person. He called this virtual shell of permanently tensioned musculature "the body armour" and started to work on it directly in his therapy sessions with patients, using direct physical manipulation of the patient and breathing techniques. Whenever he achieved a breakthrough in loosening a part of the armour, he observed that the traumatic memory contained in the respective muscular spasm was set free as well.

Reich observed that only a

3

healthy and unarmoured person can experience a full orgasm, the ultimate mobilisation and release of life energy in any living organism.

These observations of what I'd like to call the "psychological Reich" were most prominently developed in his two books Character Analysis[2] and the The Function of the Orgasm.[3] The restoration of a person to full orgiastic potency became Reich's therapeutic aim in the 1920s and 30s, thereby picking up the thread that Freud had woven, but not followed to the end. This gave the somatic foundation of the psyche concrete meaning, where Freud had become evasive and finally fled into the mystical concept of "Eros and Thanatos", Freud's poetic sublimation of what Reich was later to name POR and DOR.

Wilhelm Reich had sought to understand the genesis of neurosis and what he called the "pestilential character" of fully armoured man in the context of an oppressive and exploitative society. This led him to a very leftist political position in the 1920s and 30s. He was for a long time a member of the German Communist Party. However, orthodox Communism did not really reciprocate his embrace and in his later American years he was to see international communism as the red fascism that it really was.

From this body-oriented work, his research, driven by an insatiable curiosity and a deep belief in the power of his mind to progress gradually towards an ever-better understanding of the true nature of the universe, arrived at the discovery of what he was to name orgone energy.

His research into cancer, which he consequently described as the result of energy blockages due to the permanent contraction of the muscular "armour", led to a groundbreaking discovery.

He found that tissue cells of healthy patients had a faint blue radiance while those of cancer patients seemed to have a grey emanation. This was the threshold to the discovery of orgone.

An important step in the discovery of orgone energy was Reich's "bion" research, which started around 1939.

Using very strong optical microscopes, he found "bubbles of energy" in sand and other "non-living" matter.

It is noteworthy that around that time optical microscopy had reached an absolute peak in its development. The later advent of the electron microscope made that technology wither away. It is therefore no surprise that modern researchers have difficulty replicating Reich's findings, because an electron microscope can only be used to look at "dead" probes. Reich's findings were based on the observation of living organisms and the living energy he called orgone under extremely high optical resolutions of about 4000x.

He had a lot of this documented on film but unfortunately, when his archive was raided by the infamous FDA in conjunction with other agencies, these invaluable documents were "lost".

These energy bubbles, or bions

as he was to call them, behaved like primitive life forms: they pulsated, expanded and contracted and moved about like single-celled organisms.

When pouring a sterilised infusion of hay, he found that primitive life forms, amoebae and protozoa were forming from this organic yet totally sterile solution.

Wilhelm Reich had discovered nothing less than the genesis of life. Modern theories speak of morphogenetic fields as energy fields that have form-building power.

His experiments were successfully replicated and verified by the then very well known researcher Roger du Theil at the Sorbonne University in Paris, France, and his team.

This monumental discovery alone would warrant more than a book to be written about, but unfortunately I can only mention it in passing, and encourage you to read about it in Reich's original publications, as far as they are still accessible.

The way Reich observed it, orgone is omnipresent, and the basis of all life processes. He observed the same principle in the forming of galaxies, as on a cellular or macro-biological level.

His earlier research into psychological disorders had shown him that when this energy is blocked by traumatic memories, manifesting in constant muscular tension (he called that armouring), this energy becomes Deadly Orgone or DOR.

As the environmentally threatened world we have created, over the last few hundred years, is only a mirror of our upset and unbalanced collective psyche, the same principle applies environmentally. One could say the growing deserts on this planet are an expression of the "deserts in our heart".

Deserts of the heart – deserts of the planet.

Wilhelm Reich, who also deserves credit for inventing the first cloud-buster, demonstrated the working of DOR in the forming of deserts and developed a method to disperse DOR concentrations by grounding them into sufficiently large water bodies.

Classical W. Reich Type Cloudbuster, Built by J. Trettin, Nuernbrecht, Germany. Photo: J. Trettin

Whenever the atmosphere feels stale, oppressive or dead and when you observe a particular blackness in cloud formation you are in fact experiencing a high and unhealthy DOR concentration.

Reich successfully experimented with orgone accumulators to cure cancer patients, as he observed cancer to be a biopathy, resulting from the blocked life energy in a highly DOR infested body.

W. Reich style orgone accumulator (Orac) Built by J. Trettin, Nuernbrecht, Germany. Photo: J. Trettin

He observed that the accumulation of orgone was stimulated by a layered combination of organic and metallic material.

Reich used some type of soft board and sheet metal to build man-sized boxes, into which the patient would go.

While the results were quite staggering, Reich's devices had one decisive shortfall: They accumulated whatever energy type (DOR or OR) was present in the environment.

This was all fine in the remote part of the US where Reich had his Orgone Institute in the 1940s and 50s, but in an even more DOR polluted environment such as we have today, this may be outright dangerous. All Reich's contraptions always had to be handled with care.

By saying this, I'm not trying to diminish W. Reich's pioneering research or his integrity as a scientist. The opposite would be true. Orgonite has certain qualities that Dr Reich did not foresee and a lot of fear that's being generated by more orthodox followers of Reich, does not take these empirical findings into account.

It seems that every great man or woman inevitably and unwillingly creates their own orthodoxy, almost as if it was a systemic reaction to slowly grind down the revolutionary impulse that has been generated by such people.

From Accumulator to Generator – In comes Don Croft

Don Croft is an independent researcher and inventor who lives in Idaho, USA. Among many other inspirational deeds, he can take credit for having made the step from orgone accumulator to orgone generator. Based on the findings of inventor Karl Welz, who found out about the potential of a matrix of metal filings suspended in polyester resin to convert negative DOR into POR, he started experimenting with a new type of "cloudbuster".

Karl Welz is most probably the inventor of orgonite; at least he has used the name first. His website at the time of writing is www.orgone.net.

His interest was mostly in radionic machines, that is intent-amplifying apparatuses. His machines are apparently quite powerful.

It was Don's innovation to start using this mixture for environmental healing tools that would positively affect large areas.

Wilhelm Reich's CB had relied entirely on the resonant cavity effect, whereby the stagnant energy would be drawn into an array of large parallel pipes, directed at the sky and then preferably grounded into a large water body.

In order to achieve a revitalisation of a DOR-infested sky, the operator had to skilfully sweep the sky, to create movement in the stagnant fields of dead energy. Because of the amount of negative energy that could be attracted to the Reichian CB, operating it could be hazardous for humans and great care had to be exercised.

The Don Croft orgonite-CB, on the other hand, is much smaller, hence cheaper to build and the main innovation is that the pipes, preferably made of copper, are inserted into a base of orgonite, which automatically starts converting the DOR to POR as soon as the CB is put together.

Based on this revolutionary observation, a whole range of other devices were developed by Don and other members of the growing network of experimenters, such as the compact conical orgone converter, called the "Holy Hand Grenade", the disk shaped "Tower Buster" for neutralising the ubiquitous microwave transmitters that are a main source of DOR in our environment (more about those later), and a host of other tools derived from these basic ones.

The addition of quartz crystals allowed the energy thus created to be projected at an even much wider field.

It is important to note one big difference between the orgonite-based devices à la Don Croft and the classical orgone technology of Wilhelm Reich.

The difference is that the Croft technology is absolutely foolproof and always positive in outcome. A lot of people who have gained a bit of knowledge in the classical Wilhelm Reich research and technology are not aware of these important differences and create needless fear. It seems that every great thinker and taboo-breaking discoverer inevitably leads to new restrictive belief systems, by his followers creating a new orthodoxy from his original and challenging thoughts.

Orgonite has been used by thousands of people worldwide, who have reported positive and lasting changes in their environment.

MANIFESTED DOR: THE WORLD IN WHICH WE LIVE

The table below shows typical attributes of these juxtaposed aspects of the universal etheric energy ocean.

	POR	DOR
Microscopic life forms	Pulsating, alive	Rigid, dead
Human being and other organisms, physical	Healthy, vibrant, expanding	Sick, cancer, auto-immune diseases, contracting
Human being, psychological	JOY Independent, self-regulating, communicative, awareness of self and others	FEAR Neurotic, easy to manipulate, "pestilential character"
Political organisation	Freedom, true democracy, self-regulating small units in free voluntary exchange with others, abundance	Tyranny, direct dictatorship or fake democracy, central control, giant corporations or state monopolies, scarcity
Planet Earth	Abundant plant life, biodiversity, well watered	Desert-forming, biodegradation, drought
Cosmic	Spiral motion of planets, stars and galaxies following same "orgonotic" form principles as mono-cellular amoebae	Reich didn't talk about that, but what about dying galaxies, black holes, supernovae?
Physics	Disentropy, "spontaneous" formation of ordered patterns in chaos, implosion energy	Entropy, decay of ordered structures, explosion energy

DOR on a social level: Conspiracy theory or alternative history?

The conspiracy is not a theory – A theory does not kill people
Credo Vusamazulu Mutwa

Do you still believe that your government loves you?

Can you imagine that the Twin Towers in New York and the Pentagon were wrecked by a bunch of Arabs who could hardly fly?

Do you believe that all the new controls imposed on you when travelling or the new intrusions in your privacy actually serve a legitimate purpose, such as fighting real terrorists?

Do you actually believe that there are any genuine terrorist groups out there who were not created by one of the major secret services?

Do you believe that Afghanistan or Iraq were invaded and bombed to smithereens in order to "liberate" them or even bring "democracy" to the people there?

And finally, do you think that the sky above your head looks natural, the way it looked when you were a child?

I don't think so, because you would hardly have opted to buy this book if you held these beliefs.

Of course the belief in a conspiracy to create a one-world government is not a necessary condition for understanding the concept of Orgone Energy.

It will be difficult to accept the enormous reality of the chemtrail spraying, weather modification and mind control programmes without assuming a hidden group that follows a sinister agenda. So, while you could still enjoy the benefits of the orgone tools and zappers we're going to talk about later, a lot of what we are talking about will not be comprehensible to you.

If we want to follow the emerging consensus of a growing number of alternative historians and independent researchers, an effort for total control and domination by a small "elite" of extremely control minded people is being carried forward on all levels of human existence: Spiritual, mental, material, financial, political and military.

Many excellent books have been written about single and combined aspects of this conspiracy to move the world from a polycentric world of diversity to a "One World Government" in a "New World Order".[4]

Many people who are willing to accept that people could be driven by ulterior motives, such as greed or the will to exercise power and control over others, have difficulties imagining a long term drive towards such a goal, spanning many centuries, if not millennia. This is where the occult background of this conspiracy kicks in as an explanation. The controlling group is interlinked through a web of secret societies, overt and covert political networks, permeating think tanks, the secret services of all nations, the military and large corporations.

Now if these few people have such power, why would they have to act in such secretiveness? The answer is that open coercion has proven counterproductive to this group in many ways, more covert ways of reaching the goal had to be devised.

They have always looked for ways in which to manipulate events in such a way that "We the people" actually demand the changes that they want to bring about.

So instead of outrightly passing draconian laws that abrogate our constitutional rights of habeas corpus and informational privacy, they will create a terrorist threat like the famous "Al Qaeda" (more aptly named Al CIA-da, because it's an entirely fabricated organisation) and creates so much fear that people actually demand all those controls they would have never accepted in peaceful times.

The same can be shown for all major policy shifts.

David Icke, in one of his most lucid contributions to the debate, calls this pattern of advancing an agenda by creating a problem first, and then offering the intended new policy as a solution to the reaction of the general public, the Problem-Reaction-Solution scheme. It's based on the Hegelian Dialectics of Thesis-Antithesis-Synthesis that was so refined and brought to perfection by international Marxism.

Once you understand that most events that "make the news" because they are admitted to the controlled media, the whole charade becomes more easily understandable.

Show me a single major event or scenario of the last few years we all have recollection of, and tell me it was not manufactured and I'll probably be able to prove you wrong.

You think the Asian tsunami on 25 December 2005 was a natural catastrophe? Objection, your honour, it was an H-Bomb. The radioactivity was so high that after 2 or 3 days there were no more fish, not even sharks to eat the corpses of the victims that were floating in the coastal waters.

I personally know one of the aid workers who came in from Germany to help "clean up" after the slaughter. After they reported increased radioactivity and the conspicuous absence of all marine life in the "tsunami struck" area, they were called home, all their notes and data confiscated, and they were sworn to secrecy by sinister secret service types at their home airport.

The 9-11 hoax is well documented on the internet and in several good books by now, and doesn't really need much further explanation. Did it not astonish you how the US House of Representatives had the infamous Patriot Act ready in the drawer and passed it within days after the manufactured event, in a time so short none of the representatives could have even pretended to have studied it.

In the future, just watch: whenever a car bomb goes off at some airport, just count the days until some politician raises the question of new competences for the police, like "killing first, asking questions later", breaking into houses without a search warrant et cetera.

The game is very transparent once you have allowed yourself to notice the obvious signs.

The manipulation of the public mind works with very coarse triggers and accommodates the extremely short attention span of general public opinion.

It is obvious that this group controls the official media. There is only one news agency left in the whole English speaking world, (Reuters), and of course the other ones are interlinked. The alternative news scene is constantly infiltrated and manipulated, as well – what else are 2 million paid spies (meaning members of one or the other secret government agency) in the US to do the whole day? They can't all be hunting for terrorists, can they?

How then would such a big plan as steering 4 large airliners into different prominent targets in the best protected airspace in the world have remained unnoticed? (If you had tried to veer off course in a Cessna over New York any time before or after 9-11-2002, they would have been on to you with all the might of the US Air Force and Strategic Air command in no time.)

So brace yourself for the sad news: most conspiracy websites are run by the same agencies that they purportedly expose.

And this is how the disinformation game works: Since you are already looking for the truth, they will give you some truth but spin it in such a way that you will never get the whole picture.[5]

First and foremost, however, they will present the truth in such an overwhelming and disempowering way that you lose all confidence to ever change anything.

They will constantly overstate the power and might of the conspiracy according to Sun Tsu's (Chinese warlord and philosopher) motto: In order to beat an adversary you must first convince him that he cannot win.

This is the secret behind why millions of people have read David Icke's popular conspiracy books and yet the same shenanigans continue unhindered.

This is not a book about the "One World Conspiracy", but rather a book about how you can empower yourself to help us end it and create paradise instead, hence the title of the book.

Of course at least the outlines of this conspiracy have to be sketched out as we see them, before we get to the fun part of how to overcome this grisly paradigm.

You may take that as a statement of our assumptions of how the present world is organised, nothing more nor less.

You may also have come across theories that the leadership of this secret group trying to control all aspects of our life is partly non-human. Many people take these stunning allegations as a pretext to ridicule the whole conspiracy story.

The story of our partly non-human origins are surprisingly well documented, by the way, in the

Sumerian Clay tablets which tell the story of the Annunaki who came down to this planet some 425 000 years ago and genetically created the present human race in order for it to work for them. This story has been relayed and interrelated from many texts including Genesis in the Old Testament of the Bible by Zacharia Sitchin.[6] I do not know if all his conclusions from the extensive material he presents are true, but the timely coexistence of a reptilian race of overlords with humankind, of snake gods and human sacrifice to those gods, is so all-pervasive in all cultures, that it's hard to dismiss it in its entirety.

> "And it came to pass, when men began to multiply on the face of the earth, and daughters were born unto them, that the sons (plural, sic!) of God saw the daughters of men that they were fair and they took them wives of all which they chose."
> (Genesis 6, 1-2)[7]

Did it ever occur to you what this cryptic sentence in the Bible could mean?

It is however not really relevant for our story whether the bloodlines of these elite families are reptilian, draconian or just evil human, whatever that means. What counts are their deeds and attitudes towards us "ordinary humans", most of whom they regard as useless eaters (Kissinger is quoted as having said that) anyway. The shape and denomination of otherworldly beings changes with culture and perception, of course.

One culture's elves are the other culture's grey aliens, or yet another culture's Madindane (that's what the Zulu call them), but all cultures talk about them. Let's have a look at how the agenda of manifested DOR plays out in our 3-dimensional world...

The occult foundations of the New World Order

> ...Pleased to meet you
> Hope you guess my name
> But what's puzzling you
> Is the nature of my game...
> From "Sympathy for the devil" by Mick Jagger and Keith Richards

Interestingly, this small elite of an estimated 300 families that are said to be in control of the world's financial, military, economic and political affairs, all believe in and use magic (or rather "magick" as they love to call it), while peddling blatant materialism or sanitised spirituality in the form of the organised religions to the masses.

They are all connected through a network of secret societies that pervade all outwardly visible structures of world society. Through the minions and unwitting foot soldiers in these numerous and multifaceted organisations, the agenda of the secret core is promoted in an endless parade of seemingly unconnected events.

These people (if one wants to grant them that honorary title) engage in the most gruesome rituals, including human sacrifice, in order to boost their hypnotic stranglehold over humankind.

All this is well documented,[8] and I'm not attempting to write another book about the Illuminati, Freemasons, Jesuits or "The Brotherhood of the White Light". An important point in this context is that this group is working with exactly those aspects of reality whose existence they officially deny. Sounds a lot like "preaching water and drinking wine", doesn't it?

Materialism is for the cattle, the ordinary Jim and Jack in the street, as is organised religion and its newest version, the manipulated New Age Movement.

Masonic symbolism on the US 1 Dollar bill

What is now the difference between "Magick" and spiritual healing, between true spirituality and satanism?

The legend depicts Lucifer, who is often identified with the great adversary of God, Satan, as a fallen angel, an angel that is in rebellion against God. In his arrogance, he sees himself separated from the divine and will use all "magick tricks" to maintain that separation and draw power from promoting that same separation in others.

He will promise an individual who is willing to enter a pact with this consciousness, power over others, wealth, and success, just like the Mephistopheles figure in Goethe's most eminent work "Faust".

In many spiritual traditions this arrogant attitude of an individual mind or soul entity is called the False Ego. By separating itself from the flow of divine will and energy the satanic consciousness is casting a shadow. It can only feed off negativity in others and is thus by definition a parasitic consciousness.

In analogy it can be described as Wilhelm Reich's DOR on a spiritual level. DOR is blocked life-energy on a "proto-physical" level. Satanism is blocked divine energy on the spiritual level.

True spirituality is humility without being feeble. It is the joy of experiencing one's individuality as part of and in harmony with a greater whole, the creative consciousness that is also known as GOD.

Unfortunately many of us who are awakening to recognise a larger reality beyond the truncated views of school-book physics (the true borderline research in physics is much more exciting than that of course) are landing in the wide and sticky spider's web of the various New Age cults and new religious belief systems.

Satanism is often very well masked as spirituality and you can be assured that the purporters of this spiritual attitude will rarely confess to it openly. A few exceptions like Aleister Crowley, who was proud of it, break the rule in this case.

Getting an illuminated member of the Great White Brotherhood to confess to being a satanist is about as difficult as finding a self-confessed white racist in modern South Africa. They have all "disappeared" with the advent of the "New South Africa" and it's linguistic straightjacket of political correctness. Next time you are approached by some members of the latest New Age craze, just ask yourself the following questions:

Do they talk of an elite of initiates, only whom can understand the deeper secrets of their doctrine?

Do they make it attractive for you to join by flattering you that you could belong to such an elite?

Do they flatter you further by telling you how stupid 99% of the human herd are, and how an elite has to direct mankind's fate anyway, and again that you could be part of that elite?

You got it!

They're all in it. There's no major cult or religious movement out there that is not in part created or at least deeply infiltrated by the New World Order gang. They constantly try to do this to our spontaneous and unorganised Network, but have not been very successful so far. Maybe that is because we have nobody who is willing to play the role of the "all-knowing Guru", the source of endless wisdom.

The negative energies conjured up by magic ritual cannot be sustained in a strong orgone field. This is the reason why we continuously gift the sites of negative magic ritual with orgonite. Sensitives have continuously noted how not only the atmosphere clears up, but also souls or spirits that have been trapped by such ritual become liberated and set free. Apparently black magic uses a lot of parasitic techniques, where the energy of another soul is used to achieve certain ends. This is easily understood once you've grasped the non-creative exclusively parasitic nature of satanic consciousness.

It can – per definition – not generate its own energy and therefore needs to spoil the life energy of mankind in order to tap into the power of those entrapped victims.

Hence the mass addiction to drugs, pornography, violence and all kinds of perversions and deformations of the human psyche constantly and tirelessly promoted by this ruling and highly hypocritical elite. In their public personae, they will of course support "The War on Drugs", while actually being the drug pushers themselves, or will devise Visions of a "World without Violence", while being the driving force behind every terrorist organisation that they then venture out to "fight", in massive and inappropriate wars of mass destruction and cruel conquest.

It is a strange world out there!

Massive orgonisation of the planet will break the hypnotic spell that this group holds over mankind.

Due to the parasitic nature of their game, their power wanes as soon as the energy that they are used to tapping into is withdrawn from them.

This is well within the scope of humanity's short-term options given a sufficient degree of awakening worldwide.

We have found the extraordinary effects of orgonite on the human psyche demonstrated again and again. People disengage from fruitless conflict and become constructive and cooperative in the presence of strong positive orgone fields.

The Money Scam – Hypnosis in Action

"If the American people ever allow private banks to control the issue of their money, first by inflation and then by deflation, the banks and corporations that will grow up around them (around the banks) will deprive the people of their property until their children will wake up homeless on the continent their fathers conquered."
– Thomas Jefferson –

Money is a central pillar of the unbelievable hypnotic control structure the secret brotherhood has erected to steer all affairs of humankind comfortably from the backseat.

In fact, my own waking up process started with an enquiry into the money system.

Try this: Go to your local library and try to find a book that describes in understandable terms what money is. Like: who issues it, who determines its value, how is it created.

You will not find such a book. At least, I did not find one.

If you use the keyword catalogues you will find books about how you can learn to "make more money" for yourself, you'll find books by celebrated Nobel Prize winning authors like John Maynard Keynes or Milton Friedman about the macroeconomic management of money. But none of them goes to the root of "What money is".

The question is obviously considered naive and every professor of economics (I had and have a few in my family) will brush you off like a schoolchild if you dare ask such questions. But, like the fairy tale of "The Emperor's New Clothes", it is the child who makes the pertinent statement "but the emperor has no clothes on" that finally ends the hypnotic spell that made a whole kingdom pretend to see the beautiful clothes the emperor was allegedly wearing, only out of fear of looking stupid.

History and theory

We must lose that fear and ask the questions.

What is money then?

This ain't Money – fact #1 that worthless paper shown in the picture above is NOT MONEY ... it is the biggest sham ever created ... the IMF world bank that sits above the "FED" or federal reserve has produced what we should call "debt notes". JimCanneyScience.com

Money originates from the original form of trade, which is barter: the exchange of goods considered by both transacting parties to be of equal value. Now some goods evolved to become more universal media of exchange, because of their widely recognised value and unperishable quality.

Even goods like seashells (the cowrie shells of West and East Africa) or beads were considered money in large parts of the world for a long time.

Over time precious metals such as silver and gold assumed the widest acceptance.

The value of money was regulated by the exact weight of gold or silver contained in a coin.

Certain rulers were of course known even then to counterfeit the value of money by replacing pure gold with lesser alloys, or cheating on the weight.

So, for example, one dollar in legal money in its original sense is defined as 24.75 grains of gold or 371.25 grains of silver.[9]

Banknotes came into existence as depository receipts when gold or other real money was held in deposit by a deposit-keeping institution, the "strong room owner". Since the carrying of large amounts of precious metal coins could be cumbersome or even risky, banknotes became ever more popular.

Originally every banknote was thought to be the exact counterpart of a specific amount kept in deposit by the banker.

Smart as bankers are when it comes to maximising their own gain, they soon discovered that they could loan out some of the gold kept in deposit for their "valued clients" while these were still doing business using the depository receipts. The money had suddenly taken on a double existence!

In fact, certain rules of thumb were rather quickly established, according to which only about 10% of the value of all outstanding notes had to be kept in cash (gold that is), because so great was the trust of the public in those bankers that most people were happy just to know they had a right to the gold in the bank.

Each banknote still promised to be exchangeable into "specie", the technical term for real money, i.e. gold or silver.

Frequently bankers became too greedy and then, through one or the other incident or rumour, the trust of the depositors suddenly faltered, creating the famous "runs on the bank", when suddenly large queues of angry customers would demand their gold back to no avail...

It is interesting that the notion of money lent to their credit customers was created out of thin air. It did not exist before the banker brought it into circulation by lending the non-existing money to his debtor client.

In due course, the underlying gold standard was abandoned when certain governments were unable to meet their gold obligations from international debt transactions. In the USA the redeemability of so called "dollar" banknotes into gold was abandoned in 1933 and private possession of physical gold was declared illegal.

Some researchers say that the US then secretly declared bankruptcy and is since under forfeiture by the international bankers who had held most of those "banknotes".

Unfortunately old Grandpa who had entrusted his "Gold Eagles" to his bank was never notified of the proceedings, and was thus outrightly robbed of his gold.

Now many people think that the issuance of currency is still in the hand of the nation state.

This is not so in most cases.

For example, the Federal Reserve System is owned by the leading banks of America and is thereby a private monopoly to create money out of nothing and charge interest on it.

It was conceived in a very secretive meeting on the private Jekyll Island off the coast of Georgia, hence the name The Creature from Jekyll Island, of the very seminal book by G. Edward Griffin.[10]

Another important book on the issue is Eustace Mullins's The Secrets of the Federal Reserve System.[11]

I recommend that you read both books.

The important point in our context is that money is an unreal commodity, whose value is only upheld by the hypnotic spell of those in its command, and that a small elite has managed to manoeuvre themselves into a position where they can create money out of thin air, charge interest on it and receive real value in return in the form of collateral.

This has created a situation whereby practically all material wealth on this planet is owned by the banks, who in their top structures are controlled by the same 300 families mentioned before. We are only the custodians of the goods we have bought with money "lent" by a bank.

This is true from our houses and cars to the vast industrial empires built on bank finance.

Of course you are not supposed to see the simplicity of this giant wealth and energy extraction scheme, hence the difficulty of finding a straight answer to the simple question "What is Money?", which was the question I posed at the beginning.

You're supposed to think it's all very abstract and very scientific and not to be grasped by mere mortals.

Just think about how the mind control industries collude in imbuing that magic glitter into those worthless promissory notes that actually ceased promising anything a long time ago; look at all the gangster movies where that smart suitcase with thick wads of bank notes is shown as the ultimate "object of desire", certainly worth killing or even dying for!

Everything is done to make the possession of the largest possible amount of these fake banknotes, that are only brought into circulation when an individual or company takes out a loan from a bank, look very sexy.

Yet the truth is much closer to the final scene of the movie "The Matrix" (after the visionary book by Valdemar Valerian), where Neo and his friends discover that humans are just held in basins of nutrient liquid, connected to the matrix by plugged in cables and hoses in order to feed energy into the matrix-system, being discarded ("unplugged") as soon as their useful lifespan is over. Consider this movie a poetic documentary of the state of existence of humankind.[12]

So, the seemingly unrelated theme of money is central to the understanding of how DOR manifests in society.

It is the transmission belt by which life energy is sapped from the potentially healthy and productive lives of the general population and led astray to fuel the hypertrophic growth of negative giant complexes like the arms industry, the nuclear complex et cetera,

Fortunes of unimaginable size are then created by the hands of those at the levers of this evil construct.

Meanwhile, two thirds of the global population wither away in abject poverty, and working and middle-class populations in the first world are deprived, piece by piece, of their erstwhile social achievements now that their productive and skilled labour is no longer needed in a globalised world to create those powerful industrial conglomerates.

The natural state of humankind is that of abundance, because our productive abilities are unlimited and the joy of creating things is intrinsic to our psyche. Please note that I'm not advocating any form of socialism, but rather real economic freedom. The freedom to exchange value for value on an entirely voluntary basis.

Socialism is just another variant of the great life force extraction scheme that has played out over the millennia, and should by now be thoroughly demystified. This is especially true since we know that the Bolshevik Revolution was just as much funded by the Wall Street Bankers, as was the rise of Adolf Hitler,[13] who served a necessary role in the bigger game plan of global social re-engineering that our wannabe masters, the Freemasons, like to call "The Work of All Ages".

Interestingly, the Prophet Mohammed had a clear grasp of this situation and Islamic banking theoretically condemns the charging of interest as well as the use of "fiat" paper money, allowing credit only in the form of venture capital; that is, participation in risk and gain of another person's business venture.

Even Christianity had cultivated

that notion for a while, based on the alleged scene where the young Jesus drove out the money changers from the temple in Jerusalem.

That scene must have long been deleted from the mind of the ordinary churchgoer as well as the cleric in any of the known branches of churchianity.

Chemtrails, HAARP, mind control

'Man does not have the right to develop his own mind. This kind of liberal orientation has great appeal. We must electrically control the brain. Some day armies and generals will be controlled by electric stimulation of the brain.'
– US government mind manipulator, Dr Jose Delgado, Congressional Record, No. 262E, Vol. 118, 1974

From the above, it is clear that a small group of parasitic individuals can only retain their grip on humankind by using elaborate techniques in order to hold the majority of "lesser humans" or "cattle", as they like to describe us.

Since we as the mass of humanity are intrinsically more powerful than they, by sheer count of numbers, they can only stay in their powerful position which allows them to tap into our energies by keeping us in a permanent state of fear and distraction, by preventing us from waking up and taking our lives into our own hands. The sum of these techniques, when consciously applied, can be called mind control.

Mind control can take many forms. In essence any consistent manipulation of thought, perception or mental state can be called by that term. In that sense our education system, the media, advertising and the prevailing cultural forces work together to create a particular perception of reality.[14]

The careful orchestration of events following the Hegelian dialectic principle of Thesis-Antithesis-Synthesis, or "Problem-Reaction-Solution", is another method to create social consensus and move the world population to accept the policies of the "elite".

An example: If you want to create tougher security laws such as the US with their infamous "Patriot Act I and II", you create a horrific incident like the bombing of the World Trade Center on 11 September 2001, blame it on some Arab terrorists, and when everyone is sufficiently shocked, you pull your previously prepared draconian laws out of your sleeve and get them nodded at in an instant.

The technique is not new. It's been done again and again, most famously in Nazi Germany. The Nazis burnt down the parliament building, the Reichstag, blamed it on the Communists and rounded up thousands of opposition politicians, shooting some 500 the first night after the incident, without meeting much resistance.

History and theory

Mind control always involves fear. Induce a sufficient level of fear into an individual, and the traumatised person will accept any help that is suggested by a confident manipulator. That's how it's done on a macro-political and individual level.

Trauma-based mind control is probably much older than the Nazi period in Germany, but it is widely believed that the Nazis brought this "ancient art of evil" to a new scientific level, driven by perverted minds like that of Dr Mengele, who apparently continued his "fruitful career" after WWII, as a leading figure in US mind control programmes, like MK Ultra and MK Naomi. Trauma-based mind control uses a facility of the human mind to shut off experiences that are too traumatic to integrate into their waking consciousness. In this way a compartmentalised personality or multiple personality disorder can be created.

The victims of such treatment can be used as zombie soldiers who feel no pain, or as spies or secret messengers who will not remember their mission after their handler has snapped them out of one compartment of their consciousness into another.[15]

At least since the 1960s, the CIA has mastered the technology of beaming subliminal messages directly into the subconsciousness of the targeted person(s) or population, by modulating voice and sound on to electromagnetic carrier waves in the radio- and microwave frequency spectrum.

You can even buy meditation cassettes and CDs that use these brain entrainment methods to change your attitudes towards life by "silent affirmations", text chosen and spoken by yourself and overlaid with the musical carpet of the tape in a way you cannot consciously hear.

Another method used in these tapes is the stimulation of certain brainwaves by playing slightly different frequencies to the two ears, causing the brain to react by oscillating to the exact tune of the differential. This method is called the Holosync®[16] method. While its founder Bill Harris propagates it as a tool for personal spiritual growth, achieving the results of a lifetime of meditation in a few months or years, he also clearly states in his brochures that a lot of these techniques, especially the silent subliminal messages were developed by the CIA in the 1960s.

While Bill Harris may be well intentioned and his methods possibly beneficial on a certain level, I am only quoting this little example from my own experience (I tried it out some time ago), as proof of the ongoing concern of the secret services with methods of direct electronic manipulation of thought and emotion. This is only one of the many attempts at constructing the optimal "mind machine" that has fascinated the alternative research community, at least since the 1970s.

Many and much more sinister applications exist.

At the same time, the leading figures of the ruling cabal in the US have started salivating over the perspective of what they call the psychotronic age (an expression coined by erstwhile "National Security Advisor" to President Carter, Zbigniew Brzezinski), an age of total control over the human mind. (See the quotation above from master mind controller, Jose Delgado of MK-Ultra fame.)

The electromagnetic soup created in our atmosphere by the myriads of transmitters, some of them allegedly used for communication, others being secret weapon systems and weather-modifying technologies such as HAARP (High Altitude Auroral Research Project), EISCAT (its European equivalent), and the much higher developed Russian technologies for weather modification and mind control, are designed to achieve just that.

It is to be noted that the ubiquitous microwave transmitters, sold to the populace as necessary for cellphone communications, play a major role in this undeclared war against humankind's mind and vitality.[17]

Interestingly, we often find whole arrays of these deadly entropy transmitters concentrated in natural vortex points, often in very remote areas where no presence of any paying network subscribers could ever justify the massive "firepower" concentrated there.

For too long, the attention of researchers has been hypnotically transfixed on the well-known HAARP installation in Alaska and its European Counterpart EISCAT. The truth is that HAARP-like weather manipulation and mind control (brain entrainment, subliminal messages, et cetera), is perpetrated through the dense network of worldwide transmitter sites.

Mountaintop array above Tzaneen

Clairvoyants who can see auras inevitably see the negativity emanating from such transmitters.

While perceptions differ in their concrete visual manifestation from sensitive to sensitive, the emotional valuation of "negativity" has been consistent.

I once did an experiment with a woman who is a noted and successful psychic healer, in which I asked her to describe the aura of a particularly large cellphone tower before and after we applied orgonite to its surroundings.

Since she had never before focused her attention on these towers, she did not know what to expect.

Her description of the aura field around the untreated tower was as follows:

"A black ball, slightly flattened like a

melon, about half a kilometre in circumference and criss-crossed by grey veins similar to certain slabs of black marble."

After we had surrounded the tower with a few tower busters, her impression was very different:

"The blackness was now confined to the immediate surroundings of the microwave panels, emanating only approximately one metre from them. The previously black aura beyond that had now become a vivid display of bright and fresh colours."

The aspect of such a tower's radiation that seems to cause the negative effects is apparently not the "normal" electromagnetic radiation of longitudinal waves, but the scalar or standing waves aspect.

Such things are only beginning to be investigated by a few curious members of academic science.

Most debates about the potentially harmful effects of microwave towers centre around the question of radiation thresholds that can be measured with conventional instruments. This way of looking at it seems entirely mistaken when the effects are based on the manipulation of the etheric field rather than the raw electromagnetic vibration.

While it will be difficult to prove any of this to an entrenched sceptic, we find experiential proof in the observation of our own reaction to those towers and the often immediate changes in atmosphere and cloud patterns after treating them with orgonite.

So the proof is indirect by demonstrating how an oppressive negative atmosphere expressed visually through a dull sky, with often rippled layers of thin 2-dimensional or "flat" looking clouds, makes way for a lively and jubilant atmosphere with well-articulated cumulus clouds, when orgone generators are introduced into the area.

Characteristic HAARP ripples over Johannesburg

More rippled skies over Johannesburg

As part of their efforts to "control the weather by 2025" (as per an alleged secret study of the US-Navy), our secretive rulers have started spraying thick layers of heavy metal and biotoxin laden artificial clouds (chemtrails), which seem to augment these covert environmental weapon systems of the **psychotronic age**.

HAARP in Tornado Mode over Kampala, Uganda

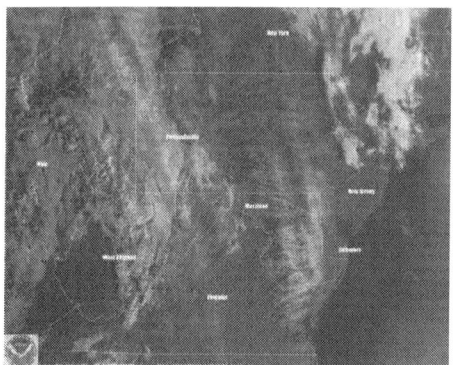

Chemtrails over Maryland, USA, Sept 2000

It is not entirely clear what the intended purpose of this vast worldwide spraying programme is, but the following aspects seem to be agreed upon by most researchers:

Chemtrails contain biotoxic agents and are at least in part designed as a cynical method of population control, one of the agendas closest to the heart of the Illuminati, who feel greatly disturbed by the multitudes of useless eaters on this planet. [18]

They seem to share this distaste for ordinary humanity with their predecessors, the elohim of the Bible who wreaked a flood on humankind in order to decimate their numbers.

Chemtrails seem to be used as a reflective screen in order to enhance the working of sophisticated electromagnetic weaponry, such as "over the horizon" and "ground-penetrating" radar.

Chemtrails most obviously create drought by binding water molecules. They work like a desiccating agent. This is despite the ongoing myth that spraying was originally developed in order to create rain.

Chemtrails cannot be confused with regular contrails that are stripes of condensed water produced by aircraft when travelling at very high altitudes. Contrails, which disappear within minutes, occur only at specific heights and temperatures and leave no slimy residue visible for hours. The often regular, but always unnatural-looking spraying patterns defy any "regular explanation".

Some researchers allege that chemtrails are brought out as a secret programme to mollify the effects of the alleged global warming. We think this is disinformation, as much as we think that "global warming" is another hoax, perpetrated in order to aid the global push for "one world government".

Luckily the placement of only one, sometimes a few more, small orgone generators (called tower busters) transforms a cellphone tower from death-force emitter to a veritable orgone generator, while the presence of an orgonite cloudbuster opens up the sky and dissolves chemtrails. Apparently by strengthening the self-healing capacity of the bio-physical system "air", the poisonous soup is transmuted into harmless components, because nobody has ever seen toxic fallout come down at places where cloudbusters do their work.

Typical chemtrail spraying in grid pattern near Freiburg, Germany. Note the characteristic polarised "halo" around the sun

HAARPed chemtrails east of Pretoria

Chemtrails over Nelspruit, SA, Dec 2003

It is interesting that a lot of people, probably the majority of ordinary people, do not "see" the chemtrails at all.

This seems to confirm the theory that our seeing is very much informed by our belief system, and far from the mere physical recording camera-like machine that school book science wants to make us believe it is.

A contemporary record by one of the first Spanish conquistadors in South America said that the local Indians did not see the sailing ships of the Spaniards at first, because they had no concept of such strange beasts.

We seem to shut out those elements of reality for which we have no concept or explanation.

I often test relatives or acquaintances in this respect, and find that they may even "see" the chemtrails in their full beauty, but then at least shut down any notion of them being anything extraordinary even if they are clearly so different from the sky of our childhood.

It seems also that we shut out any perception of realities that would cause too much pain to acknowledge.

Halo around the sun, indicative of strange substances in the atmosphere

So it is plausible that large numbers of people are only beginning to notice these strange phenomena, now that the worst is already over.

Those of us in the orgone network who have been watching chemtrails for years now, have noticed that they are changing in character.

The really bad ones look yellowish, like billowing smog, while recently they are becoming increasingly white.

We think the massive proliferation of cloudbusters, completely unmentioned by the controlled mass media, has already taken the brunt out of that programme and its deadly intentions failed to materialise.

Now that so many disinformers talk about chemtrails, it's already yesterday's news.

Most "chemtrail websites" are run by government agencies which are trying to exploit the failed, but ambitious programme, at least for some fear mongering.

If your discernment is sharp enough, you could at least visit these websites to see some good chemtrail photos, in case you're not so sure what a chemtrail looks like.

Just do not buy into their doomsday mood; that's the mind control aspect of these fake "truth investigators".[19]

What happens to the chemtrails when an orgonite cloudbuster dissolves them?

We honestly don't know, but from the experience of thousands of participants in this worldwide "unorganisation", we can calm all fears that the muck would simply fall out of the sky and increase the toxicity on earth's already burdened surface. That has never been observed, in many thousands of cases of sky cleaning with orgonite.

We do not know if the saturation of the atmosphere just lets the aerosols decompose into their possibly harmless elementary constituents, or if something even much more fundamental happens: an "alchemistic" transformation of matter into energy.

Many of us believe that is the case and that also, in reverse, matter is created out of nothing by orgone energy.

We especially often sense that water vapour seems to appear out of an empty sky and forms into healthy looking cloud as we go along and orgonise a larger territory. The only other explanation would be that such moisture was previously bound by microwave induced atmospheric heating.

Since a lot of what we experience borders on the miraculous, I tend strongly towards the "alchemist" explanation. After all, quantum physics and mysticism finally concur that matter is energy and energy is matter.

ORGONE AND RELATED FIELDS OF RESEARCH

"A true scientist does not confuse theory with reality and does not try to dictate what nature should be like"
Stanislav Grof – The Holotropic Mind

Alternative healing

Practically all genuine healing traditions agree on some kind of energetic or spiritual view of life and human nature.

It is common practice to channel energy towards the patient by laying of hands, mental focusing, and working with crystals, plants, prayer or other means.

Another line of healing traditions emphasises the stimulation of life energy by teaching the exercises that are thought to remove energy blockages and connect the practitioner to the cosmic source of life and wisdom. Qui Gong, Yoga, and Tai Chi are only a few examples.

Even traditional herbalism is mainly based on the intuitive powers of the healer who feels the resonance between a specific herb and the condition his patient is in, and then determines how to treat him.

Medicinal approaches that acknowledge the prevalence of an etheric realm that precedes and underlies material manifestations of disease or health are often referred to as vibrational medicine.

Not surprisingly, a lot of the very active members in our growing planetary healing network have a background in the healing arts.

Orgonite tools are compatible with and can complement any genuine alternative healing modality.

Even with accompanying conventional medical procedures and protocols, however critical we may be of most of them, it will speed up the healing process and mitigate some of the destructive effects of allopathic interventions.

We have received a lot of unexpected and spontaneous feedback from people who were suffering from various ailments and felt better when exposed to orgone energy. I would like to talk more about this, but our experiences in this field have not been systematic and our real focus has been on environmental healing. There is space for a whole book about personal healing with orgonite to be written by someone who is dealing with person to person healing issues on a regular basis.

Some of the energy sensitive participants in the worldwide orgone network have invented special healing applications for orgonite, such as the "Saint Buster's Button", or SBB, which is based on a special coil design.

On all our expeditions in Africa we have sought contact with the traditional healers, the sangomas. Often we were able to donate a cloudbuster or other orgonite to one of these spiritually and energetically highly sensitive people.

We have always found that they spontaneously feel the energy produced by the devices and without any explanation see the full scope of applications this energy can be used for.

This ability to feel energy is still widely present in the African population despite all efforts by missionaries and the paradigms of technical civilisation to eradicate it.

The acknowledgement of a supernatural realm is nothing special for most Africans whose traditional culture was deeply rooted in the dialogue with the spirit world.

I will talk more about some of these encounters in the chapter about our expeditions.

Free energy

It is obvious from the above that the idea of orgone energy, or a "living ether", is intricately linked to other advanced scientific concepts.

Conventional science negates the possibility of drawing usable energy from the Ether. Yet numerous inventors and scientists have discovered and described processes that suggest that just that is happening. Not surprisingly, the establishment has consequently suppressed the most viable inventions, as they would have posed a threat to the ruling petrochemical cartel.

There are, however, persistent rumours suggesting that exactly those inventions that were ridiculed in public are secretly used by the deep black core of the secret services and military organisations.

It is widely alleged that Nazi Germany had developed operational free energy generators known as Kohler-tachyon-converters and that they had usable anti-gravity engines and flying disks, similar to those seen in UFO sightings the world over.

These technologies were passed on to the Russian and American military industrial complex after World War II.[20]

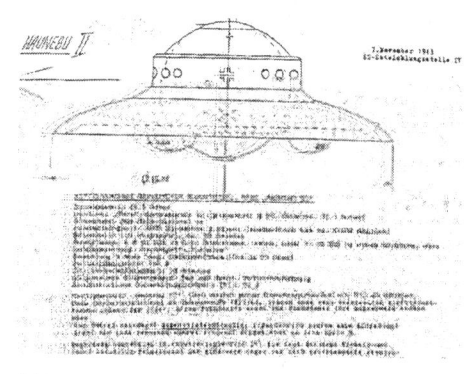

Did this ever fly? Cross section Haunebu II. Allegedly at least 17 of these anti-gravity disks were produced and successfully tested

If this is true (and I'm quite confident it is), it would essentially make the official NASA Space Programme appear as a Muppet show for public consumption, which it probably is.

This is not the place to refer to the whole breadth of the free energy discussion, of course. Anyone who is interested in the theme should read Gerry Vasiliotis' excellent book Lost Science[21] in order to get an idea of what the true state of the art in energy generation is like. We are living at least 100-150 years behind the potential technological development that has been withheld from us. It does not matter whether we talk of Zero Point Energy, Torsion Fields, Quantum Fluctuation or Orgone Energy. These concepts are all different approaches to describe an undeniable reality: That the visible world, or rather world of our random sensory perception, is but the tip of the proverbial iceberg, nothing but ripples on the surface of an indefinitely deep ocean of energy and information.

The important thing in our context is that the so-called elite has withheld these technologies from the general public and prevented their large-scale application at household level. Many inventors, such as Bill Muller in Canada, were able to reliably harness the etheric power by constructing generators that ran at over unity. (They put out more usable energy than had to be put in to drive them.) Bill was on the brink of mass-producing small table top units the size of an external hard drive that would have supplied a whole household with electricity, before he suddenly died.

Also think what I'm thinking? They just always die whenever they are ready to seriously challenge the existing paradigm.

Don saw Bill and has seen his machines at work. I had several extended telephone conversations with him. He was a highly qualified electrical engineer who had been designing large turbine generators for Siemens in the 1960s, among them those that are still powering Zambia and Zimbabwe in the Kariba hydroelectric power station.

He told me that he had several large units successfully supplying mining operations in the polar regions of Canada. Of course Nicola Tesla needs to be mentioned, the genius who brought us AC technology that is now the basis of all power generation and distribution grids, but was dumped by his sponsor Westinghouse, when it dawned on the industrialist that his far-reaching inventions would empower the consumer to generate his own energy, free of charge.

How could he (Westinghouse) have turned that into a profit?

Tesla reportedly drove around in a black Packard convertible that he had converted to "free" (non-entropic) energy.

It was an "auto-mobile" in the truest sense of the word.

We could live in unprecedented wealth, free of fear of manufactured energy crises and with a drastically reduced impact on the resources of our planet – be it raw materials that are presently used to manufacture burning fuels for the obsolete entropic technology we are still forced to use, or the pollution of oceans and the atmosphere.

There is certainly no need for atomic energy, the ultimate in scalar pollution. The true danger of atomic energy is not so much the actual radioactivity that could be technically controlled, but the output in extremely negative DOR that cannot be contained by measures adopted to prevent radioactive fallout.

Interestingly, it seems that the radioactive chain reaction cannot take place in a strong positive orgone field.

Sufficient quantities of orgonite placed around nuclear power plants can neutralise the DOR output. If orgonite is placed into the cooling circuit, it allegedly stops the nuclear reaction.

While I haven't seen that happen myself, the following anecdote may serve as an indication: A member of our orgone network in Australia had it publicised.

Wilhelm Reich had a running model of an orgone motor that went missing when the FBI burned all his manuscripts after having murdered him. How sad for a man who had just escaped the murderous regime of book-burning National Socialists in Germany to the perceived Home of the Brave and Free, only to be murdered for his scientific beliefs and have his books burned Nazi-style by the murderous thugs of the FBI and FDA. Many researchers say that National Socialism was in fact introduced in Germany and the USA simultaneously in 1933, only the decoration was a bit different. Surely the gold standard was abrogated (which means that the State defaulted on its gold obligations and thereby de facto declared bankruptcy), and the constitution of the US suspended pretty much like what Hitler did in Germany.

Wilhelm Reich's son Peter, who wrote an autobiography of his childhood, mentions that a small version of the orgone motor was permanently placed on the backrest of their family car, constantly producing kinetic energy, without using any known source except the etheric energy ocean.

The free energy revolution is overdue, and will happen as soon as the majority of the population worldwide becomes aware of its potential reality and demands it to happen.

So why isn't Greenpeace promoting this?

Sadly the organised environmental movement is so heavily manipulated by the ruling elite that the words "free energy" do not even feature in any of their pamphlets.

The very best they have to offer is solar cells, wind power and limitless fear of the future(!).

Noble as many of their members' and followers' motivations may be, the established environmentalist paradigm serves the agenda of the controlling elite, rather than empowering change.

It is strange, then (or rather not so surprising), that so many of Greenpeace's leading activists and functionaries find themselves moving on to highly remunerated positions in the corporate world, last but not least in the petrochemical industry.

That's why typical "green" activists are hostile to any mention of "free energy" or "over-unity physics". Apparently they feel threatened by the prospect of a bright future with abundance, rather than fear as its defining aspect.

Don't they all just love to make us feel bad?

Luckily the research into free energy does not stop, despite the total lack of official or corporate funding, and the inventors have learnt a lesson. Those who were killed, ostracised, socially and economically ruined, had all made one common mistake: they had the naïve belief that you invent something that solves a lot of the most pressing problems of humankind, patent it and get rich on the royalties. In other words: they believed in the system.

Unfortunately, the system did not reward that belief.

The new generation of inventors has drawn a lesson from that experience: all development is shared as an open source project.

This is definitely true for the orgonite network, where Don Croft has published all his inventions for free perusal, without even trying to turn them into something proprietary for himself. This may well be the secret of why we are still alive and the network ever-expanding.

It just doesn't pay to kill any one of us (although I'm sure some of the guys in the secret elite would love to do just that), because we have no secrets, and the only effect it could have would be an enormous confirmation of what we're doing, even if at a gruesome price.

The undeniable reality of the paranormal

What was life? No one knew. It was undoubtedly aware of itself, as soon as it was life; but it did not know what it was.
Thomas Mann, The Magic Mountain

I do not claim to be an expert in this field, but the book would be incomplete without mentioning the link between orgone energy and the PSI phenomena.

The phenomena of extrasensory perception, telepathy, time travel et cetera have been snubbed (at least officially) by the scientific establishment, especially in the 20th century. Nevertheless, these phenomena are facts of life. There is not a single cultural tradition on this planet that would not boast a rich experiential knowledge of PSI phenomena. Contrary to popular belief, all major military and economic powers have done extensive research into this area.

If what Wilhelm Reich called orgone is nothing but the unlimited potentiality of consciousness, able to manifest into matter or action, if the linear flow of time is an illusion as quantum physics and relativity suggest, then these things sound a lot less unscientific than you might have thought at first glance.

The Soviets have invested billions of roubles (before their economy and currency became greatly devalued in the late 1980s) in this research.

In 1939 the Soviet scientist

Semyon D. Kirlian discovered a method that allowed him to photograph what he called the bioelectric fields of plants and animals. This technology was developed by the Soviets into an art of its own. They produced stunning photography showing, among other things, that the bioelectric fields continue to be present after a leaf has been cut or a limb amputated.[22]

We believe that what Kirlian photography was able to visualise through the technical medium is nothing but the bio-energetic field or aura that many sensitives can perceive directly without the help of machines.

The Eastern Bloc researchers went much further than that by scientifically testing telepathy and – of course – its potential military applications. Psychic mediums were trained to send short messages in Morse code to another medium in a submarine submerged under the polar ice cap. The messages were repeated a few times and could be decoded with the help of mathematical statistical methods without error.[23]

The CIA has used trained psychics for espionage and other purposes, and the technique of remote viewing has been developed to a protocol that can apparently be learnt by very ordinary people, like me and you, who have not shown any special psychic abilities before. If you do an Internet search on "remote viewing", you will find that it's being taught by a lot of Ex-CIA and other guys. It's not a big secret any more.

If you have seen the movie "Minority Report" with Tom Cruise, consider that to be a documentary.

Most interestingly the Russian and Czech researchers who were interviewed by Ostrander and Schroeder, referred to Wilhelm Reich's orgone theory, orgone being the medium in which the instantaneous transmission of thought takes place.

As orgone is assumed to be mass-less energy, very similar to what advanced physics calls the quantum potential, transmission of information in this medium has been observed to be instantaneous and not bound by the alleged cosmic speed limit of the speed of light, postulated by Albert Einstein.

The concept of distant healing is very familiar to any shamanic tradition worth the name, of course, as most of you probably know.

Affecting a person or the outcome of certain events over a distance is the daily bread of hundreds of thousands of traditional healers (sangomas) in Africa. I have met a few genuine ones and have no doubt that they know what they're doing.

You will not be surprised to hear that in our experience orgonite greatly enhances the potential for distant healing, as it makes the "sending person" more aware of their own energies.

Orgone activists who are concerned not only with healing their environment on a physical level, have developed a technique of group healing sessions over the Internet. These have become known as Chatblasts, because ordinary chat software is used to

31

bring the group together.

Chatblasts are used to go after the overt and hidden members of the ruling elite and neutralise their negative intent before they can create new horrible events like 9-11 or the artificial tsunami that devastated Java on the 25th of December 2005.

THE ARSENAL OF THE PEACEFUL ORGONE GUERRILLA

What it's all made of: Orgonite

Orgonite is a matrix of metal particles suspended in resin. Normally the mix should be 50/50 by volume. Other than the layered structure of organic and metallic substances in Reich's original ORACs, which concentrate orgone inside a box, this matrix has a generally vitalising effect in all directions. Our explanation is that it works like multiple ORACs in all directions, thereby converting stagnant (DOR) energy back into spiralling positive energy flow. This is the secret of the user-friendliness of all devices built with orgonite; they cannot concentrate DOR!

This is often hard to understand for people who have spent considerable time researching the classical devices invented by Dr. Reich. So, some of the more orthodox "orgonomists" (every great thinker unwittingly creates his orthodoxy after a while), have issued misguided warnings against the deployment of orgonite devices, thereby completely misrepresenting what orgonite devices achieve and how they work.

The Don Croft Cloudbuster

Orgonite CB from Orgonise Africa

The Don Croft-style orgonite CB or chembuster consists of 6 copper pipes 28mm (2 3/8") in a circular placement. Length approx. 1800 mm (6'). These are mounted in an orgonite base of approx. 9l (2 gal).
We use normal household buckets as moulds. Each pipe has an end cap at the bottom and a double terminated crystal mounted in that end cap. The crystal works as an amplifier of the energy exchanged through the pipe.

Strong positive effects have been observed for distances of over 150 km, after placing a CB.

Unlike the Reichian CB, the Croft

CB is not so much meant to be used for active weather manipulation, but rather as a general healing tool that needs no attendance or operating. It will just create a positive orgone field in its wider surroundings, stimulating self-healing processes on all levels: climatic, biological and mental (!).

Contrary to what many people think and even publish on the Internet, an orgonite cloudbuster does not need to be grounded or even to stand on soil. Frequently we find alterations to the original design that are promoted as being "better" than the original design by Don Croft. So far, very little of this has been demonstrated to be true.

We recommend that you stick to the original, which is amazing in its simplicity.

The Holy Hand Grenade

The Holy Hand grenade

The somewhat warlike name, "Holy Hand Grenade", is borrowed from Monty Python. (The holy grail)

An HHG is the perfect, personal orgone generator for house and garden, but can also be used to revitalise natural vortices or neutralise strong DOR emitters in the environment.

It is made from an orgonite cone, and has 5 crystals to draw in and diffuse energy.

Four crystals are placed in a cross formation at the bottom (tips pointing outward, if single terminated), and one in the top, pointing upward. Originally the HHG was designed to neutralise microwave towers as well, but it was soon found that for most simple microwave towers, much less is needed and since there are so many of these towers, we have to use our resources sparingly.

A Holy Hand Grenade is very powerful. We have had strong visible effects by placing 2 of them at more than a 2 kilometre distance from an inaccessible mountain top array in Uganda.

The Tower Buster

The Tower Buster is the standard ammo for all applications in the life of an "orgone guerrilla".

It can be used in any place where negative energies need to be revitalised.

Originally devised for neutralising cellphone towers, it is great for water gifting, busting of Masonic halls, police stations, prisons, ritual murder sites, soiled natural energy vortices, battlefields, concentration camps, cemeteries, churches, radio and TV stations and other places where daily indoctrination and mind control take place.

Typical TBs

Put a few around your house and garden as well as on your TV screen, computer monitor, electrical and water inlets.

The tower busters shown here are made in simple muffin forms and weigh approx. 3-4 oz. (100-120g).

Plastic cups can also be used, or almost anything else that will hold a bunch of metal shavings and some resin until it is set.

The crystals used here can be of low grade and breakage is absolutely fine. We also put amethyst and often pyrite dust inside, as that makes the energy stronger.

One or 2 TBs hidden near a normal microwave tower will normally be enough to neutralise it with visible and instantly noticeable effects.

Either dig it in with a small garden shovel or find a nice undisturbed hiding place. The environment will say "Thank You".

It is really a universal tool!

We have probably distributed more than 10 000 of them on our various expeditions all over Africa.

The effects are just amazing

The Earth Pipe

Earth pipes are a recent addition to the arsenal. Their main purpose is the neutralisation of threats from underground. Whether you believe in aliens or not is up to you, but there's a lot of DOR already coming out of the underground military installations of your own government.

The earth pipe is a hollow copper pipe, approx 13" with a 5" orgonite plug.

A single terminated quartz crystal with a special coil is inserted, pointing from the plug towards the hollow end.

Earth pipes in the making

The pipe is driven into the soil with the hollow end pointing downward.

Wherever you notice particularly nasty energies and there is no visible source for that above ground, caution demands hammering a few earth pipes into the ground.

The Etheric Stick Hand Grenade

The ESH is similar, only we embed it in the muffin form we also use for TBs.

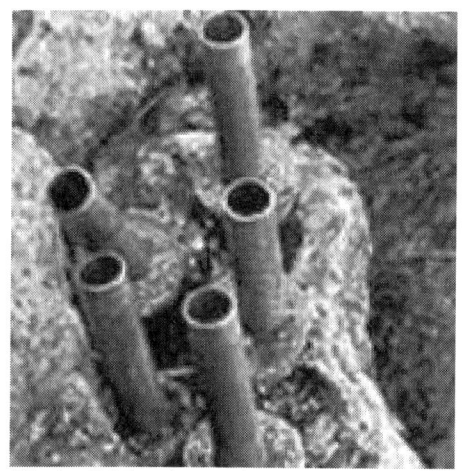

Etheric stick hand grenades

It's a copper pipe half filled with orgonite and is especially used for water gifting, that is, re-vitalisation of water bodies, rivers, lakes, the "seven seas", and so on.

It has a nice balance for throwing. The effect of the orgonite seems to be amplified by the resonant cavity of the hollow pipe section.

This is apparently a similar effect to what happens in the pipes of a cloudbuster

The "etheric stick hand grenade" is in fact a further development of the earlier "pipe bomb" that was just a piece of copper tube half filled with orgonite.

I came up with the idea by accident, when making pipe bombs, because I found it easier to make them when the bottom end was already closed because it was embedded in a TB.

It is useful that they then not only have better throwing properties, but they also seem to act faster than the mere "pipe bomb" because of the additional orgonite.

The Orgone Zapper

This list would not be complete without mentioning the orgone zapper, which has become an important tool in the orgonite community. Of course this little device would warrant a book of its own, but I think that book should be written by Don Croft, who developed all the principles of the orgone zapper in his famous Terminator II model.

The zapper is a simple but very effective bioelectric device. It is based on the lifelong research of Dr Hulda R. Clark who has published her findings in the book The Cure of all Diseases and other subsequent books. Dr Clark, like many other researchers, has found that a weak current of pulsed DC kills parasites in the body.

This includes all types of worms, bacteria, viruses and fungi.

Dr Clark, a biologist and natural healing practitioner, has studied parasites all her life and the zapper was only the last step in her evolving treatment philosophy.

She arrived at the conclusion that practically all diseases are caused either by parasites or toxins.

The US Center for Disease Control (CDC) has found that the average American carries a weight of 500g of living parasites. Toxins in our food, household chemicals and the environment weaken the barrier of colon against penetration by intestinal worms and other parasites.

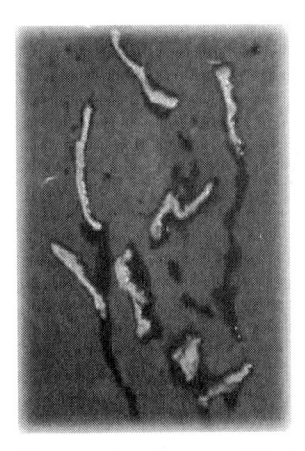

Photograph of worms killed in the first few minutes of zapping during a colonic irrigation treatment. Photo: Don Croft

Major sources of toxicity are dental amalgams, which should be removed immediately and replaced either by gold fillings or modern compound ("white") fillings.

Zapping has been shown to be effective in connection with cancer, HIV/AIDS, herpes, organ transplant rejection, viral hepatitis, sinusitis, warts, psoriasis, influenza (the genuine one), general weakness of the immune system, PMS, and many other conditions caused by parasites.

History of bio-electrification

Apart from Hulda Clark, other researchers have arrived at similar conclusions. In the fall of 1990, two medical researchers, **Drs William Lyman** and **Steven Kaali,** working at the Albert Einstein College of Medicine in New York City, made an important discovery. They found that they could deactivate the HIV virus by applying a low voltage direct current electrical potential with an extremely small current flow to AIDS-infected blood in a test tube. Initially, they discovered this in the lab by inserting two platinum electrodes into a glass tube filled with HIV-1 (type 1) infected blood. They applied a direct current to the electrodes and found that a current flow in the range of 50-**100 microamperes** (μA), produced the most effective results. Practically all of the HIV viral particles were adversely affected, while normal blood cells remained unharmed. The viral particles were not directly destroyed by the electric current, but rather the outer protein coating of the virus was affected in such a way as to prevent the virus from producing **reverse transcriptase**, an enzyme needed by the virus to invade human cells.

Reverse transcriptase allows the virus to enter a human **T cell** line (called **CEM-SS),** and commandeer the DNA reproduction machinery. After using the host cell to reproduce itself into thousands of new viruses, the swollen host cell (now called **syncytia** or giant cell) will burst and spew the contents into the bloodstream or lymph system. This is how the virus spreads. Lacking reverse transcriptase, the HIV virus can't invade the host cell and it becomes vulnerable to destruction by the body's immune system. (The details of this experiment can be read in Kaali's patent application.)

All these widely published effects of zappers can be achieved with a simple zapper, without orgone components. These simple zappers are also often used to power interactive devices like the succour punch crystal or various wand designs as described in the next chapter.

An Orgone Zapper has the added benefit of subtle energy components that produce a healing energy field, aiding the organism in the process of regaining health by strengthening its own bio-energetic field (aura).

Don Croft has described the two aspects of the orgone zapper thus:

The zapper cures, orgonite heals

Orgone zappers can be equipped with different electrodes, which may have different benefits on top of the already impressive results we have observed with the standard orgone zappers. We have tried copper – which is also used in Croft's Terminator – with great success, as well as silver and gold.

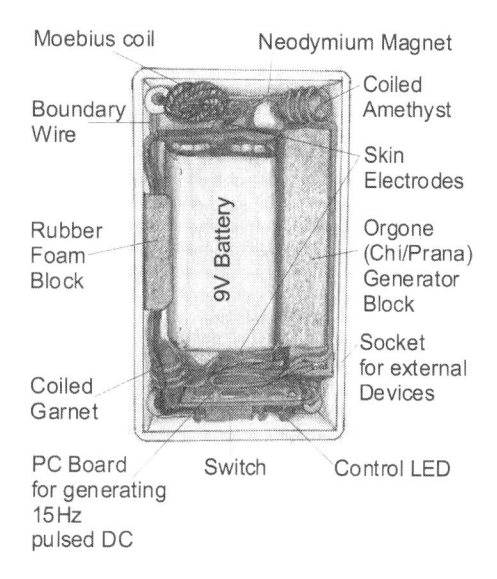

Diagram of orgone zapper components

Application of the zapper

It is recommended that the zapper be worn for at least 30 minutes in one session per day, the upper limit being dictated only by one's own feeling of comfort. It is essential to wear it every day, for at least 6 weeks, to kill off all parasites and their passenger bacteria and viruses completely.

Should you develop an uncomfortable (itching) feeling, remove the zapper and place it in a different position. In some cases after long wearing, slight burn-marks have been seen to develop. These are an indication of an over-acidic body. In this case please consult a nutritionist or read appropriate books or websites for advice on an appropriate change of diet.

Some sources do not recommend wearing the zapper while sleeping.

On the contrary, I have personally had best experiences with wearing the zapper under the foot, especially in cases of any acute infections like developing flu or a cold.

It is also highly recommended that the zapping treatment be accompanied by immune-system-boosting herbal supplements such as Sutherlandia, Moringa, African Potato etc, as well as through cleansing the intestines of parasite infestation.

Zapper confirmations

Zappers have been successfully used for at least 7 years now, and the anecdotal evidence is overwhelming. Little has been done in terms of systematic clinical studies yet, which may have to do with the status of the zapper as a product of alternative medicine, shunned without further investigation by established medicine.

In fact, I started making zappers after I saw a friend who had been diagnosed with cancer of the thyroid and was scheduled for surgery for the complete removal of the thyroid gland. She lost her cancer within 6 weeks of wearing my Don Croft Terminator.

It was just gone!

I'm getting a lot of similar feedback, but please remember: this is not considered evidence by the international medical and pharmaceutical cartel.

Since November 2003, we have been in contact with a group of medical doctors in Uganda. They have already provided some clinical data and we expect further confirmation in the near future.

This is what we have received so far:

Dr Paul Batiibwe, medical superintendent of Kiboga Provincial Hospital has a group of 44 AIDS patients who are using a zapper under his supervision. The treatment was started in November 2003. All of the patients had tested HIV positive and had other AIDS symptoms to varying degrees.

The treatment was supposed to continue for 6 months in total, after which a series of blood tests would be conducted.

Since blood tests are very expensive in Uganda, most hospitals rely on clinical reports for the evaluation of a patient's progress in healing. Some of the patients receive additional herbal supplements. All are advised to follow a healthy diet and avoid toxins.

The clinical reports are already showing great improvements in the group and Dr Batiibwe is very optimistic about the outcome of this study. Expect a bombshell!

Dr Sekagya, dental surgeon (they have the same training as medical doctors and specialise only in the last year at university), and traditional healer and president of the Traditional Healers Association (PROMETRA) for Southern,

Eastern and Central Africa, has treated 2 psychotic patients with zappers with great success. This is not surprising, when you are aware of Dr Clark's findings that schizophrenia and psychosis are caused by brain parasites.

Dr Kayiwa has treated a female private patient diagnosed with AIDS and with HIV positive blood test results. The clinical symptoms (skin lesions, et cetera, low energy, low appetite) have disappeared and the test results are now NEGATIVE.

Many more anecdotal confirmations were relayed to me during my short stay in February 2004 by people to whom we had given zappers in November.

In recent months the case of Mr Nathan Kagina has created some excitement in Uganda. He was on the brink of dying from AIDS when he started using an orgone zapper (a Don Croft Terminator). Within 6 weeks, he had recovered completely and is now responding to blood tests as HIV negative. His case was published in all major Ugandan newspapers, and has led the Health Department to acknowledging the zapper as a legitimate treatment for HIV/AIDS. Nathan Kagina is a Ugandan citizen who recovered completely from full blown AIDS, using one of our zappers. Here is his story:

Hello,

Yes, I am Nathan Kagina and I did promote the Terminator on National T.V., Radio, and Newspapers [here in my home country of Uganda].

The response and requests for more information and availability is overwhelming. Uganda has a population of about 30 million people and 20% are now living with HIV/AIDS and need this treatment.

The government chemist, Minister of Health, Dr Grace Nambatya Kyeyune, has now included the ZAPPER for HIV treatment in Uganda, officially, on the basis of my own research, testimony and case study.

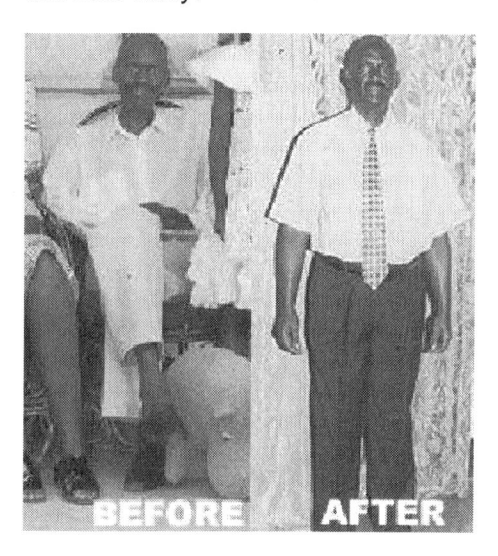

The Zapper is amazingly the most important scientific discovery since the Atomic Bomb but based on laws of magnetism.

In just six months of using the Zapper my viral load fell from millions per sample to an undetectable level.

This is bad news for the drug cartel and good news for millions living with HIV/AIDS, world-wide.

Thank you for your quick response and for your offer to give me a couple of Terminators.

Attached, find photos taken on the point of death (a memory photo with my wife and children) then the second photograph, after recovery.

Thank you DON for saving my life!.

Kind regards,

Mr Nathan Kagina, P.O. Box 16264 Kampala, Uganda

Email: nathan_kagina@yahoo.co.uk

Tele: +256782690197

History and theory

When Nathan wrote this letter to Don Croft, he believed that he had used one of Don's Terminators. We later learnt that he had used one of ours, which of course makes no real difference.

He had been treated by Dr Rushidie Kayiwa who, among other doctors in Uganda, has been using Don's and our zappers successfully to treat AIDS and other serious conditions.

In the long run, the truth cannot be suppressed, however hard they try. If it works, it works.

Since zappers are not registered medical devices in most countries, usage can only be on an experimental basis with no medical benefits promised whatsoever.

The harmlessness is pretty well established after tens of thousands have used zappers worldwide, and electrical stimulators with much higher voltages and currents have been registered as safe for use in all countries.

Interactive Tools: SP-Crystals and Power Wands

A while after the growth of the gifting network, active gifters complained about increasing molestation by all kinds of agents on their tours. Apparently a lot of electronic surveillance and psychic interference was going on.

Since Don had already used Mobius coils as a scalar field generator in his zapper designs, it was a logical step to wrap a larger Mobius coil around a crystal and pulse it through a zapper circuit.

This set-up was tested by many sensitives in the network and proved to have very helpful properties.

It created a white noise type of scattered scalar electromagnetic field that cancelled out most modes of electronic surveillance and psychic interference.

On the other hand, it excited the crystal to vibrate at such an intensity that even a relatively insensitive person like myself could feel it.

If you have ever played an electric guitar and used one of the many distortion gadgets, you will know that a rectangular wave has unlimited overtones, thus creating vibration over the whole frequency spectrum.

SP Crystal

This was found to enhance the usability of the crystal for distant healing and energy sending purposes.

Since the hypothetical "other side" was resorting to increasingly mean occult tactics to stop our budding effort from succeeding, it was found that we needed to "strike back" on the etheric plane.

This was the birth of what we now call "chatblasts".

Chatblasts are Internet-based sessions of several people. In order to be successful at least one or, better still, 2 or more accurate psychics have to be present in such a session.

We identify targets in the occult hierarchy of the New World Order and blast them with energy, often neutralising them completely, or at least their evil intent.

Somebody else will hopefully come forward with an account of this new and successful type of etheric warfare. In the meantime a lot of episodes from the Ethericwarriors chatblast moderated by Don Croft can be found in Don's Internet Forum.[24] A very accurate psychic in our network, who calls herself Dooney in the forums, has opened her own psychic coaching website where basic blasting techniques can be learnt.[25]

The Power Wand is a further development of the principles already explored in the SP-Crystal technology.

A very large crystal, preferably longer than 160mm and about 40mm thick, is coiled with 6 or more moebius knots. This is then embedded in an orgonite matrix contained in a large copper tube. (We use 76mm diameter, 300mm long.)

Compact PW with external zapper

Additional hematite and garnet beads give it more power, as does an additional large amethyst crystal next to the Quartz crystal's tip. Of course the theme can be varied, and over time we have made smaller wands in different sizes that can easily be carried around in a coat pocket.

We call them Miniwands.

II. THE QUESTION OF PROOF: DOES THIS REALLY WORK?

Which science do you mean? (A reflection on principles)

"As we have seen, the basic tenet of quantum physics is that we are not discovering reality, but participating in its creation"
Michael Talbot (The Holographic Universe)

I am often asked by interested people, or outright sceptics, whether I can prove what I say about the wonderful effects of orgonite and, yes, I accept the necessity of proof. Before we get to the actual proving part, a short excursion into the nature of science is necessary to clarify some very basic concepts and common misconceptions about science and what constitutes scientific work.

Until about 1930, most fields of science were still wide open to debate. Intelligent discussion took place between private scholars and academics, independent researchers and entrepreneurial inventors.

At that time some basic concepts were still undecided, such as is there an ether? – a question that was interestingly answered affirmatively by Isaac Newton, who is widely regarded as the inventor of the mechanistic world view.

Of course each time had its established dogmata, but with hindsight we can see that none of them ruled for ever. The truth about science is that it's no more and no less than mankind's collective attempt to understand the world in which we live.

At least in my time of going to school, we still learnt some basic principles of scientific honesty. Let's have a look at how the scientific community upholds these values.

We were told that a single experiment can prove a whole theory to be wrong, even if it's the presently held belief of the majority of scientists. My feeling is that findings that contradict present scientific belief systems are just declared non-existent, at least in public. For example: the UFO-phenomenon, psychic abilities and extrasensory perception, healing successes of diseases deemed "incurable" with non-conventional methods or successful demonstrations of free energy devices that tap into the unlimited reservoir of non-entropic energy.

We were also told that science is free and that every person is entitled to conduct his or her own research into whatever pleases his or her mind.

The freedom of science was said to be intimately linked with the freedom of speech, and guaranteed by all major constitutions of (so-called) democratic countries.

The reality is that an impenetrable cartel of interlinked institutions today decides what is acceptable science and what is "lunatic fringe".

For "professional scientists" who depend on institutional funding in order to do their research and maintain a living, it has become very dangerous to veer outside the box of allowed thoughts and concepts.

The effective and all-encompassing censorship goes further, of course, because only devices or procedures that can be described and tested in the language of "cartel approved science" can get certifications that enable them to be traded or advertised publicly.

This means that all inventions or observations that have been confirmed by the sound observation of sober and mature people are virtually non-existent, as long as they are not approved by the ruling octopus of thought control.

It is a devilish loop of self-reinforcing power, suffocating and eliminating all dissent without too much effort.

The fact is, however, that the evidence of suppressed phenomena, as mentioned above, is irrepressible. An increasing number of people are becoming aware of spiritual and non-mechanistic aspects of our reality that need explanation and ask for reconciliation with our acquired knowledge, as taught in schools and universities.

When you read older scientific texts, regardless in what discipline, you will also notice that until the onset of World War II, a different scientific method was still widely practised: intelligent observation and speculation!

The rule of the mechanistic double blind test was not yet firmly entrenched.

It is obvious that mainstream science has been following an ever more dissecting and isolating trend towards simple provable facts, away from looking at "the bigger picture".

Statistics have become the new venerated idols. Has this increased our understanding of nature? Toxic medications for AIDS or cancer are presently approved on the basis of (often manipulated) double blind studies that show a statistical short-term improvement in 55% of all tested cases, while 45% of cases showed no improvement, and close observation of any person so treated would show that these medications contribute to the deterioration of the patient's general health and energy status, often causing their premature death quicker than the untreated condition would have.

It seems that the mechanistic world view has enabled us to build brilliant machines, nano-robots, computers, disposable ink cartridges and a whole civilisation of throw-away consumption to go with it, but totally obscured our vision of who we are and what we are here to do on this planet.

Observations and confirmations

When we flick a switch in our house and the light comes on, we have gotten used to the idea that the flicking of the switch "causes" the light to come on. Of course we have heard about electricity at school, or maybe we have even studied electrical engineering at a university. However, in reality we know very little about what happens to all those electrons (another metaphor science has invented) in the wiring that connects our light bulb with an electricity generating power plant, or an even more abstract entity called "the power grid". We do accept "causality", because we have experienced the coincidence of "switch flicking" and "light going on" many times.

A spectator from another civilisation who has never heard of "electricity" might rightfully doubt that the two events are linked, because he has no concept to describe it. This has often been observed wherever people from so-called primitive cultures were suddenly confronted with the refinements of modern civilisation. They would not accept our "civilised" explanation and would rather scream in panic or be extremely impressed by the obvious presence of powerful spiritual forces.

Those of us who have done extensive healing work with orgonite have developed the same familiarity with the effects our actions inevitably have on the environment. If each and every single case was looked at in an isolated fashion, as an entrenched sceptic would do out of sheer habit, these observations would be ascribed to coincidence. Only in the continuous experience of similar changes, again and again, can something like proof be established. In order to understand what's happening, one has to return to an older understanding of scientific work.

It can best be described by the following sequence: observation, intelligent speculation and verification by repeated observation.

The effects of orgonite manifest on different levels and can therefore be demonstrated in different ways. The list below is probably incomplete, but will give you an indication.

- Visible perception of cloud changes after gifting
- Visible dissolution of chemtrails
- Significant weather changes over a longer period
- Increased plant growth and animal health
- Subjective impressions after revisiting an area that has been orgonised previously
- Aura photography
- Perception of energy changes by sensitives
- Behaviour changes: people becoming more friendly and constructive in their dealings with each other. Reductions in crime and violence.

Cloud changes

Cloud changes are most dramatic in situations where the condition before gifting is worst. That is, in highly DOR-infested environments, like massive microwave transmitter arrays, radar or military installations.

Here is an example of how the

Observations and confirmations

sky is affected by HAARP activity and how it quickly transforms as soon as some orgonite is placed near the source of the interference.

Some rural HAARP array before busting...

...and after

The stunning transformation above happened on our Kimberley tour in January 2005. It is exemplary, and you will find many such examples in our expedition reports further down.

Dissolving of chemtrails

This dramatic transformation of a sky that was completely stuffed with a HAARPed up soup of sprayed chemicals happened within the breathtakingly short timespan of 30 minutes. This was over the city of George in the Western Cape province, Easter 2005. Again, it's only one of many examples.

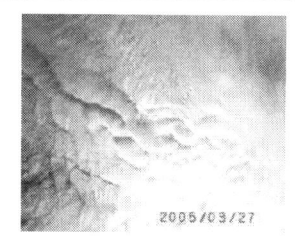

HAARP above George

HAARP dissolution after 5 min

After 10 min: Cumulus forming from dissolving HAARP-carpet

Another 5 min later

After 20 minutes: mostly gone

45

Significant weather changes over longer periods of time

When we started our large-scale busting activities, drought warnings with forecasts of potentially 10 million dead from starvation were the order of the day. (See page 92 ff)

Through strategic intervention in sensitive spots, we were able to prevent this scenario from unfolding.

Since then, we had a constant build-up of more and more abundant rainfall in the larger region. Some were spectacular, like the all-time record rainfall in Namibia, the year after we did our "operation desert rain". The rainfall was the highest since the beginning of meteorological measurements about 150 years ago.

Similarly spectacular were the results of our Western Cape tour, where the weather was so perceptibly changed (in fact restored to its "pre HAARP" pattern) that a resident told me 2 years later how he had noticed the change back to normal about Easter 2005 when we had done our tour. (See page 167 ff.)

For a more in-depth discussion of the rainfall patterns in relation to our busting activities, please also look at pages 212 ff and 229 ff.

I am presenting the whole of our expedition reports as a body of evidence for the profound and consistent changes that massive and large area orgonisation yields.

A lot of the change is difficult to prove with hard numbers. You will feel a general freshness in the atmosphere, an increase in the number of days with beautiful skies with well-articulated cumulus clouds over the foggy and hazy days. In addition, the days with smog are becoming much less frequent over large industrial centres.

Increased plant growth and animal health

We have found that wherever we planted sufficient amounts of orgonite, plant growth always exploded.

Anecdotal evidence can be gained from the fact that we lived in three different houses when we started our orgone activities, and always took over the gardens, which were in a somewhat neglected shape. Soon after we deployed our customary overdose of orgonite, birds started flocking in and plants suddenly grew to enormous heights.

Friederike with giant sunflower, early 2006

Some members of the orgone network have done comparative

studies with HHGs in flower or vegetable beds. The plants close to the orgonite always grew faster and bigger.

The most obvious beneficiary of this effect is, of course, the farmer.

Let's hear it in the words of James Moffet, accomplished organic farmer from the Free State province of South Africa (see also page 104):

"We positioned the CB in the garden with instructions to point the array at developing clouds. Within the week, the first rain fell, breaking the drought and these continued regularly until late May when our rain ends for the summer season.

The Moffet family with the CB in front of their farm house

While Georg stayed with us, he treated numerous cell- and radio-phone towers in our area by placing his orgonite discs at the bases of the towers. The impact of this drive has been amazing as mentioned above, in terms of rainfall, which we also experienced at Kirklington. Further to that I have seen a definite improvement in human, plant and animal health on the farm. This was aided by placing orgonite discs all around the perimeter of Kirklington and seeding dams with the discs. The biggest visual impact has been on the farm community, including myself: a new openness, combined with renewed trust and a phenomenal feeling of love has entered and permeated our lives. The result: a farm filled with happiness, joy, sharing and love. Our thanks to Georg and Friederike."

Subjective impressions after revisiting an area that has been orgonised previously

One of the best possible confirmations one can get is to revisit a previously treated area after one year, at exactly the same time of the year.

Apart from the changes around the places where we've lived, we've had that chance twice so far and the results were stunning in both cases.

The first was a revisit to the Kruger Park exactly one year after we had done the adjacent areas and left a CB at Timbavati, a private concession bordering on the Park. (See page 98)

When we had arrived there first in December 2003, all was bone dry and the bushveld seemed to be dying. A year later, just before Christmas 2004, we paid a visit to nearby Skukuza camp and found the whole area lush and green. The difference was just stunning. Wildlife seemed to prosper and we were even washed away in our tents by a hefty 65-mm downpour.

A similar observation was made in the Matatiele area, which we had thoroughly gifted in January 2006 (see page 203). We passed through the same area at the end of December of the same year, just before New Year. The changes and the gratitude of our local contacts were amazing.

With the wide areas we've covered on our expeditions and difficulties in communication with most of the local people we meet on our trips, it is not easy to keep tabs on all developments, but these two may serve as an example.

Aura photography

Gerald Bini from Australia has managed to capture the energy emanation of a simple HHG on photographic film, just by using highly sensitive film in a completely darkened room.

Aura photo by Gerard Bini

Perception of energetic changes by sensitives

Many people can see auras. This ability is actually much more widespread than generally assumed. One can even train that capacity by means of certain meditative exercises.

I have come in contact with many sensitive healers since we started this activity.

Most prominently, I once asked Caroline, an accomplished intuitive healer, to accompany me on a busting expedition around her area.

There was a giant round concrete tower with several platforms speckled with different microwave transmitters just a few hundred metres behind her property.

I asked her to describe her impression of the radiation around that tower.

She described it as a flattened ball of blackness, not unlike a large melon. The ball of blackness was crisscrossed by little light grey veins, similar to pieces of black marble with very light veins.

We approached the tower and surrounded it with TBs.

While approaching the still unbusted tower, Caroline was experiencing anxiety and shortness of breath.

After we had surrounded it with the orgonite, she said those symptoms had stopped.

Retreating some distance and looking back, she described the following new picture:

The blackness was now confined to the immediate surroundings of the panels. The wider aura had assumed a positive colourful radiance.

On another day I took her out to some hills in Pretoria that were rumoured to be extraterrestrial underground bases.

Now you may or may not believe

Observations and confirmations

in such beings. For some sensitives they are a clearly perceptible reality. They seem to reside on a different frequency range to our normal reality and hence are perceptible only to sensitives who receive impressions in that higher frequency range.

Whether they are really extraterrestrial, or just other dimensional, may be a futile question. All cultures before the onset of western rationalism had contact with and various accounts of such beings.

These little wooden depictions of what modern Ufology calls "grey aliens" abound all over Africa. These come from Cameroon.

Some of them are negative and some positive.

These were apparently of the negative variety.

As we approached the place Caroline reported great activity and apprehension, much like a beehive that's under threat.

When we went to the top of the hill and placed some orgonite, the activity subsided completely.

Apparently, negative other-dimensional entities cannot stand positive orgone energy.

Similar observations have been made and reported on various internet forums.[26]

Behaviour changes

A little anecdote may illustrate this aspect of orgone energy:

Two or 3 years ago we left a cloudbuster with a man called Christo. He runs a horse trail operation in Mpumalanga, in a small village near Nelspruit.

He used to run this jointly with his long-term girlfriend Merle, who is also an avid horsewoman.

As happens in life, somehow their intimate relationship fell apart and over time they were estranged, but they were still stuck with the jointly owned business that they had built up together.

Christo and his CB

Exactly at that time we asked Christo if he would host a CB for us, because we wanted one in that area. He agreed and we planted it in his veggie garden behind the

49

house. We have been going there for horse riding over the years and revisit the place at least once or twice a year.

On our next visit we noticed that Merle was gone and Christo was living there with his new girlfriend (who, by the way, is an intuitive healer).

He told us that he felt the cloudbuster had changed the energy of the place so much that it suddenly became easy for him and Merle to let go of all thoughts of revenge that are often typical for couples who are breaking up.

She found a new partner, settled into a new life, and allowed Christo to continue his horse riding operation, which he runs with excellent skill and all his heart.

All business issues were settled amicably.

This is only one of many similar stories I have heard.

I know it may sound like a tall order to you, but I feel that the new spirit of optimism that permeates South Africa has something to do with the blanket cover of orgonite we have established there over the last 5 years.

When I had finished the basic coverage of Johannesburg in 2003, the incidents of serious crime dropped by 13%, for the first time in years in the city which is often dubbed the "murder capital of the world".

The general observation is that orgonite has a distinct effect on consciousness. This is the reason why we constantly gift places of bad mental energies. Prisons, police stations, Masonic lodges, places of mind-controlled religious worship, places of human sacrifice and places where great wrongs or acts of barbarism have been committed, such as battlefields, concentration camps, et cetera

We have also found that placing a few orgone generators in any work environment can transform the place greatly.

Three years ago, a friend who works for a major software and network company in Johannesburg, placed some HHGs in the access flooring and server room of that company.

The room where he worked had been painted in grey and beige and made an oppressive impression on me on previous visits.

When I came back a few months after the gifting, they had repainted the office in "happy" colours and the general atmosphere was cheerful. Even the tone between the employees seemed to have changed.

Just a coincidence? Of course every single anecdote can be dismissed as just that. I would be stupid if I denied that.

The only way for you to find out is by trying it yourself.

And this is the foremost truism of this whole movement:

Don't believe anything I say or anything anybody else says – try it out yourself!

BUSTER'S DIARY: THE ORGONISE AFRICA EXPEDITIONS

How it all started

During the years 2000 to 2002 I started developing an increasing interest in alternative history and border sciences. As with most people who are ready to accept this type of information, reading was at first chaotic, and discernment between revelations of truth and disinformation had only just begun.

I started replicating free energy experiments with varying success. Among these I stumbled over Don Croft's cloudbuster information on Stephanie Relfe's website **www.metatech.org**.

Strangely enough, I had been familiar with the work of Dr Wilhelm Reich since I was 14 years old, but while his psychological work had left a great impression on me, I had never known what to make of his latter orgone research, because it seemed so far out to me at the time.

Now here was something simple and straightforward, an instruction to build a powerful new type of cloudbuster for relatively little money.

I started corresponding with Don Croft and got 3 of his excellent orgone zappers of the Terminator II model from him.

I was fairly impressed with those zappers when a 60-year-old female friend, who had been diagnosed with cancer of the thyroid, was completely cured within 6 weeks.

I know that people go to prison nowadays for making such claims, but Norma's cancerous growth was completely undetectable after 6 weeks of zapping and taking a bouquet of herbal food supplements.

Thus encouraged, I decided to build one of Don Croft's orgonite CBs.

The results far exceeded my expectations.

A few minutes after the resin of the CB was set and the pipes stuck in, I started noticing changes in the sky. A ring of beautifully articulated towering cumulus clouds was clearly forming around a circular, radiating blue hole.

After approximately 2 hours, this hole started to "implode", meaning that it suddenly filled up with thick, dark rain-heavy cloud, and a sudden downpour began.

The initial blue hole had been approximately 3-5 km in diameter.

I was able to observe this visible hole for months from as far as 40 km from home. It seemed also to affect the atmosphere in a less tangible way. Everything seemed to be more alive, invigorated.

At the time a small community of CB experimenters was already exchanging their experiences on a board on the Internet. In quick succession Don came up with new applications for orgonite.

First the Holy Hand Grenade, then the Tower Buster. The neutralisation of negative energy and mind control functions of the increasingly widespread microwave transmitters came into focus for the group. It became clear that a CB could only unfold its full energetic healing potential when the microwave transmission towers in its wider surroundings were neutralised with tower busters or other orgonite devices.

The new activity of "gifting" was born.

We started hiding orgonite next to those microwave towers, still shy and with a pounding heart.

I built more CBs and started visiting alternative healing fairs, where I offered my first creations for sale. There I got some early confirmations from energy sensitive healers who were visiting or also exhibiting at those fairs. They could indeed feel the energy emanating from those tools.

The following articles are published here pretty much as they were written at the time. Most of them have been previously published on my website www.orgonise-africa.net as well as on www.ethericwarriors.com.

Zimbabwe, September 2002

Our first Orgonise Africa CB outside South Africa now stands in Matabeleland in a small farming village, about 100 km southeast of Bulawayo in the homestead of Kenny Ngwenya.

He had taken an interest in the CB in our garden where he came to work once a week. When he told me he wanted one at home in Zimbabwe, I immediately agreed and suggested we go there together.

Kenny, his brother and me

It was properly inaugurated by a feast that involved slaughtering and consuming a goat, and drinking lots of African sorghum beer.

Dancing and singing went on the whole afternoon under the able guidance of Mama Ncube, a sangoma (traditional spiritual healer) and one of the famous rain queens of Ingelele.

We believe we must work with the traditional healers who have been conducting rainmaking ceremonies for millennia.

Ingelele is a part of the famous

Matopos hills, which have been regarded as holy forever.

Mama Ncube

They abound with the most beautiful cave paintings by early Stone Age Bushmen that can be dated back to more than 10 000 years ago.

San painting in the Matopos hills

Every year in August rainmaking ceremonies that are attended by thousands of people are conducted by the rain queens.

We were not allowed near the holy place this time by the custodian sangoma Abraham Ndlovu but, with our new friend Mama Ncube, we hope to put a CB right there, where I assume a very strong energy vortex exists.

I guess in Africa one has always to look where the African people conduct(ed) their ceremonies in order to find the energy spots.

The rainmaking cult of the Matopos was a focal point of anticolonial resistance by the Matabele people.

Not by coincidence, Cecil Rhodes, the "illuminated conqueror" for the British Empire of much of southern Africa, chose a fantastically picturesque site for his burial, right in the middle of the Matopos. (This after crushing the Matabele and banning them from much of the terrain by making it a National Park for white Rhodesians.) His grave was fittingly honoured by a gift of two beautiful red HHGs.

Cecil John Rhodes's grave

Of course we hid them in some nearby shrubs after this photo-op.

May his spirit be posthumously orgonised and the arrogance and destruction brought to African culture by the British Empire he represented be remedied.

There were not many cellphone towers in Bulawayo, so with our limited ammunition of about 12 TBs we took out about 50%, I would say. There were none in the countryside yet.

Zimbabwe is a wonderful country, despite the political tensions. People are very helpful and friendly. Rural people live pretty much in the traditional African way, even if they have "one leg in the city" or in South Africa.

The drought is terrible, though, and pushes large parts of the population to the edge of survival. The so-called "El Nino Phenomenon" (we think it should be named El HAARPo) has been present since 1996.

Some clouds and a fresh wind showed up after the first Zim-buster was installed, but the demonstration effect of some good rain was not granted.

Nevertheless, when we left, humidity and cloud cover were building up and by the time we departed from Zimbabwe, 6 days after installation, a hefty rain came down further south far into South Africa. In the meantime it has rained in the area. We'll have to watch it for a while in order to arrive at any decisive conclusions.

It will need more than one cloud-buster to break a year-long drought, and we hope we'll be able to work on building up a grid.

Vendaland, December 2002

We went to Venda on the evening of the 3rd of December 2002, just in time to witness the solar eclipse on 4th December. A group of Pretoria businessmen had tried to market the event as a major attraction and had set up several viewing sites in cooperation with the tribal and municipal authorities. We had arranged to stay with a traditional Venda family as guests in their home.

We brought a CB and a box full of about 70 TBs for the trip.

Our welcome was warm, although we arrived late. Our host, Richard, lives on a small (4 acre) farm plot.

In traditional African fashion, the homestead consists of several separate huts, all except one round with conical roofs. Connecting walls form different functional areas, like your "lounge", "kitchen" et cetera; quite a functional design.

Walls and even the external floors are artfully patterned with different clay pigments, the floors with combed patterns of cow-dung.

The Venda are direct descendants of the old Zimbabwe culture that created the enigmatic stone monuments of Great Zimbabwe. Their language is a derivative of Shona and they have preserved their cultural heritage far better than many other South African language groups.

Under apartheid they were an

independent homeland and enjoyed more international recognition than many others of these artificial entities. As far as I know, they boasted embassies in Switzerland, Sweden and other countries at that time.

Star patterned wall in the neighbourhood

The climate is subtropical and the natural vegetation lush and green. A small plot like Richard's – after feeding the extended family – produces surpluses of maize, mangoes, tomatoes, papaya, ground nuts and various other herbs and vegetables.

Traditional dance performance

To the great disappointment of the locals, the white visitors in their 4x4 vehicles all flocked to one site, where they stayed entirely among themselves, an unfortu-nate and typical occurrence in South Africa.

We were, at times, the only spectators for whom about 60 women in beautiful traditional dress performed their ceremonial dance. Sadly – we don't know if it was the massive load of orgonite in our vehicle, the eclipse, or just a coincidence – the sky was overcast from the morning of the 4th onward and when the eclipse occurred, accompanied by the clapping, singing and dancing of the Venda women, it was more like somebody dimming the light in a theatre. Quite eerie for a moment, but it went past very quickly. A light drizzle started coming down after the eclipse. In the afternoon we went on a very interesting sightseeing tour, guided by Richard and his brother Leonard, who is a school teacher and studying for a master's degree in public administration.

We had great talks and won some new friends. Our staying with a traditional African family caused quite a stir in the area and we received courtesy visits from the local councillor and the chief's wife (official state authority and traditional tribal structures exist in parallel in many of the rural areas).

Children in front of our holiday home

The friendliness, hospitality and courtesy of all the people was overwhelming. Our children had great fun, playing with a large gang of some 20 neighbourhood children.

The body of evidence

We handed our cloudbuster over to Richard, who was very pleased and surprised, as none of this had been arranged beforehand.

We hope it will do some good work up there. It was raining intermittently after putting the CB up and also most of the way back to Jo'burg.

Note the astonishing density of towers in this remote area. At that time we were still very stingy with our TBs and actually only bust towers, nothing else. Wherever you see a blue dot on these early pictures, there is actually a death force transmitter, aka "cellphone tower".

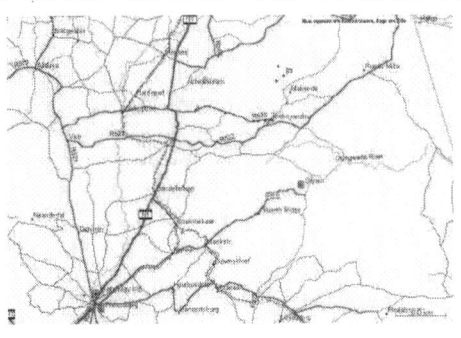

Blue dots represent busted towers. The flag symbol represents the CB.

On later trips we would become much more generous with our gifts, including rivers, streams, and other places of significance in our standard gifting programme.

Free State, December 200

In early December 2002 I had a most amazing trip to the Free State province. The purpose of the trip was to deliver a CB to our first farmer client, Ed von Maltitz near Ficksburg, close to the Lesotho border and the Drakensberg mountains.

Ed is a well-known right-wing politician and close to the AWB, or Afrikaner Weerstandsbeweging.

I do not associate with a lot of his political views, but acknowledge that he's driven by a genuine love of (his version of) Africa and is a fine, upright and honest human being, to say the least. His honesty and bluntness have earned him the respect of many black people in the country, both from the general and the political ranks. So let's suspend all judgement, especially as the cultural and political background is a bit too complex to grasp outside South Africa.

He's certainly got one point right: destroying the farmer will result in destroying the country. And that is exactly what is happening.

I sincerely believe that he will eventually come out of the right wing corner and take a lot of folks with him, thus contributing immensely to our growing "planetary rescue team" with his honesty, ability and insight.

Certainly an interesting man to meet and a very warm and welcoming host as well.

Enough of this. I needed to refer to his public standing before somebody else does and uses this information out of context.

Ed v. Maltitz in full Camo and his CB

One of those HAARP needles surrounding Ed's farm

Ed has been severely affected by weather control for 22 years and always been very outspoken about it. He phones in to a lot of radio shows worldwide and speaks about these issues. He's collected a lot of evidence as well.

I've seen the planes buzz over, unmarked of course.

They do little chemtrails. Much more of it seems to be a kind of "HAARP with wings". But Ed has photos of chemtrails as well.

He also has 5 emphatically evil towers surrounding his farm.

To put it briefly: he's up against real evil.

According to Ed, yearly precipitation was about 150% more before weather control experiments were started.

These South African government experiments were quite widely publicised at the beginning. Allegedly, they were designed to *create rain*. But strangely, they produced the *opposite result* right from the start.

They called it "cloud seeding".

I have even heard about this from a simple black man in Bulawayo, Zimbabwe.

We busted some 50 towers on our way down, all of Ed's HAARP needles, and put a CB on his ground.

A lot of dramatic stuff happened in the atmosphere, stuff I've never seen before.

Rain was still reluctant to fall over his property, apart from a few drops, but Ed (who has been looking up to the sky all his life) said it looked very good. On our way back it rained (starting with a hailstorm) all the way along the busted route.

Actually, it was a discernible strip of rain with blue sky and cumulus cloud at the fringe.

That was a most exciting result. I felt sure it must have rained on Ed's farm as well, but it didn't. He says that his place and the area around is the apex of all South African weather and that's why they're concentrating their efforts so much on his farm.

The result was that he was effectively bankrupted over the years, losing his 2000 ha farm in the process.

When rain cloud is building up, a plane always moves in, sometimes at 1 or 2 minute intervals.

After the CB was installed and the strange towers (which have no apparent justifiable function –other than creating a weather barrier) were done, we had thunderstorms building up in a semicircle around with strangest horizontal lightning discharges (also known as sheet lightning). At times it was so dramatic that I was reminded of descriptions of the last days of Stalingrad.

My feeling is that lightning has a lot to do with the orgone dynamics in the atmosphere. We would see dramatic lightning more often in the future, wherever a CB was newly introduced and started to heal the atmosphere. On the other hand, we would observe that lightning that had often been very violent over Johannesburg and Pretoria, would become much softer after we had brought out sufficient orgonite in this area to neutralise most of the DOR transmitters there.

We also saw strange rays of "blackness" coming up from the ground from a distant position. No way of mistaking sun rays, as they converged to a point on the ground.

Also, I think I really saw pure DOR very clearly for the first time. This was the day before at sunset.

The next day everything looked very different. The sky was clear and fresh, with good cloud build-up and a first hint of rain in the early afternoon. A lot of swallows were buzzing around some rocks on the property. Looking at the sky, one could also see the orgone as Wilhelm Reich has described it (white streaks and sparks, minute but visible).

All the blackness was gone. Great numbers of swallows were back in the area, diving happily up and down. Ed had pointed out that one of the symptoms of weather control was the disappearance of most of the birds...

The most amazing thing happened then, witnessed by my wife and myself: A white unmarked plane disappeared into a cloud and didn't come out. The droning noise stopped. The cloud was isolated, blue sky around. There no way the plane, which was moving fast, could have disappeared naturally. I wouldn't believe it if I hadn't seen it..

Ndebele Tour, July 2003

The Ndebele people, an offspring of the Zulu nation, are widely known for the colourful painting of their houses in geometric patterns.

Ever since a cultural event, sponsored by the Alliance Francaise, had brought us to the Ndebele village of Mabhoko, we'd been in loose contact with Angelina Ndimande, a painter par excellence.

We decided that Mabhoko would be a great place to put a cloudbuster and, of course, to neutralise all cellphone towers on the way. Mabhoko is about 90 km north of Pretoria. Amazingly, Angelina was not at all surprised when I phoned her about this. She immediately knew who we were and seemed to have no problem accepting what I proposed to her, namely to bring her a device that would hopefully help to bring more rain to her community. We were shocked to see how many towers had proliferated in the approximately 24 months since we last travelled on that route.

The stream of blue points going north-east out of Pretoria shows the suspicious density of towers. The flag is the new CB near the words Elands River. On white-owned farm land you will still find the old-fashioned pattern of a tower every 35 km on the major regional roads. This is not so in the "locations" or previous "native homelands".

Always in clusters of 3 and with a breathtaking density, the population certainly gets its daily dose. I was particularly shocked by the implications this has for our activities because it means that our busting is so far behind the real need and we must inspire more people to help us in this effort.

Map of the trip

I realised on this trip that we just cannot handle it alone.

On arrival in Mabhoko we first visited Esther Mahlangu, the world famous Ndebele painter who has exhibited the world over and has her works hanging in museums in Europe, the USA and Japan. We had a chat with her and left her a nice HHG as a gift.

Esther is also a traditional healer and was at that time involved in the initiation ceremonies of the young boys entering manhood. So her time was limited.

The body of evidence

Esther Mahlangu, Kevin and Friederike

We met Angelina at the Ndebele Foundation, a beautiful cultural centre which has been built and decorated in the characteristic Ndebele style.

Kevin in front of the Ndebele foundation

At the Foundation there is accommodation for tourists, who can participate in painting classes. Another activity is that all the accomplished painters (traditionally only women) teach classes to the village children. Artefacts, paintings on cardboard and paper, as well as various beadwork items and painted objects are available in a little shop.

After we had been treated to a cup of tea and shown the new facilities at the Foundation (last time we were there, it was still under construction), we went to the car and got out the CB.

I explained what it was and encouraged Angelina to feel the energy. She immediately adopted it with all her heart and showed her joy and gratitude in a wonderful serene way, that I've found so often with the more traditional African people. This is the reason why I prefer to work with these wonderful people. They know intuitively that this stuff works and don't need lengthy explanations because their energy sensitivity is still largely intact, despite concerted efforts to change this. For those of us white intruders who show respect for and genuine love and interest in their traditional culture and spirituality, they will always open their heart. Angelina told me that her grandfather was a sangoma (traditional healer) which didn't astonish me the least.

There was much more non-verbal understanding than anything else and it was of the most amazing kind. Nothing we said or did seemed to surprise her in the least.

Angelina – The light is shining through her!

Angelina is a very loving and bright person. I've not come across anyone like her anywhere else.

The CB is going to stay at her home and is surely in good hands there.

We went home deeply touched and happy:

Angelina, we love you!

Encounter with a remarkable man

African Depiction of Truth – Credo V. Mutwa

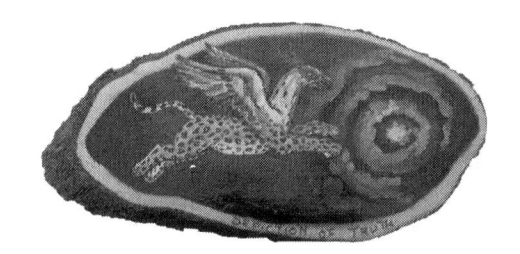

*"My child, the truth is a fearsome beast,
A beautiful beast, part eagle and part leopard.
It cannot be caged, nor can it be buried in a cage.
It cannot be hidden, but will emerge even after thousands of years."*
Credo V. Mutwa

On Friday, 27 June 2003 I was finally able to fulfil a long-held dream.

Thanks to the generous sponsorship of a forum member, I was able to donate a CB to Credo Mutwa, the official keeper of the history and healer of the Zulu nation.

I had been in contact with him since October 2001, visiting him a few times after a trip north to a place called Gianni, in connection with a later abandoned project to create a cultural village and conference centre.

Credo had been very reclusive of late and has limited contact with white people to the absolute minimum.

He has been very ill with old-age diabetes and was generally in a sombre mood.

I feel that it is the general state of affairs of his people and his culture has invoked an almost holy anger in him.

However, the prospect of bringing him some gifts gave me the courage to try and probe this veil of silence.

I had also – since the previous October – had a T2 zapper donated by Don, together with a letter from Don and some photos of Carol's trip to Kenya to hand over.

So, I was very excited when I finally got an appointment for 3pm on that Friday. I was also quite anxious.

What would the wise old man say about all these gadgets I was planning to show him, and the strange activities I was going to tell him about?

The CB was very well received and will stay in position, at a long overdue location, just west of Pretoria in a still rural area.

I showed Credo the Power Wand and he confirmed the strong energy emanating from it, but he didn't really know what to do with it.

His main interest instead focused on a giant SP-crystal, which I had brought as another present.

He asked me to press the tip of the crystal to various parts of his skull and forehead. He reported different very strong reactions at the various spots.

At the back of the skull he said it triggered strong visions. In the middle of the skull (the position of the fontanelle, or area where there is a space between the bones in a baby's skull) he said it felt as though the energy was streaming into the brain as if through a giant open hole.

Other spots reactivated memories, and sensations of taste or hearing.

He then asked his assistant Virginia to conduct an experiment with him. Pressing the tip of the SP to his forehead, he asked her to hold a corresponding crystal (not SP) to hers.

He then concentrated on transmitting various thought forms to her, which she received with 100% accuracy.

He was very reinvigorated and excited about all this and what I told him about our activities.

(By the way, this experience proves Don's point about none of the established inventions becoming obsolete, just because something new is coming up...)

After these experiments, Credo said something very moving and encouraging to me: "You are going far into the future – may I come with you?" Of course I said yes, not believing what he'd just said. At least he was not contemplating his own death any more!

Credo showed me a photo of a device he had built many years ago which apparently produces a strong healing energy field and measurable "free energy" effects.

It is a globe of strong copper rods, with various crystals, a bowl of brass filled with marula juice and a coil around the foot.

The device was able to light up the bulb of torchlight at a distance and the coil would get hot when the marula juice was poured in.

It is not a chemical battery, though, as some might think.

This knowledge has been handed down over millennia. ("The Zulu kings loved to dabble with electricity", Credo said to me on another occasion, a long time ago.) Credo refers to it as "the holy knowledge".

We agreed to build two specimens of this beautiful device together – one for each of us – very soon.

I left in singing and dancing mode, in the hope of this happening soon.

After this astonishing and special afternoon, I visited Credo a few more times. I often brought him crystals which he used for various experiments and the etheric machines that he builds.

early one afternoon.

First we went to a nearby scrapyard in order to find some additional parts that were needed.

House of the moon in Naledi, created by Credo V. Mutwa

I also brought different orgonite tools and left them with him. He referred to them as "those holy things".

Credo rummaging in a scrapyard for usable parts

Credo wolding

One of Credo's protective guardian sculptures, welded from scrap iron

Eventually he told me to bring some iron reinforcement bars and different sizes of crystals to build the Tladinyana devices mentioned earlier. This I did with great excitement, arriving at his home

The Tladinyana (the name means "little lightning" in Sesotho) is originally a Sotho (the people who inhabit the country of Lesotho and large parts of South Africa) design and was used mainly for etheric healing purposes.

It radiates a perceptible orgone field and also has a measurable electric effect. As I mentioned earlier, Credo had told me that the first one he had built some 20 years earlier was able to cause a torch light to shine without batteries.

The outer shell is almost finished

It's done

I assume that at that time torches were still made with metal casings, which would act like a capacitor in a static electric field. I was not able to replicate the effect with a modern plastic torch.

But a simple volt meter showed electric charges of up to 1 volt on different places of the metal cage.

This is difficult to explain in terms of conventional knowledge of electricity because all parts are one solid body of iron and should electrically short themselves out.

I believe that the effects noticed have something to do with static electricity, which is in fact closely connected to orgone or etheric life energy as Nicola Tesla demonstrated a century ago.

Credo allowed my to keep the Tladinyana we made together in exchange for all the other gifts I had brought him and it is now one of my most cherished possessions.

My Tladinyana

While we were sitting together on these extremely delightful afternoons, the idea was born that we should write a book together.

The theme was to be "The secret knowledge of the Zulu". I would have asked questions and recorded

Credo's answers and would then later edit the whole thing and produce the book.

Stone circle at Naledi, created by Credo Mutwa

We got around to the first chapter, which was about the role of prophetic dreams in traditional Zulu society.

Credo is the best story teller I ever encountered, and he can talk "print ready material" for half an hour at a time. It really is amazing. In that first chapter, which I still have, I did not have to change so much as a comma in the text.

Unfortunately while this was in progress, people around him began to block my access to him.

Most notably, at the beginning, by a certain Warren, an ex-mercenary with one of the infamous private security firms that are involved in so many African coups d'etat. He had somehow managed to put himself in control of Credo's worldly affairs, after originally being appointed as his bodyguard by a well-meaning American woman who had also donated a monthly stipend of 2000 US dollars for Credo, and bought a farm and a car for him. The bodyguard was hired because there had been attempts on Credo's life as a result of all the knowledge he was making public.

Somehow Warren ended up living on the farm bought for Credo and I don't think too much of his money ended up in Credo's hands either.

It is the tragedy of this formidable and highly gifted man that he always relied on white people to organise aspects of his worldly affairs. This has led to very unhealthy relationships and tragic disappointments on Credo's side.

For example, the rights to all his books, even future unwritten ones, have been appropriated by a certain woman. Credo has apparently never seen a penny in royalties from any of his widely published books, most notably the wonderful Indaba, My Children a collection of tribal mythology and oral history.[27]

Other highly recommended books by or with him are Song of the Stars[28] and Profiles Of Healing – Vuzamazulu Credo Mutwa: Zulu High Zanusi.[29]

Credo has gained a measure of fame among the alternative research community through his 6-hour interview with David Icke, in which he elaborates on traditional Zulu knowledge of the reptilian origin of the "Gods" and ruling bloodlines on earth. I can also highly recommend this video.[30]

A small chapter in this book cannot do this great man justice and the main reason for mentioning our encounters is because they have been very important to me in my development and in the unfolding of our continent-wide healing activities. Credo's books and his presence and insights in those brief moments we were able to share have inculcated a deep appreciation of traditional African spirituality and culture in me. This is not only for their power and beauty, but also because all this knowledge is vanishing fast and it is tragic that the younger generations of Africans know less and less of their own sacred traditions, especially on Credo's level of initiation into the true mysteries of this continent.

On our first trip together we went to an ancient Venda settlement where remnants of fortifications and paved places were still accessible, totally unprotected, as well as iron smelting furnaces.

Credo sat in front of the entrance and sighed sadly: "Oh, if it all could come back!"

He had seen the life that once thrived there unfold before his inner eye.

Despite all setbacks, in his strange, fruitful and inspirational life, Credo has managed to travel over large parts of the continent and confirm the unity and connectedness of all African belief systems as being essentially one and the same from South Africa to Uganda.

I have a small collection of Africana Books – accounts by early white explorers. More often than not, Credo has met these people and been to the places himself.

In one of the books I showed him he immediately identified the picture of a beautiful Zulu woman with elaborately braided hair as his Mother(!).[31]

Often when I think of him I am moved to tears of love, joy and despair, all mixed together in an intangible emotional turmoil.

"Oh if it all could come back!"

Africans are still under deep cultural shock from the advent of Western materialist culture. Only 150 years ago, they were still living in a world where the supernatural was fluently entwined with the natural, and spiritual entities were perceived to be as real as any natural phenomena.

Since the white man, the Mzungu, came and quite violently routed these beliefs and declared their age-old perceptions as null and void, Africans have taken their culture increasingly underground, losing much of its cohesion and protective value.

Nothing will bring the old Africa back as it was, but my hopes are that it will resurface after some time on a new plane of consciousness.

Africans today want to enjoy the perceived benefits of Western culture, including advanced telecommunications, cellphones, the Internet and, of course, the new shiny vehicles that Western civilisation has brought to this old continent.

But sometimes when I am travelling in the urban and rural slums in which the majority of black Africans reside nowadays, with their of ramshackle corrugated iron shacks and dotted with the ubiquitous microwave transmitters, the landscape littered with plastic bottles and bags, the signs of modern mass production, and I compare that with the dignified image of a traditional Zulu homestead of which there are very few left in South Africa, I ask myself:

"Is this really progress?"
Recently a hopeful new trend has developed amongst the children of the black elite, the ones who have succeeded in moving about in the Western "jet set".

They go back to their grandmothers and seek initiation as sangomas (traditional healers).[32]

I believe that African spirituality is irrepressible and will make it's important contribution to the development of humankind in the 21st century.

Human evolution is often compared to movement in an upward spiral. Whereas we may came back to the same point on a circle, we will do so on a different plane at every revolution of the spiral.

I am an African optimist.

Obstacle course to the Makgaben, July 2003

One of the 3 sponsorships we originally received for Namibia (that trip had to be postponed) allowed us to deploy a CB in another outlying rural area in South Africa.

The area is called the Makgaben and it is a so-called "tribal area".

Our friend Kevin had frequently visited this area 12-15 years before, amongst others with US actor Val Kilmer, but foremost with a man called Adrian Boshier.[1]

Adrian Boshier was possibly one of the first "white sangomas". After spending weeks and weeks in the bush repeatedly over many years, he gained the respect and trust of the traditional African people and was let in on many secrets. He discovered much about ancient settlements and other human artefacts that proved a much earlier occupation by black Bantu people than conveniently assumed by the white settlers who often liked to claim that they arrived almost at the same time as the Bantu. (One of those apartheid myths.)

On their trips Boshier and Kevin had always linked up with a headman (chief) named Samson, who led and accompanied them into the wilderness of the Makgaben (some 80 km northwest of Potgietersrus).

Those were the days, my friend, I'd thought they'd never end ... but end they did.

The obstacle course started with the fact that our late departure and heavy infestations of ugly towers

---

[1] A great account of the life and work of Adrian Boshier has been written by Lyall Watson: **Lightning Bird**. Also, Credo Mutwa, who met Boshier repeatedly, writes about him in **Indaba My Children**.

(that had to be neutralised) slowed us down so that we reached the target area only after dark, at approximately 8 pm.

Apparently familiar landmarks had changed to the extent that Kevin couldn't recognise the spot.

We drove way past it, still scanning the perimeter of the road. When we realised that we were lost we spoke to some white farmers on the road.

They had neither heard of an area called Makgaben, nor of a headman called Samson.

Things started getting mysterious. We drove back, me already slightly irritated.

And then it happened:

The strip of grass to the left and right of the road was used by the local population for grazing cattle, and some smaller herds were out that evening.

One of the cows suddenly decided to cross the road and – BAMMMM! – I hit it. It was moving so fast that I cannot even remember having seen it run over the road; it must have been hidden behind another cow.

Zuuusch, the radiator blows, the lights go off, silence.

Middle of nowhere.

We step out unharmed but confused. The Pajero is a mess. The cow lies 5m in front of us and is dead. (Luckily I don't have to slaughter it.) Traffic whizzes by mercilessly. All the white people shoot by without stopping. Quite scary, because we haven't managed to put up any warning signs yet, and the dark mass of the cow is still lying there.

Some friendly black people finally stop, offer help, consolation and cigarettes, which were appreciated in our state of shock.

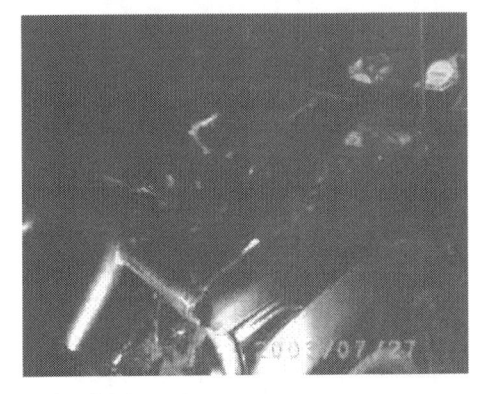

Right after impact

They help us drag the cow off the road and then amazingly I manage to start the engine and hobble the car off the road like an injured animal.

Later at the towing yard

We were towed some 150 km to Pietersburg, where we spent the night in the car in the towing service's yard. So shocked must we have been, that we didn't even notice that the windshield was missing.

In the morning I thought that

someone had pinched it from the yard while we were sleeping.

Undeterred, however, we got into a rented VW Polo and went back to complete our mission. While busting some towers in Pietersburg, recently renamed Polokwane in an attempt to erase white memory, we were greeted by a widely visible X sprayed in the sky. I couldn't help thinking that some bad boy was displaying a strange kind of humour, trying to say something along the lines of "gotcha".

Giant sprayed X – one cannot deny that "they" have some sort of dry humour

Well, we'll see who's gonna get whom in the end.

All ideas of a great hike in the wilderness were abandoned. Let's just find this Samson and give him the cloudbuster.

We went into the area again and in the daylight we finally found the man, but only after an extended search and at a totally different place than Kevin remembered.

In his memory the place was still indigenous Africa with traditional huts and an original African lifestyle.

Not so any more. Development had brought wide and straight gravel roads, ugly rectangular cement-block houses and a general aesthetic deterioration. Samson's homestead had been moved about 30 km from where it had been, away from the road and into the bush.

Finding Samson was the real shock. He is still recognised as the headman, but what had happened to him? He had almost lost his eyesight, and worse: he had lost his memory!

The only white person he could remember was a man from a big mining company who had been negotiating mining rights with them after platinum had been found in the Makgaben!

He didn't know the name Adrian Boshier or remember Kevin. Totally blanked out!

The final place for the CB

We talked to some younger men who were staying close by and found a very friendly man who was keen to be the custodian of the CB for the time being.

At least we could leave the CB in the area in good hands

We left feeling very strange; Kevin probably more affected than I because a world that he had known and loved had disappeared forever.

We were of course wondering what was going on there:

The destruction of a once vital and strong man; the total memory loss of the area; and the idea of throwing cows in our way to halt our advance. (A healer friend told me I had been "blanketed" for a split second in order not to notice the danger in time, but of course there are more banal explanations, like my anger and frustration at not finding the place etc ...) Then there was the looming encroachment of the mining company.

Traditional Africa and each and every memory of a time different from ours is wiped out at a breathtaking speed, turning the once proud owners of the land into a destitute mass of slum dwellers, disposable on any whim of the moment as useless eaters. We went home quite shocked and depressed and it took me quite a while to get over this.

Somebody really didn't want us to get there, for sure!

Uganda, travelling with the Don, November 2003

In October 2003 I learnt at short notice that Don Croft was planning a trip to Uganda in November. I asked if he minded if I came along and he agreed. Don had been in contact with various Ugandans for a while so that we were immediately among friends. The trip was an overwhelmingly positive experience.

I am using Don's own report and that of our friend Dr Batiibwe, because I couldn't improve on their narrative, even if I wanted to. All text by Don or Dr Batiibwe is set in italics. Any comments by myself are in straight text.

Proud to be a Muzungu
(By Don Croft)
Actually, I'm proud to be an American, but 'Muzungu' is the regional term for any Europoid like myself. It's not derogatory at all and apparently the word is used similarly to the way Western cultures use the term 'ET.' I love it when little kids here run up to me and say, always genuinely, 'Hello, Muzungu-how are you?' I sort of feel like a visiting spaceman, as not many Muzungus are seen in these parts. A black person is 'mudugavu,' by the way.

I've wanted to visit Uganda for most of my adult life, ever since learning from some expatriot American friends, who lived here before Idi Amin's well-funded rampage, about the gracious, talented, witty, culturally rich and resourceful people here. Winston Churchill had named this country 'The Pearl of Africa' during his visit here after World War II, and while he may have been eligible at the time for hanging due to his war crimes, his compliment was right on the mark, I can tell you.

During the course of this monologue in several parts, I'll introduce you to four of my Ugandan friends/team mates who have been instrumental in facilitating these very productive efforts on behalf of orgone and zappers, both preceding and during my too-brief visit to this wonderful country.

Certainly not least, you're probably already acquainted with Georg Ritschl, who accompanied us during the first two weeks of this East Africa gifting exposition. Dr Paul Batiibwe, who has, ten minutes ago, frankly told me that he can't figure out why I'd want to mention him at all (I told him that I'm no more worthy than he is, so 'Please don't worry about it.') may be considered the clinical, overall scientific component of this team and is currently my host and the coordinator of the field-testing work for three crowd zappers.

He routinely 'gifts' with Holy Hand Grenades, Towerbusters and Etheric Pipe Bombs during his travels whenever he encounters deserving sites and has been working extensively with Kizira, who has reluctantly agreed to let me refer to him as a 'witch doctor.'

I'll have an awful lot to say about Kizira, of course, and the unique working relationship he has with Dr P. He's one of those very rare individuals who have fully committed to applying a rare, composite gift of healing, high psychism, courage and exemplary spirituality, not to mention a profound knowledge of an extensive regional herbal pharmacopoeia.

Kizira checking out some gifts that we brought along. Photo: Dr Batiibwe

Under the circumstances, I was unable to come up with a more descriptive reference for Kizira than 'witch doctor'. (My hope is that I'll be able to purge that term of the old Hollywood and dime-novel connotations that incite apprehension.)

You can't conceive a more gentle soul than Kizira's.

Dr Rushidie Kayiwa is the fellow who laid the groundwork for our visit and made it possible for us to get right to work. This very well-rounded, well-travelled (he's fluent in English, Arabic, Finnish, Swahili and a host of regional African dialects) and well-connected physician has consistently astonished us all with both his resourcefulness and his power of friendly persuasion. Nobody ever, apparently, taught Dr K that he has limitations.

Don, Dr K and me (from right to left) Photo: Dr Batiibwe

He was the first to greet Georg and me at Entebbe International Airport after one of his close friends, who prefers to be referred to as our 'Secret Supporter' had us ushered past customs. 'Secret Supporter' had been regaled by Dr K with tales from 'The Adventures of Don and Carol Croft' on www.educate-yourself.org and obviously wanted to see our tricks first-hand. Dr K had previously given our very open-minded and inquisitive Supporter several zappers, which were subsequently distributed to trusted associates and relatives in the upper echelons of Uganda's establishment who had then gotten profound healing from diverse maladies in a short time.

Georg Ritschl of www.orgonise-africa.net graciously joined me for the first sixteen days of our multinational orgonite/zapper initiative and after our first night in Uganda we made for our Secret Supporter a couple of cloudbusters, then we got very busy busting towers the very next day, using our host's side yard as an orgonite factory for the ensuing two weeks and, of course, keeping him fully updated on our progress.

German Georg is a tower-busting fury on two legs and he also heroically participated in Uganda's mainly unregulated (by Western standards, at least) traffic 'system' throughout. He rather reminds me of the cartoon character, The Tasmanian Devil, in fact, since he rarely stops moving and planning. Thanks to his tireless efforts (and the use of an intrepid 1978 Toyota Landcruiser, compliments of our magnanimous and curious Secret Supporter) we busted essentially all of the HAARP and entropy transmitters from Congo/Rwanda to Kenya in less than two weeks and deposited the two cloudbusters in key positions in Kampala and Kisoro. Kisoro is the district that lies in the southwest corner of the country and includes a small population of gorillas and some borderline-surreal, jungle-clad towering volcanoes and dizzying roadside vistas.

After the final round of busting, last Friday, the equatorial skies over populous Southern Uganda are now uniformly pristine again. It's always refreshing to look at white, billowing cumulus clouds in an azure sky rather than the sad aerial constipation that's come to characterise the skies over most of the world's population centres since the northern hemisphere's autumn of 2001...

There are no chemtrails to speak of in Africa, except the intermittent, half-hearted ones they've lately squirted out over Johannesburg, South Africa, in beleaguered response to the good job that Georg and a few associates have done to severely insult the extensive HAARP and electronic entropy network throughout much of southern Africa.

Kampala, the capital of Uganda, is built on a procession of lush, verdant hills at the north shore of Lake Victoria and on each and every hilltop the disgusting, parasitic World Order has erected HAARP and entropy arrays. If anyone wishes to go to Africa or to any other lovely, remote area in order to escape the debilitating effects of the World Order devil-worshippers' deadening new electronic matrix, he would be grievously disappointed (unless he moves to Uganda, of course). When we got here the skies over Kampala were mostly whited out by local HAARP transmitters, which push atmospheric moisture up above the altitude where rain happens, as we've seen elsewhere. Dr P's cloudbuster is located a hundred miles west of Kampala and, of course, no cloudbuster is likely to disable the whiteout-we have to bust all of the local HAARP transmitters to get that happy result – but it has been raining sufficiently in Kampala regardless of the parasitic, global scheissvögel, thanks to his effort.

The nice thing about doing this work in Africa is that there's so much vitality in the land, water and atmosphere that it must surely take two or three times as much energy from these unsavoury Illuminati tecchies to get even minimal ugly effects in the sky, and those effects are usually localised, at best, in Africa except around Johannesburg, where there's apparently enough human misery and electronic/industrial molestation to maintain some pretty ugly skies for periods of time, in spite of Georg and friends having busted all or most of the towers in the metropolitan area by now.

My heart surely goes out to Georg, who periodically develops new methods for busting a big, blue hole over Jo'burg, only to see it get covered over again within a few days by the obsequious whiteness as HAARP regroups from his latest assault.

Thanks to his efforts, though, we have a new range of orgonite 'weapons' that we can deploy against the enemy of humanity. I'm particularly fond of his 'Stielhandgranate,' which is an etheric pipe bomb whose orgonite end is embedded in a towerbuster, and his prototype Orgone Howitzer, an orgone tecchie's delight.

Many of the lakes and rivers in Uganda are now graced with some of Georg's offerings.

The Stielhandgranaten feel awfully good to throw, by the way, though one is left with a slightly nagging feeling that it would have been more appropriate to 'pull the pin' first. His 'Orgone Howitzer' may be the proper antidote to the remote HAARP and groundwave transmitters that are still plaguing Jo'burg and Pretoria. Stay tuned to www.orgonise-africa.net for further reports on that, of course.

As in the case of Vancouver, Canada, perhaps, most of this incessant urban whiteout that occurs in spite of extensive gifting of urban HAARP and entropy transmitters may be getting accomplished by a combination of underground facilities (Extremely Low Frequency groundwave transmissions, sans towers) and scalar transmissions from remote HAARP arrays. This, in fact, apparently causes the Illuminati to overextend their reach in this case, which presents us with some intriguing opportunities if we're willing to exploit them.

Dr Paul Batiibwe had constructed East Africa's first cloudbuster six months previously and that had perhaps forestalled a severe drought and famine which had apparently been slated for this region. Due to the vitality here it only takes a minimal effort to cancel the worst effects of the World Order's atmospheric/electronic raping and plunder. Dr P did that on the eve of the equatorial June-July dry season, which then turned into a wet season. When Georg and I landed here in mid-November we were treated to such brilliant hues of green that it came close to hurting our eyes. I'd never encountered this phenomenon, though I'd travelled extensively in tropical regions.

Carol and I had busted all of the new HAARP and entropy transmitters that we encountered during our travels in Namibia two years ago. The Illuminati had then just initiated their ugly, global display at the time, so I'm sure that we were only seeing the first of their efforts in that region and there hadn't been enough of the new transmitters on the ground for them to have established the high-altitude whiteout that you and I have come to know so well where sufficient transmitters are still functioning in close proximity to each other. I bet you enjoy wiping that hideous crap from the sky as much as we do. Could you have conceived how much fun this would be before you ever heard of tower busting and cloud busting?

Another feature of Africa's vitality is the ease with which one can accomplish 'sky sculpting' with an ordinary cloudbuster. We had a chance to play around with that near Kampala in our host's side yard with the two CBs before we planted one, upright, in his garden and delivered the other one to a garden in Kisoro District.

In this case, I followed Dr Reich's recommendation to point a CB near an existing cloud in order to draw rainfall from that direction. I did it towards clouds that were in a downwind direction in order to demonstrate that rain can be gotten that way and I kept the other one pointed over Kampala in order to suppress the still-existing whiteout until we finished disabling the nationwide, east/west HAARP network after our visit to Kisoro. Our host was quite impressed and I felt like some kind of wizard, though I slyly didn't let on that this doesn't work as well in my country, where the more sluggish, ambient orgone matrix still needs a lot of healing and revitalising.

HAARP in tornado mode over Secret Supporter's house before Don started playing with the CB

Before I left home, I got kind of fat because Carol had warned me that East Africa is a place where tasty, nutritious food is scarce. She was right in her assessment, at least, regarding the nearby section of neighbouring Kenya, where she'd spent some time in a pestilential area in 2001, demonstrating the crowd zapper in a village clinic.

What she couldn't have known is that the difference between that little area and this country is quite profound. She was literally restricted to her cramped quarters after sunset due to the prevalence of aggressive, violent, male voodoo terrorists ('night runners') and that locale was generally ravaged by a combination of near-genocide by the World Order, HAARP drought and the residual fear-based magical traditions, an army of homeless, starving AIDS orphans and rampant illiteracy. But Uganda, although essentially identical in terms of natural resources and climate, has a long-standing tradition of good family relations, mutual assistance, self-reliance and literacy, which is probably why it has survived a series of British-instigated, bloody dictatorships with general magnanimity and confidence. I've long felt that the Illuminati are jealous of the Ugandans, as they apparently were of the Biafrans, hence the destruction of that progressive Nigerian community by the Illuminati's bloodthirsty, rapacious proxy Nigerian regime in the early 1960s.

I must say that I've rather been in a glutton's paradise here, because while the traditional foods in Uganda are delicious, varied and filling, I'm actually losing weight without having to exercise. I actually feel bad for Carol and wish I'd had to suffer here at least a little bit for her sake. I'm hoping that my recently acquired taste for fried locusts will get her past some of this. No, they don't taste 'like chicken;' they rather remind me of roasted pumpkin seeds.

By the time Her Royal Highness, the scaly Whore of Babylon, had thrust the similarly cannibalistic Idi Amin Dada at the peace-loving Ugandans, gave him a trunk full of blank checks, an unlimited supply of bullets, a huge walk-in freezer for human meat, and a full array of the latest torture implements, the Western world, fortunately, was no longer willing to condone genocide in Africa, so that syphilitic, brutal psychotic and former British Army

Sergeant Major, was unable to fulfil his genocidal mandate from the City of London.

AIDS, which is, of course, yet another deadly Illuminati bid to reduce the Africans to a 'manageable' population, is far less rampant here than in neighbouring Congo and Kenya, by the way. In frustration, after President Yoweri Museveni's grassroots 'Movement' successfully supplanted the most recent, well-armed and limitlessly financed proxy-monster head of state here in 1986, the banker trolls in the City of London immediately and drastically devalued the Ugandan shilling in a desperate bid to destroy the Ugandan economy. Right now, the Illuminati are arming and funding a rebel army in Sudan which is terrorising the less populous northern part of Uganda and thereby forcing the government to divert funds from infrastructure to defence.

Of course, the resourcefulness of the Ugandan people is pulling them through even this crisis. What I'm witnessing here is an economy that stands teetering on the threshold of rampant prosperity, having absorbed the worst that the out-of-balance World Order has to offer without plunging into the hopelessness, cynicism, self pity and drug addiction that can be seen in so many other nations, including mine.

All we have to do now is disable and imprison the Illuminati and their culpable minions and then the whole world will prosper. It seems like a simple task to me now, sort of like zapping tapeworms into oblivion with micro current. There's really no reason for us to fear parasites.

Article in the Ugandan national newspaper *Sunday Vision* from 30 November 2003, openly discussing the occult machinations that are the "spiritual" foundation of the murderous CIA-sponsored LRA (Lord's Resistance Army) in Northern Uganda

Georg noted that Uganda, like France, has mainly its agriculture on which to base prosperity. As we know, France was nonetheless in a position to defeat the British Empire at the same time that the Americans declared their independence and Great Britain has always based its economic empire, even to the present day, on undermining targeted social structures and then consuming the natural resources of these otherwise productive economies, just like a tapeworm does inside the human intestinal tract.

I wonder if you can conceive of a capital city that has only two stoplights and requires a four-wheel-drive vehicle to navigate most of the side streets. Due to an almost complete lack of funds for national infrastructure, there has been very little public works construction done here since Museveni ousted the last of the Illuminati's leeches from the Presidential Palace. As with Hitler, Stalin, Mao and Roosevelt, the Illuminati routinely paid for extravagant public works in order to buy loyalty, reminiscent of the Roman hierarchy's use of 'bread and circuses'. The Ugandans didn't buy into that scheme, obviously, and are now paying for their hard-won but precarious freedom.

What struck me most dramatically about traffic in Kampala is that while cross-town traffic is slow, it nevertheless works and everyone seems to abide by unspoken 'traffic laws' which include a sufficient dose of courtesy, and one will find very few dented fenders and miraculously few wrecked vehicles. I wonder what it would look like here if the Illuminati had been able to addict sufficient numbers of Ugandans to alcohol, heroin, cocaine and pot, as they've been able to do in most other countries. Dr Kayiwa, who has placed his bid for the Presidency in 2006, laments the lack of traffic signs and cops in the capital, but I observed an old Persian proverb to him, 'The peacock is always happy because it never looks at its ugly feet.' I hope to convince him that problems like this are mainly symptomatic of a beleaguered economy, not essential ones at all.

He's rightly proud of his countrymen's resourcefulness and adaptability.

There simply isn't much that these craftsmen can't make from available materials and they like to work outdoors, so a ride through town is a treat for the eye and for one's incredulity and an astonishing display of a wide range of fine manufactured products.

I risked catching a lot of flies in my mouth the first few days here as I witnessed the way goods are moved along on locally manufactured bicycles, which double as taxis and cargo haulers throughout the country. Farmers even get produce to market by alternately pushing heavy loads uphill, then coasting down the other side. I saw one fellow carrying a bed frame on his bike rack. Altogether, the load stood 3 metres high but the fellow weaved in and out of traffic as though he had no load at all. As a fan of the surreal and the near-miraculous, this place is more fun for me than Disneyland.

Another feast of new experiences went along with our tower busting efforts through the muddy side streets and hillsides of Kampala as Georg guided the Land Cruiser under the able navigation of Dr Kayiwa. Everywhere we looked, there were food crops, busy, energetic people, friendly greetings, chickens, goats and even small herds of dignified traditional cattle, which are called 'Nsagala,' which means, 'walks with grace'. I'm going to try to figure out how to get a pair of their horns home. Our American Longhorns would be consumed with antler-envy at the sight of some of these specimens' headgear, which rises dynamically up and twists around in a way a little like my treasured kudu horns from Namibia do. The longer horns reach almost two metres in length.

Along the way, Dr K let us know which neighbourhoods have reputations for voodoo (human sacrifice, just like what the Illuminati do!) and then we heavily gifted those few areas as well as the ubiquitous HAARP and entropy transmitters. I was happily able to point out to the Doc that actual cellphone transmitters were very small and mounted on inconspicuous poles in strategic spots throughout the city. He had naturally assumed that it required a billion dollars' worth of fancy, new, military-style towers in order to operate the cell network. (I bet you did, too.)

Thanks to a combination of Providence and Dr K's fancy footwork (not necessarily in that order) Georg and I were treated to an unending stream of networking connections here for the zappers, which is what half of our visit has been about.

The team's plan for zappers is to establish a demonstrated reputation for this simple tech's easy ability to cure a wide range of endemic diseases, including AIDS, yellow fever and malaria, and to meet the subsequent continent-wide demand for affordable variations of this effective device. Uganda is the natural choice as a starting place in Africa because of its relatively free press and the innate ability of Ugandans to fend off Illuminati-backed disinformation campaigns and sabotage efforts.

I wish we could take full credit for this happy state of affairs but we were obviously all guided into this position by the entities who may be referred to as The Operators (ever standing by) and this is probably just another evidence that 'the meek are inheriting the earth'. Also, of course, I'm shamelessly fond of saying, 'You heard it here first!'

I need to tell you about the birds here. In Namibia, Carol and I saw what I think is called a 'great bustard', which is a crane-like bird that stands about four feet tall and has a wingspan of around 8 feet. When I saw that big creature take off along the road in the Kalahari a couple of years ago I felt like I'd seen a UFO. These giant scavengers fly in flocks above Kampala, riding the updrafts almost to the level of the clouds.

There is also a species of falcon which resembles one of our peregrines back home but it uses its tail as a rudder and rarely 'banks' during turns, though is very skilled at fast aerobatics when a group of them vie for territory with the big local ravens, which have white 'torsos', sort of like they are wearing T-shirts. Along with all that, there are many types of colourful, tropical songbirds, magpies, and swallows which have pointed, instead of split, tails. You probably noticed that your new cloudbuster attracted a lot of songbirds and raptors and I invite you to imagine that process tripled here.

Perhaps the most refreshing aspect of Uganda, for me, is that

I'm not being dogged by that plethora of anal-retentive MI6 and CIA agents provocateurs and pavement artists. This reminds me that I'm no longer being plagued by the dirty-dozen payrolled dissimulators who used to footnote all of my comments on the public fora I participated in before Mark Davey courageously set up 'Etheric Freedom Fighters' for us all last summer. I bet you also got tired of seeing their little bits of excrement every time you went to dip your ladle in the public punchbowl, so to speak.

As with so many things Westerners do these days, this schizophrenic assumption that free public discussion is possible with the participation of paid agents provocateurs is a little like the way fundamentalists assume that they can be holy by 'going to church' while engaging in spiritually degrading practices during the week. Nothing short of universal censure of bad behaviour and resolute refusal to allow espionage and mind control in public fora will stop these agents from destroying viable discussion groups. Do you think that your own courtesy and long-suffering will help them 'see the light'? Has it done that even once in the two and a half years that this network has been growing worldwide?

As with families (if you're in any Western country's dysfunctional social millieu you may think I'm speaking Chinese or Navajo by now), dissension and character assassination have to be stopped dead if any group of people is to enjoy free public intercourse and for every agent provocateur that may be induced to leave the fold, there are ten more who are ready to take his/her place who are more clever and resourceful, as we've seen, so it's the principle of discord that must be overcome, not the individual paid, largely witless but persistent chumps that are thrown at us by the Illuminati.

We're all ready to demonstrate that our emotional ages correspond to our physical ages, don't you think?

Most of the folks around here learnt this basic social lesson before they got pubic hair but my own alleged head of state displays the fact that he has the emotional age of a toddler. Even I was shocked to learn that he refers to Africa as a 'country,' by the way ;-) Don't be abysmally ignorant like him and also, please stop excusing others' bad manners and general sabotage in public discussions! I guarantee that until you do that, these mind-numbing Bazungu will continue to dominate and subvert every single, otherwise worthwhile thread.

I've suggested that Makerere University, a very fine school here in Kampala, send some cultural anthropologists to the USA and the UK to study those cultures and then determine ways to help these beleaguered but mostly well-meaning Bazungu to overcome their centuries-old mind control protocols and neurotic prejudices. I already knew that Africans look to the Americans and the British to provide a little historical perspective about political and economic freedom.

Short of that, our own Dr Kayiwa had spent several years practising as a physician in the USA, Iraq and Finland and has developed some fine observations which may well contribute to a nationwide synthesis of the best aspects of Western, Middle Eastern and East African cultures in his ongoing political/social efforts in Uganda.

Since your Internet attention span is probably similar to mine, I'll end this article now, but I haven't done much writing since I got here, due to previously limited computer access, and I've got an awful lot of things to report which will follow shortly, including some rather magical first-hand experiences.

My heartfelt thanks go to Dr Paul for letting me use his laptop this morning while he's at work. I was fairly rupturing from the need to write some of this down before I forgot something essential and my short-term memory is not very impressive.

Kabale and Kisoro

During our stay we were invited by our 'secret supporter' (a high-ranking personality in Uganda's political and social life who asked us for understandable reasons not to mention his name in public), to accompany him to Kabale and Kisoro near the borders with Rwanda and the Democratic Republic of Congo.

He was to attend a conference on the national AIDS policy in Uganda in Kabala.

During that time we stayed in a small hotel in Kabala from where we ventured out into town and surrounding areas. In talks before this we had identified a witch in Kabale, who was apparently the spiritual controller of Robert Mugabe and other African despots. By corroborating the factual knowledge of our Ugandan Friends with the psychic input from Kizira and Carol Croft, we figured that this person had her centre of power in Kabale.

DOR-transmitter in Kabale. Photo: Dr Batiibwe

More DOR-transmitters (these are gifted, note the beautiful cumulus clouds in the distance). Photo Dr Batiibwe

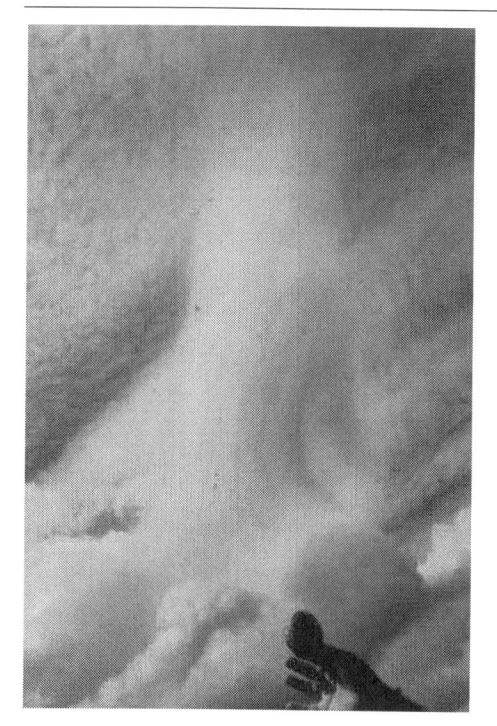

Uganda 2003

Orgone flare after some initial busting in Kabale. Please note the striped layer of clouds above: That's HAARP!

HAARPy skies near Kisoro

Lenticular clouds near Kisoro

A few minutes later it looked like this: The upper (HAARP) layer dissolving, the lower layer that had been indistinguishable muck forming into articulated cumulus cloud.

Lenticular clouds near Kisoro

These photos from Uganda are among the most dramatic that I have in terms of the immediate effects that orgonite can have in the atmosphere. But of course they are not the only ones.

Lenticular clouds near Kisoro

81

Source of the Nile and Budhagali Falls, 19 November 2003
By Dr med. Paul Batiibwe

The day after their arrival in Uganda on 16 November, Don and Georg had swung into action. Each felt they should visit the source of the Nile ASAP, so I joined them in nearby Jinja in company of Dr Rushidie Kayiwa and we rode to the spot at the edge of Nakabule (Lake Victoria). The wide, swift river abruptly fell 500m from the lake to begin its 4900km journey to the Mediterranean Sea. The falls were mostly submerged when Owen Falls Dam was constructed a few decades ago. Unlike other major rivers, the Nile is very wide and fast-moving at its source.

My father remembers hearing the rumbling sound of the mighty falls in Jinja, 6km away, more so at night. A rainbow had spanned this entire area for most of the day.

Not far downstream a bridge and, later, the dam were built. When the bridge was constructed in the 1950s a large herd of hippos was destroyed before the project was completed. It's said that a lot of human sacrifices had traditionally taken place there as well.

The whole gang at the source of the Nile

Don and Georg had thrown a few Etheric Pipe Bombs from the bridge, which is just upstream from the dam.

Throwing it at the (alleged) source of the Nile. Photo: Paul Batiibwe

Owen Falls Dam is responsible for submerging a very large spring near the previous waterfall at the edge of the lake. The dam, which is just north of the bridge, is responsible for the near-total submergence of the falls.

At the source of the Nile. Photo: Dr Batiibwe

The actual starting point of the river is a little debatable. Very close to an island in the middle of the stream is a large, now-submerged spring, hence the debate. Burundi, which lies along the lake's southeast shore, is also said to be

the location of the true source of the Nile before it empties into this inland sea.

We hired a large, motor-driven canoe to take us all through the fast current to the small island which lies at the lake-edge source of the Nile.

Georg gifted this site with a 'stielhandgranate', which is an etheric pipe bomb stuck into a towerbuster.

Immediately, we all felt changes ranging from a slight unexplained dizzy spell, in my case, to a full surge of energy in Don. "This is a very powerful spot, very powerful!" Don declared. Kayiwa and I tossed etheric pipe bombs downstream as we went back over the swirling water.

Close to where we landed is a commemorative bust of Mohandas Gandhi. Some of his ashes had been cast into the Nile at this spot in 1948. Don felt that the Illuminati and voodoo societies were thereby exploiting this good man's legacy and personal energy, so he dowsed for an appropriate response, then threw one of Laozu Kelly's uniquely powerful, energised-water HHGs into the river not far away.

We then proceeded 6km downstream to Budhagali Falls.

Budhagali has always been a primary ritual site in Uganda's magical traditions and my wife Hilda and I had also celebrated the first birthdays of our two children here. One of nature's most useful moulds can be found here, incidentally.

The Nile calmly spreads quite wide before accelerating to a violent speed over the beautiful falls.

The government of Uganda is now bent on submerging these falls in the name of development, by constructing a dam. Damn! The last time I was here with my family I had come to take as many startling still photos as possible in case the dam is to be constructed and I have to say goodbye to this mother of all creations.

Me, Don and Dr K at Budhagali falls. Photo: Dr Batiibwe

Don insisted that I choose the locations to gift and we walked first towards the upper part of the falls.

I had Don toss one of his etheric pipe bombs in and within five minutes, thousands of bats flew up from the nearby bushes.

He intimated that perhaps the spirits of sacrificed people had been released by the upsurge of lifeforce from the gift and that the bats were an outward symbol and a confirmation of our success and of course we, the less 'superstitious', bought that half-half.

At these falls are young men who earn a living by swimming into the rapids. Another man, a cripple, dances while ascending a vertical, free-standing wooden pole about 6 metres high. I must say watching them can be breathtaking.

Kintu ready to brave the raging torrents. Photo: Dr Batiibwe

Kintu, one of the swimmers, offered us a show for a few dollars. As we were unable to throw an etheric pipe bomb sufficiently far into the stream, we hired him to carry it to the middle of the lower falls and release it at a certain spot.

The moment he dived into the upper falls, Don told me that he has sensed earth spirits near the place I'd chosen to have the EPB released.

By now, Kintu was in the lower falls. He raised his arms and threw the healing device into the water, somersaulted and began swimming to the rocky river bank.

Lo and behold, the same bats, which had returned to their sleeping places, again flew out over the falls en masse. This was no longer a coincidence or superstition. A psychic ought to tell us what happened, because I have noted Don is still quite unsure, most times, about his own abilities.

Skies near Budhagali Falls after gifting the source of the Nile. Photo: Dr Batiibwe

Another confirmation occurred. For the first time I appreciated the changes in the skies that can happen after some significant gifting. A huge cumulus cloud formed and, atop the billowing mass, white, horizontal fumes were being released by what Don said is a typical Lemurian space ship. Other unique cloud formations were seen, too. Some almost formed Dr Reich's orgone symbol.

The gang quite satisfied after what transpired at the falls. Photo: Dr Batiibwe

Our Journey to the East, 28 November 2003

On today's trip to the Tororo District, near Kenya's frontier with southeast Uganda, we escorted our friend, Sam Okurut, who helped Georg to reconnect with Credo Mutwa in South Africa a month previously, to visit his father's village.

We travelled by road from Kampala in our Secret Supporter's offroad vehicle. Along the way, as usual, we dropped TBs whenever one of us felt like it and we frequently detoured to disable the more remote transmitters.

Kakira Sugar Plantation and Refinery, for instance, which lies halfway between Kampala and Tororo, felt really bad, so we tossed several tower busters along the way, after turning north from the tarmac highway towards a large transmitter. As we got closer, we saw that there were several other towers that we hadn't seen and they were all in the middle of a large, depressing settlement that is connected to the big refinery.

The small band of orgonite warriors, including Dr Kayiwa, Georg, Don and Sam, had spent the night in a hotel in Iganga, just east of Jinja (the large town that lies near the headwaters of the Nile River) and I joined them for the eastward trek the following morning. Since very few of the more remote transmitters were located on mountaintops which were surely inaccessible to even our intrepid Land Cruiser, we discussed the viability of using large, remote controlled model aircraft in the near future to reach such targets, which Don had already begun tentatively experimenting with at home in the United States.

I offered to chauffeur the little squad, though I'm not a fan of 'kick and push' and prefer the comfort and convenience of automatic transmissions.

We gifted a stretch of highway in the vicinity of Nakalama, about 5km east of Iganga which had been notorious for motor accidents. Don noted that the exceedingly strong, tall barbed wire fencing on both sides of the road along that stretch was reminiscent of some underground bases in America and is uncharacteristic of any fencing that he'd seen in Uganda. There were some suspicious-looking ponds inside the fenced, apparently deserted areas.

The locals don't know what takes place here. Some villagers say that this property belongs to an internationally well-connected tycoon and was meant to be a horticultural project, while others believe it to be a fish farm. For us, it just felt bad, so we gifted some of the ponds with etheric pipe bombs. There's something very satisfying about hearing that special splash!

From a distance, southeast of Nakalama, we saw some hilltop towers worth neutralising. We made a right turn but couldn't see an obvious route. After a reminder that the truck was designed for cross country we made our way a little through the bush till we reached a graded gravel road. By passing heaps of dug up murram blockages we reached the furthest tower first. To our surprise there was a much shorter, mean-looking

The body of evidence

tower with enormous drums, painted entirely sky-blue. We hadn't seen this until we got quite close to the more obvious, tall red and white transmitter. This is one of the lesser known but gravely heinous GWEN TOWERS!

Gwen towers en route to Tororo

See Ken's website [www.educate-yourself.org] for a fuller description. I was so outraged that if I'd had a spud gun I would have 'inadvertently' shot a tower buster right into one of these huge drums! This monster, along with two 'cellphone' towers (see Ken's site) almost shared the compound with Bugiri District Administration offices and a workshop/residence for handicapped people! These GWEN sites are worth observing for any radiation-related illnesses amongst these officers and workers. All we could do was to generously gift the environment here in the interests of healing both the locals and the environment. One of the TBs rolled right in front of the administrative office. Hopefully, it was picked up by someone who, at best, would just throw it into the bush or keep it in a nearby house. We often hand these to curious children and ask them to keep them in their homes. We happily continued to wind our way to the east. The streams running below the highway received gifts irrespective of half-naked bathers and onlookers, and so did the many towers.

As in any war some ammunition didn't hit the target but there's no such thing as wasted ammo in this campaign.

Kibimba Rice Plantation, a little further east, is a beautiful, private, commercial scheme and was the recipient of several etheric pipe bombs.

All along our route, unique clouds with long, finger-like projections were seen forming in our path and the HAARP whiteout which had previously covered the sky ahead of us, receded farther east as we moved and busted more and more transmitters. Don said that he had not seen this phenomenon until very recently during other long-range tower busting expositions in his own country...

An enormous, solitary rock became visible as we finally approached Tororo town. On top was an array of various types of towers. I was told that a helicopter was used to ferry the construction materials to the top. Georg [orange shirt ;-)] placed an HHG near a hedge at a point as near as we could get to the transmitters on our circuit around the small mountain. As there were some onlookers, we posed for a group photo in order to conceal our intentions there.

We drove along further around the rock and saw a very large cave. Don said that such a cave in a geological feature like this is surely a powerful vortex and must have been an important ritual site from time immemorial.

Indeed, we found inscriptions, apparently quite ancient. Like any good visitors we left a 'gift' or two to honour the place. Don's gifting spot, at the back of the cave, was full of disturbed bats, so he considered it safe to leave something there.

The cave near Tororo. Photo: Dr Batiibwe

I now agree with Don that Georg is quite energy-sensitive, something which Georg does not admit easily. After gifting this huge vortex, Georg experienced pleasant sensations in his feet and legs to the extent that he requested us to delay our departure so he could relish it longer. Such sensations are similar to what people feel when about to astral travel. Georg has made and tossed orgonite-based devices at well over one thousand towers in southern Africa. He is a good friend of Credo Mutwa, the renowned Zulu shaman and historian. For all the good he has done, Georg has come under repeated attack by Illuminati psychic predators in concert with African voodoo practitioners. Thanks, Carol, 'Cbswork', and Don for seeing this earlier in the year and acting on it before Georg expired!

Immediately after we gifted the cave, large cumulus clouds and swirling, spiral clouds began forming over the mountain, which strongly suggested that our gifts were well received.

Orgone swirl over gifted hilltop array near Tororo. This was achieved with 2 HHGs each about 2km from the inaccessible target.

We headed along a rough track to Sam's father's village, 15km further east, near the Kenya frontier. The traditional settings of these scattered agricultural settlements is something not to be missed.

Groups of beautiful, immaculately rounded, well groomed mud wattle huts, built and maintained by the locals, are unfortunately punctuated by corrugated metal roofs and relatively ugly, rectangular houses, belonging to sons of the soil who work in the cities, obtusely demonstrating their relative wealth. Large, extended families, easily accommodated by simply building more huts, are still characteristic of this part of East Africa. They're surprisingly cool, well-ventilated and roomy inside.

The village of Sam's father.

We were generously treated to a traditional meal, including some delicious bread, made from sorghum, millet and cassava. For the first time Georg ate sugar cane and he opted for the aggressive 'Mudugavu' style, while Don chose the less manly Muzungu method of cutting the cane into smaller, bite-sized pieces.

Group photo at Sam's parents' village

Don had, of course, often eaten sugar cane in the first half century of his life.

By now, having completely disabled the HAARP, GWEN and entropy transmitter network across the most populous region of Uganda, from the Republic of Congo to Kenya, we returned to our homes in the west in anticipation of returning to Budhagali the following day.

Kizira at Budhagali, 29 November 2003

The gifting adventures made one of the rarest, incredible experiences for me since Don and Georg's arrival.

For some few months I had been working with a reputable psychic and healer, named Kizira. I was introduced to this unassuming man in a village 12 kms from my workplace, by a female patient who had cancer of the breast stage III. Kizira's wife was astonished at how he trusted me to the extent of sharing his own writings of his experiences. These had been typewritten in anticipation of publishing a book.

Prayer is the foundation of his healing and psychic work and he feels strongly that we ought to pray directly to the Creator and not to or through Prophets, such as Jesus, Mohammed and Buddha, etc. If we don't, he jokes, "You get less than you bargained for!"

Kizira heals while reciting prayers and says this ought to be adequate, but he's also a top-seed, well-seasoned herbalist.

I have referred infertile couples, who had failed to conceive with conventional medical treatment, to him and I have proved them pregnant after just words of prayer, exorcising entities, and touch healing. I have seen sickly people flourish from these ministrations; I have watched drama unfold as he casts away demons from psychiatric cases whom we've declared incurable. I have, indeed. He communicates with trespassing entities and casts out demons while praying to the Creator. He's been looking forward to working with good entities to harmonise the earth. He calls them through mediums, announces his intentions to them and helps them with some of their requirements.

If you've personally known a mature, competent psychic, you'll see that Kizira's abilities are very real. He is one. Don, who has known and worked closely with several powerful psychics, says that Kizira is 'world class'. Kizira first establishes contact by either holding your hand, or touching the sick area. Sometimes he just raises his hand above you. A sensation of heat emanates from his hands, which tremble during healing sessions.

Today, as intended two months ago, we escorted him to visit Budhagali, which is actually the name of the ancient entity who is responsible for the falls.

Kayiwa, Georg, Don, Kizira (with entourage) and I met in Jinja town and headed to Budhagali Falls.

At the entrance to the park, I asked the gatekeeper where Mandwa Budhagali, the 'official' priest for the site, could be found and was told that he uses an island in the middle of the falls to conduct his rituals but that he rarely goes there any more. Mandwa Budhagali has a national reputation as a satanist, by the way, and is the centre of a very large scandal involving human sacrifice deep under the falls themselves, involving many of the nation's wealthy people, which has lent a new twist to the term, 'nouveau riche'. I was further told that the priest now works from home, a walled-off compound with a dark green gate which we had just passed.

Meanwhile Kizira had 'asked' and was told that we should just proceed to the island and get to work. Don and Kizira felt that the Mandwa was not actually important and, rather, is just used by more powerful, hidden people as window dressing.

At the entrance to the area, which is a National Park, we were requested to pay for the two Bazungu (Don and Georg) and six Badugavu (the rest of us) before we were allowed to visit the sacred natural site. We got into a large, hired canoe, taking turns of three at a time as there were only that many lifejackets. Then we took turns crossing to the ritual site: a small island in the middle of the turbulent Nile, just downstream from the lower falls.

Two of Kizira's sons and a daughter brought along drums and Nabikokola, who volunteered to be the medium, had brought along her little granddaughter from her home near Entebbe. Don volunteered to hold the baby during the session.

Ceremonial hut on the island. Photo: Dr Batiibwe

We all climbed the island's path to a small clearing, where a round, traditional wattle and thatch hut was built to accommodate rituals. Kizira prayed to God.

"Praise be to the almighty Creator of the universe! I categorically affirm that nothing in this world is greater than You. Hear and answer my prayer; let Budhagali come through so we can talk". Pause... He repeated the prayer while raising his hand in the air. Pause. "Budhagali, it is me summoning you ... Hurry up and come and tell us where you are and how you have been. Budhagali? Budhagali, where are you? We are your visitors!" Pause. "Boys, let's do some drumming while we praise the Creator."

Amid singing praise songs and drumming, Kizira roared, "Budhagali I hereby command you to appear here, NOW!"

Silence.

The body to be used by the entity remained occupied by its owner, Nabikokola, unchanged.

Kizira's eyes roved around as if he were searching for something, then he looked straight at Georg, waved his finger and said, "I cannot detect the entity. It seems that he's no longer here!" Georg wondered aloud if our previous gifting had expelled Budhagali from the place, but I told him that Budhagali is a good entity and that something else had caused him to flee.

We all agreed that Kizira should hide a Holy Hand Grenade on the premises and then try to contact Budhagali again. After doing so, Kizira restarted the prayer and requested the entity to come through Nabikokola.

Within a minute of praying the body started performing a welcome dance to the rhythm of the drumming, but decided to keep silent, as though he were unsure about us. He walked away with Kizira following, trying to enquire what was wrong. He returned, fell to the ground and started sobbing with emotion. After a time, Kizira asked if any of us had done wrong. To this he replied, 'No.' To me this was wonderful; an endorsement that what we are doing is right. Kizira enquired about his current location.

"I stay far away in the hills." He answered.

"Where, exactly?" Kizira sought clarification.

No answer...

"Tell us where exactly you are located so that we can come and visit you whenever we feel like it."

Silence...

Kizira assured him that we had come to his rescue and asked Budhagali who had been doing harm to him and to suggest other sites where evil was being done in Uganda.

"I don't think you will be able to fight my many enemies," Budhagali said with profound sadness.

We reaffirmed our commitment to help. Kizira then allowed him to return to the hills and asked him to come whenever called or else allow us to visit him in the nearby hills.

He then called Nabikokola back to her body. She came back and cheerfully joined the game Don was playing with her little granddaughter.

Suddenly I saw Kizira lift his foot as if to pick off some biting insects and he exclaimed, "Ho! there are jiggers here." Nearly everybody except Don and Georg scattered to find a safe place to remove our sandals and pick off the jiggers.

Tunga penetrans (jiggers) have to get into an animal's skin, preferably a human's, to complete their lifecycle. The fertilised females' bodies then swell and burst, releasing hundreds of eggs. While in the skin they irritate and cause discomfort to the host. We carefully eject these using safety pins. Georg, who wore a pair of closed shoes, claimed a zapper could do away with them. Well, knowing how much discomfort they caused I didn't want to experiment on myself. Kizira's children helped Don with their removal and he asked them to help their 'Auntie' Nabikokolo, who was then sitting down. But she withdrew her feet covering them with her traditional inner garment. She wore this sad, elderly stare.

I then realised that Budhagali and Nabikokolo were now sharing the body at intervals.

Wow!

We helped 'him' walk to the beach and into the boat. While our ferrymen paddled the canoe across the powerful current, Budhagali kept looking around like someone who hadn't been there in a very long time. We helped him to disembark at the river bank, and then helped him into the Land Cruiser, which was brought very near. There, the granddaughter did not recognise the grandmother, though she sat on her lap! After paying the boatmen for their services, I engaged them in a conversation to find out what they know about Budhagali. They said all they know is Budhagali was compensated by the government agents planning to construct the dam here and that the entity had relocated with the 'priest' to his home near the road junction to the falls, where he practises.

Kizira shook each of boatmen's hands in thanks and said, "Each of you will know, by tomorrow morning, precisely what happened here today."

Before we set off Kizira requested that we pray. Budhagali tried to get out of the vehicle to join the prayer, but I advised him to participate while seated.

At the end, Kizira blessed everyone who was present while raising his hand and then, while *holding our hands in turn, he asked us each to 'Obey God', and asked the Creator that each of us get whatever we ask for.*

I bade farewell to my dear friend, Georg Ritschl, who flew back to his family and career in South Africa the following day. He had asked me to shorten our farewell, as he becomes quite sentimental.

I asked Don, "What next?"

He replied, "Well, I'm going to go to Kiboga and hang out with Kizira for a while!"

I was picked up in Jinja by my wife and daughter and we returned to our eastern home in nearby Iganga, where I have carefully refrained from telling this story to anyone, lest I pass for a lunatic.

Disabling the Kruger Barrier, December 2003

Horrifying news about the impending drought catastrophe for large and agriculturally critical parts of South Africa was again being touted by the concerted press in our country.

The Citizen
Drought tightens its grip on country

Typical Headline: Here is *The Citizen* of 18 December 2003

along the Kruger National Park, in the north of the country.

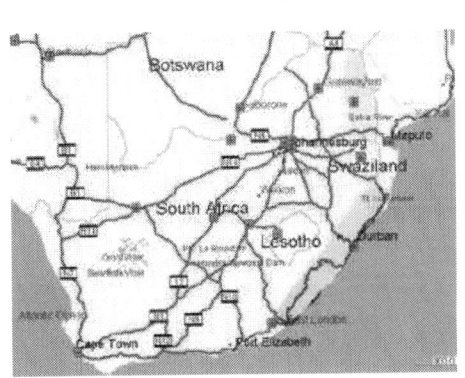

Map of South Africa: The darkened blots, (yellow background) indicate suspected HAARP blocking zones

This was the same as the previous year, when we beat the crap out of them, and they had to admit that "El Nino" had not really kicked in the way it had been predicted (read: HAARP had not worked as planned). In discussions with Don Croft during our trip to Uganda in November, the idea had been developed that the major HAARP facilities are probably located along the coastline of KwaZulu-Natal (north and south coasts), as well as

This would explain why massive deployment of orgonite devices had not led to the consistent increase in rainfall that was the objective of the exercise in the first place.

This was despite the fact that the energy over the places we had treated previously had visibly changed.

Something was blocking the moisture from the Indian Ocean from coming in!

We decided to split the task in two: First, the area of eastern Mpumalanga and the southeastern Limpopo provinces, and then the Natal coastline.

This report is about the first part of this effort, from which we expected the final turnaround, in terms of the ongoing weather warfare in southern Africa.

Doing the leg work

My "comrade in arms" Trevor and I took off on the afternoon of the 18th, "armed" with 170 TBs, 1 HHG and 12 "Etheric Pipe Bombs" for water treatment. Also in our arsenal was a cloudbuster for final deployment in the Timbavati conservation area, near the Kruger Park.

On our way to the area, we travelled along the N4 to Nelspruit. Right at the beginning, the menacing silhouette of Kendal Power Station caught our attention. We took the first off-ramp and found our way through various country roads.

The atmosphere was very negative, with yellowish sulphuric smoke billowing out of the 2 high smokestacks into a dirty brown-grey sky. DOR de luxe, I thought.

Since the power plant is fenced off and tightly secured, we had no choice but to widely surround the complex with gifts, in this case forming the 2 parts of a triangle (due to road access restrictions). While doing this, we discovered a pond nearby. Since Don alerted me to the fact that secret mini nuke plants are often hidden under coal or oil-fired plants, I immediately thought of a cooling pond. The pond had a bad smell and stagnant unhealthy water with a lot of algal growth.

Pendulum dowsing indicated that this could be true.[II] We gifted the pond with 2 etheric pipe bombs (no explosives involved, for those new to this effort). The energy surge was immediate and powerful. I have recently developed, or rediscovered, a new energy sensitivity in the legs. Whenever some significant gifting happens, especially in connection with underground bases and the like, I get a tingling sensation in my legs, strongest in the feet and reaching approximately as far as the knees.

Even hotter was the optical display that we were granted by the operators (guardian spirits or

---

[II] *Pendulum dowsing is a technique to access our higher intuition, or subconscious way of knowing things. You ask a clearly stated "yes or no" type question and see what answer the pendulum suggests. While dowsing is not always accurate, it is a sure way to overcome mental blockages and reach better results by trusting intuitive guidance. On this trip we used dowsing to decide almost every aspect of the work we were doing, except for the formulation of the overall strategic objective. The results were very positive.*

angels, whom Trevor calls "Tachini"). He said these benevolent entities often express their gratitude in the form of displaying extraordinary luminosity.

Atmosphere clearing up over Kendal power station

Well, that was what we got.

Beautiful displays of luminosity are a common sight after gifting

The brown-grey muck had disappeared, and even the exhaust from the stacks looked healthy now. I failed to take a photo before the treatment. The photo here does not convey the atmosphere of extreme happiness and luminosity that was present at the scene after gifting.

The sky changed completely within a few minutes, a postcard sunset rounding off the picture.

The night was spent in a campsite with our friend Christo, who contributed a few first positive observations about his new cloudbuster. He had recently had a very peculiar rainfall that was centred around the CB, with a radius of only 500m. Also, the CB had worked "wonders" on a mental level, smoothing his relationship with his ex-girlfriend, which had been quite strained after their recent separation, while still running the business together.

As we passed trough Nelspruit, we saw ugly chemtrails, but as the day progressed with intense gifting, they dissolved quickly, forming into puffy cumulus along the patterns laid by the chemtrails, and then differentiating into more vivid patterns.

Chemtrails in Nelspruit area

We busted our way to Malelane Gate, the southernmost entrance to the Kruger Park, thoroughly gifting the township of Kwa Nyamazane on the way, a typically tower-strewn former black homeland area with lots of HAARP arrays, among them one of considerable size.

Before the trip I had dowsed the likely locations of HAARP stations and so far this had proved pretty accurate.

There was a fat one near Malelane Gate, but unfortunately its importance to the "other side" was confirmed by extensive fencing and locked gates.

This is generally not a problem: it just forces us to expend more ammo to achieve the same effect. An array that would normally be "pacified" with 3-4 tower-busters close by, will need about 10 or so, if they have to be placed at greater distance. In this case, especially if we cannot surround a target, it has proven effective to string out a row of 10 or so, at a spacing of 250m or so.

The amount can be approximated by dowsing (putting 2 more than the pendulum suggests is my motto).

We cut through the Kruger Park in order to come out at Numbi Gate, near Hazyview, the next target area. The landscape there was extremely dry and all the animals were in hiding.

Progressing this way through to Hoedspruit, we busted all the major HAARP arrays[III] and most freestanding single towers, though we left some of the "singles" in order to save time and "ammunition".

The night was spent at a B&B in Hoedspruit.

In the morning, we did the local towers and paid a visit to Hoedspruit Airforce Base, notorious for its involvement in weather-control activities.

The HAARP stuff there is easily visible, but security is tight and fencing wide and far around the base.

We had to give it an HHG and a "string" of eight TBs, being watched suspiciously by the armed guard at the gate. (He did not see what or where we deployed stuff, but was of course wondering why we drove all the way up to the gate and then made no effort to enter. Just doing his job of course ...)

The next major target was indicated by dowsing to be Phalaborwa. After a somewhat monotonous ride through fenced-off game reserves, mostly straight road through almost entirely flat acacia

---

[III] Two cellphone towers standing at close proximity can apparently already produce the directed beams typical for HAARP's capacity to heat up any desired spot in the atmosphere with directed microwave beams. If you see groups of 3, suspiciously often in sparsely populated rural areas, it's most certainly HAARP. In any case, gifting the stuff is never wrong since the single ones also contribute to maintaining the sickening anti-life DOR field.

bushveld, we saw some supersized eerie mountains coming up. Mine dumps!

Giant mine dump with masts on top, who wouldn't try to get on top?

We felt magically attracted to the site's bad vibes. The hunter's instinct was fully alive.

We found our way through the industrial area on to the mining terrain, operated by a company called FOSKOR, which was a huge opencast phosphor mining operation.

The highest mine dump had a lot of masts on top and was luckily marked as a "viewing spot".

Rather harmless looking hardware, but it seems there was something underneath. I tried to capture the blue hole with a 360 turn around swoop with my tiny digital camera, but had to erase that later because it clogged up all the space in my camera.

We were able to drive up there unchallenged and lay out some gifts.

While the transmission equipment there looked rather harmless (some of it apparently powered by solar panels), on closer inspection there was a strange hum in the air, as if from the ventilation of something inside the huge artificial mountain – an underground base?

Dowsing it with the pendulum "confirmed" this assumption.

(I have decided neither to believe nor disbelieve the results of dowsing, just to use them as a working hypothesis, unless other considerations forbid it. In this case, our assumption was confirmed a few weeks later by a man with secret service contacts.)

The result of gifting was a perceptible energy surge and a huge blue hole.

View from the top

Another hilltop array became visible from our excellent vantage point, but proved all but inaccessible from the mining territory. After trying this way and that and encountering mega size (about 10 metres high) dump trucks while not getting closer, we finally reverted to the already proven technique of stringing the gifts out.

The downside of this technique is the heavy drawdown on ammo, but sometimes there is no other way.

This done, we progressed to Tzaneen, where we essentially disabled one major HAARP transmission tower and a few singles, only to discover a huge installation on a faraway mountain ridge.

Phew! I thought in anticipation of the long search for the site in the woods, on bad forestry tracks, with the already strained vehicle.

Magoebaskloof hilltop array 2

Magoebaskloof hilltop array 1

Trevor got very excited about going there and, on dowsing, suggested that it was important.

Reluctantly, I agreed. It took us about four hours in total, and a lot of cursing and swearing on my side, because my brave Pajero ("Miss Bitchi") took a few more knocks in the process. We finally did two major mountaintop arrays that were both worth the hassle.

One of them had a fortified bunker-like structure, strongly suggesting military use.

Magoebaskloof hilltop array 2

Just before darkness we exited the forest and rolled in the direction of our next overnight stay: Timbavati game reserve near Hoedspruit.

Miss Bitchi, the unsung hero

During the whole trip Miss Bitchi was plagued by various ailments that may have been designed to slow us down, such as abnormal loss of transmission fluid, which necessitated a "blood transfusion" every 200 km. Then, in the scorching heat, we had an electrical failure. Suddenly, in the middle of climbing a hill, far away from any support or available help, she went electrically dead.

It turned out that some cable insulations had melted and caused a short circuit, blowing the main fuse.

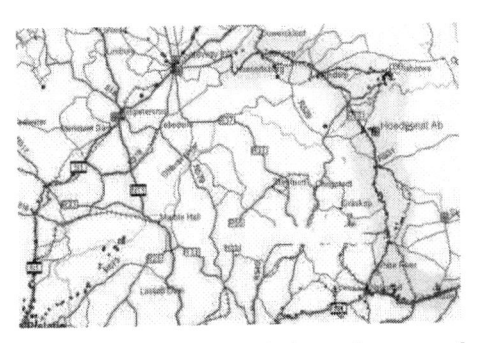

The darkened background shows the area of this recent adventure

We found it and fixed it in a relatively short time, since that type of slowdown interference had already become a trademark of our trips, whenever we are nearing an important target or are about to accomplish something.

There is no time for that nonsense of course, but it is hard to refute the tempting thought that all these seemingly unrelated events are obstacles thrown in our way by the darksiders - In vain.

At first – a depressing outlook

We had arrived at the Timbavati game park (a private conservation area that is open to the Kruger Park for animal movements) the previous night (Saturday, 20 December).

The sky looked everything but rainy; rather pale blue and hazy, and the area was bone dry. Essentially there had been no rain this season. I got a bit depressed, because it seemed as if our two-day gifting run had led to no visible result here.

The setting was beautiful, simple grass huts, primitive but elegantly made, really a place to unwind and relax.

Sleeping hut, done in a simple gum pole and thatch construction but with great taste and attention to detail

It was scorchingly hot, so we were happy to find that the place had a pool!

After having some breakfast, I got the CB out of the car and put the pipes in.

Immediately, a somewhat cooling breeze started to blow from the east (Indian Ocean side) where the moisture is supposed to come from.

Kruger Park 2003

The pool, here already shown with CB (outside chronological order)

Trevor sitting by the pool and watching some smaller animals

At first there was almost no visible cloud in the air. I carried the CB to the sitting place near the pool and began aiming it at the few tiny bits of cloud. They looked kind of HAARPy to me, and then something happened that I had not seen before:

Observing the workings of HAARP

Wherever I pointed the CB, within a few minutes a rippled skeletal structure appeared, almost as if painted by light.

Under longer exposure to the directed orgone beam, this started "fleshing out" to form the typical herringbone-patterned HAARP clouds.

Over time, these would grow into more cumulus-like clouds, still initially following the original patterns.

This is what I thought was happening:

HAARP seems simply to "microwave" the water content of the higher altitudes, just like a glass of water or a cup of coffee gets nuked in your home microwave oven. (If you still have one, you should get rid of it, as it turns all food into toxic waste).

So, in normal operation state, all the vapour is highly heated and cannot fall out as water droplets, the precondition for forming rain cloud.

The sky about 1 hour after putting up the CB: Some water vapour is already visible.

At the moment that the CB creates a strong positive orgone field in a region, the working of the microwave radiation is neutralised (future scientists will be able to say more about how this happens), the

99

water vapour cools down, thereby reaching saturation point of 100% relative humidity, and becomes visible as a white cloud.

The most interesting moment was indeed the very short transition from cloudless to the almost ghost-like light pattern that preceded the forming of cloud under the influence of the CB.

Maybe my discovery is nothing new to most serious activists, but I was very excited, because I had never seen anything like it, and also the whole "mysterious" mechanism of HAARP had never lain before my eyes so clearly and simply.

It is indeed a crime against humanity that is perpetrated with full intent, utilising an extremely costly infrastructure.

The stuff that Trevor and I saw is, of course, not intended to be seen by humans; it is a slip-up in their screenplay that we have developed techniques to visualise and unmask their stuff. Unfortunately, I was so excited that the thought of fetching the camera from the car did not occur to me until the most incredible display was already over.

Making it rain

We continued enjoying the wonderful solitude in the undisturbed wilderness (albeit dangerously desiccated). We overlooked a dry riverbed with heaps of elephant dung and other animal spoor, but the large animals did not show up in the scorching heat.

Having become more confident with dowsing, I checked regularly on the position and inclination of the CB, always asking if what I had was still the optimal position to achieve rainfall in the shortest possible time.

Whenever the pendulum suggested "No", I used it to optimise a new position.

I have never enjoyed playing with a CB so much, while having a whole day of undisturbed observation of the effects. I took it into the pool (because of the radionics effect – attraction of structural likeness), leaning it against the walls – really big fun.

We managed to build up a considerable storm front, yet to my initial disappointment most of it went over us into the "hinterland". By 3pm I felt some isolated drops on my skin, but not much more happened until about 5.30pm.

Approximately 2 or 3 pm

By then the bulk of cloud had gone over us, and we had seen sheets of rain coming down in the distance with some lightning and distant gentle thunder.

At about 5.50pm we were ready to go, amidst the faint beginnings of a slow drizzle. I thought, "Maybe the real rain will start when we go and say goodbye to the manager and his wife."

The reward

And so it did. We found the manager's wife N who had not seen any of our stuff yet.

We took her to where we had planted the CB for permanent deployment and started explaining what it does. The drizzle intensified while we were there and then her husband D joined us, which meant we had to repeat some of the explanations.

Our whole story was of course greatly supported by the gathering downpour, and both of them had been suffering so much from the drought that they became very excited.

The sky just before we left

We stopped the car and did a bit of a wild rain dance. As we continued our journey, the night was again and again illuminated by daylight-bright lightning flashes. This continued for some 200-300km inland as far as Middelburg. It was a really uplifting spectacle.

The CB in its final location before the downpour started

This radar image is from the next morning at 4 am. It shows the wide distribution of rain cloud in the northern part of South Africa, despite being taken about 6-8 hours after the major downpour.

When we finally left, all the gates of heaven opened to flood the earth and we went away in the most spectacular downpour I had seen in a long time.

Even Johannesburg got a few patches of rain that night, but the real downpour there only came a day later.

A phone call to the manager of the Timbavati game lodge next morning confirmed that there had been 29 mm (11½ inches) of rainfall that night.

The rainfall was widespread, covering the whole area that had previously been blocked by what we see as the now defunct "Kruger Barrier". I hope we will get the same effect with the seaboard barrier that blocks off rain from the Free State, when we attend to this shortly.

This new type of strategic busting is certainly the way to go, in order to get "more bang for the buck". It is just so much fun to get confirmations like this.

Update 17 November 2004

We went back to the Kruger Park for a long weekend, mostly for recreational reasons. (The family permitted only the tossing out of "thingies" for drive-by towers, without detours.)

What a change we found since the last visit.

The time before we had been there in late December, normally the height of the rainy season, and it was bone dry, near dead – until we busted it, of course (see report above).

This time, more than a month earlier in the spring season, it was green as I had never seen it before.

They had already received 10% of their annual rainfall before we arrived, and another massive downpour with frightening lightning and thunder almost washed our tents away.

Really great confirmation of effective change here! We were all very impressed.

Disabling the coastal barrier

December 2004

In pursuit of our concept that the current drought conditions may be maintained by a row of HAARP arrays along the coast, designed to stop the inflow of moisture from the Indian Ocean, we planned a camping trip at the coast for the whole family.

This was to round off the results of our recent foray along the border of the Kruger Park.

We took off on 31 December and headed first for the southernmost part of the coastal stretch.

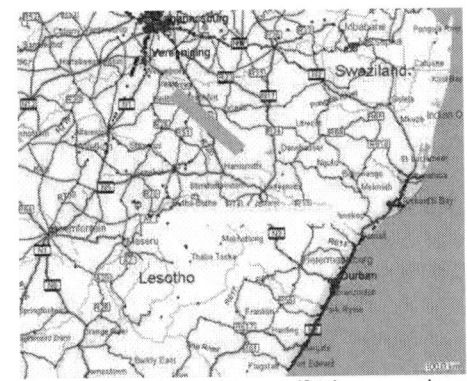

The map above shows gifted area along coastline in yellow. Gifted sites are blue dots. The ochre bar indicates estimated extent of chemtrails.

We carried 260 TBs and 36 etheric pipe bombs, of my stick handgrenade type. The latter have proven extremely effective in water gifting. On our way down, we saw the most gigantic block of chemtrails I have ever seen. Visible as an unnaturally straight fog bank from at least 30 km distance, the spraying reached as far as the eye could see.

The area looked particularly barren and has probably been subjected to such treatment for quite a long time. Busting all towers along the main highway between Durban and Port Shepstone on our way down, we also gifted all intersecting rivers with our etheric stick handgrenades.

I thought that putting the devices into fresh water would preserve them for longer, and since the road is pretty close to the shore, all the orgone charge would be distributed out into the sea anyway.

Large etheric stick hand grenade 35 x 350 mm. We also used 28 x 280 mm.

We had good rains already on the first night and pristine weather thereafter, with occasional showers. What was even more gratifying: A lot of rain fell subsequently in the hinterland; huge thunderstorms over Estcourt and along the Drakensberg mountain range.

The North Coast was not as easy, and we felt we had to come back.

Other than on the South Coast, where the concentration of towers is only along the coastal strip, Northern Zululand is heavily infested with full-blown HAARP arrays.

Blue hole over gifted tower array in Zululand

We did the highway through Durban; just everything that was in reach without exiting the highway, and the whole coastal strip up to Saint Lucia.

This included the agglomeration of Empangeni/Richards Bay that proved heavily tower-infested.

I had dowsed the major HAARP points, since I wanted to be more strategic about my targets, but could not resist the temptation to bust everything that came in sight.

Surely that coastline could be much strengthened by the presence of a few CBs, and certainly Zululand could use a lot more busting.

Build-up to thunderstorm in St Lucia

No wonder they put so many towers there, when you think what a proud and independent-minded folk the Zulu people have always been.

We were finally awarded a dramatic thunderstorm, although the rain measured was only 15 mm in St Lucia. Durban apparently had more.

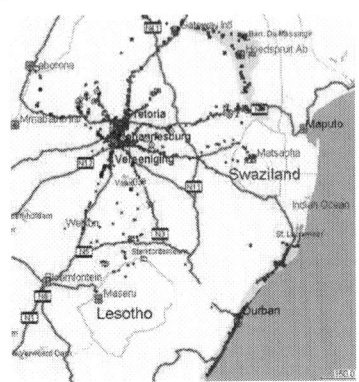

Map above shows the combination of our 2 recent forays highlighted in yellow.

The whole area was still a drought catastrophe area, with extremely low dam and river levels.

Given that the whole of December only yielded 17 mm of rain (it is normally more than 100 mm), our little storm was a good start, at least.

We will have to come back with more devices soon, because if we do not stop the drought now, another planting season will be lost.

The situation is actually better than shown here, since Trevor has also busted the road down from Johannesburg around Swaziland, so that in fact the two yellow areas are almost connected.

Free State busted again – confirmations galore

From 8-12 February 2004, we did another foray into the Free State province of South Africa, following reports of ongoing drought.

We had brought 2 cloudbusters to be donated to local farmers in the much-affected area along the Lesotho Border, from Ficksburg to Ladybrand and Maseru, the capital of Lesotho.

Our previous trips there had improved the situation, but not yet led to the expected breakthrough.

Our dear farmer and vocal warner about weather control, Eddie von Maltitz, had still not had sufficient rain. More "firepower" was definitely needed in the area.

We took approximately 400 TBs and about 30 of our new etheric stick handgrenades. I was accompanied by my friend Kevin, a seasoned overlander who is always ready for an interesting adventure.

A friend had given us the address of an organic farmer in the area, JM. We left early on the Sunday morning. A quick detour took us via Parys and the deep level gold mining operations around Welkom/Virginia.
This was where the magic started!

Energy swirls developing as we bust along

After busting many towers near mineshafts in this area, we saw wonderful vortices and swirls developing in the air.

One particularly big one seemed to be very far to the east. Shaped like a slow tornado, it was like a giant cone standing on its tip.

A nagging question beset me: Could this be Eddie's CB, so far held down by overpowering DOR from the mining area?

Beginning of vortex forming far away

Could our work here have had an effect over 70 km? We had placed it there in December 2002, but it had never really unfolded its full potential. This would be an explanation as to why people sometimes do not get the expected results from a CB immediately, before maybe neutralising a faraway source of DOR.

It's getting stronger

I trained the GPS to point at Eddie's place and – wow! – it pointed directly at the giant swirl!

The body of evidence

This would mean that the vortex had become alive because of the gifting work we had done here — about 100 km away.

The vortex from much closer up (hours later)

Our assumption was confirmed as we drove further south. The GPS arrow still pointed at the swirl ...

Interesting swirls on the periphery of the giant vortex

The heart of the vortex

Our little guest cottage at JM's farm

We spent the night at the wonderful farmhouse of JM. Our animated talks over a lovely improvised dinner revealed concurring ideas about almost every topic we touched on. J and his wife V are very well versed in the influence of subtle energies on agriculture, fertility, weather et cetera.

Big HAARP tower in large multi-tower array

The next day was spent busting some towers in the area, among them 2 formidable multitower HAARP arrays, with difficult access via hard-to-find dirt roads and partly over private farmland, which caused Kevin some understandable anxiety. We extended our foray into nearby Maseru, the capital of the mountain kingdom of Lesotho.

Blue hole forming after the array is busted

In the late afternoon, we delivered the second CB to a friend of JM, RVR who was chosen on J's suggestion to be the recipient of the second CB. This was "to space them out a bit" (that was how the good J had already taken in the whole story). The meeting was brief because we were late and he had some urgent work to do. He called us later to say that he was very excited and wanted us to come back the next day for some longer explanation of what this was all about. We decided to stay a day longer, do some more work in the area and go back to them in the course of that day.

Hole blown into HAARPy cloud with cloudbuster at RVR's farm

On the morning of the 10th, we visited Eddie von Maltitz, who had some interesting new political plans and was otherwise very much his own enthusiastic self. Since he had been observing the devastating effects of weather control by the dark side since the 1970s and had suffered personal economic ruin from it, he was watching our efforts with an understandable friendly scepticism. Convincing him that our stuff works was a major objective for me as, once satisfied, he would bring many of the more conservative farmers along.

Chemtrail whiteout near Eddie's farm

Chemtrails dissolving

who live in apparent isolation so far from the major centres.

In the late afternoon we went back to JVR, where we had a chance to give a bit of a demonstration as to how to disperse HAARP ripples with the cloudbuster.

The day ended with a wonderful vegetarian meal of tasty organically grown farm produce.

On the 11th, we finally left for home, knowing that a great part of the work was still ahead of us.

HAARP array on hilltop near Thaba N'chu. Note the rippled cloud. It dissolved right after we had finished with the town, including this array.

Driving through the countryside, we found that after our dramatic (weather-wise) arrival, the other side was launching an all-out, "no holds barred" attack to suppress the good energy. We found the whole area covered with thick parallel rows of chemtrails. Luckily they did not last.

We went on busting and visited another interested farmer in the area, with whom we had a very interesting chat. It is amazing to see how well informed a lot of these independent, rugged people are,

Busting our way through the area on different back roads, we went through Thaba N'chu, former capital of a so-called homeland for Sotho-speaking people, through Botshabelo to Bloemfontein, capital of the Free State province.

Both Thaba N'chu and Botshabelo presented an absolutely crazy amassment of microwave transmitters, confirming our impression that these are always concentrated threefold in mostly black areas.

The intended suppression of the

black people's strong spirituality seems to be the main reason for this.

We did Bloemfontein, noting that apart from a very impressive array on a prominent koppie called Naval Hill, there were far fewer towers in this neat Afrikaans-dominated town than in the much smaller townships of Botshabelo or Thaba N'chu.

While we were busy, rain clouds were rapidly forming and rain started to come down heavily.

The trip back to Johannesburg (tossing out our last TBs to neutralise some towers along the highway) was through an intense "cats-and-dogs" downpour with low visibility that lasted as far as Kroonstad.

Subsequent enquiries a few days later revealed that our new farmer friends had gotten less dramatic effects, but nice drizzles every evening since.

We shall have to watch for the longer-term changes in atmospheric conditions.

I am sure that JM will take up the fight by himself and finish the work in his area and beyond.

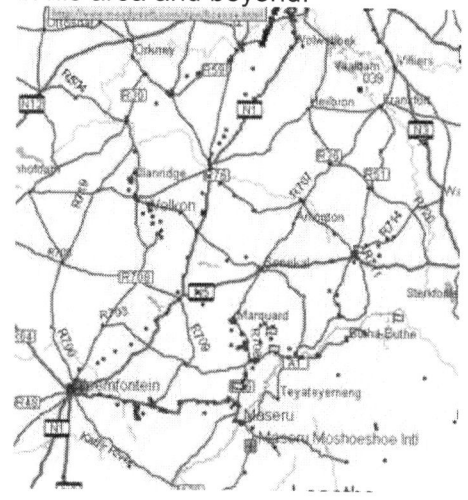

Free State busted – blue dots indicate gifted sites, flags indicate cloudbuster positions.

From paradise to Masonic Street and back

Over Easter, we visited our new friends Vanessa and James, the organic farmers in the Free State (see report: Free State busted again II), to spend some restful days and to exchange some ideas. What a paradise on earth they have created on their farm!

Once more, we found how compatible the principles of organic farming (based on an understanding of life processes and subtle energies) are with our experiences.

Since the farm had previously been attacked (it was more like a warning, since nothing was stolen; the office door had been broken and the desk messed up), possibly engineered by some agrochemical interests opposed to organic farming, we ringed it with about 30 TBs. James told me that after we placed the CB in mid-February, not only did they get abundant rain, but also the cattle looked much healthier. James feels that this is a direct result of the improved energy, not just the better feeding through improved growth of grazing pastures.

In his office I saw a copy of

Farmer's Weekly of 26 March 2004, with a map of rainfall in percentage over a long-year average. Amazingly, the areas showing above average rainfall matched very well with the areas we had so far treated with orgonite. The untreated areas, with the exception of the eastern part of the Western Cape, are still showing catastrophic drought conditions.

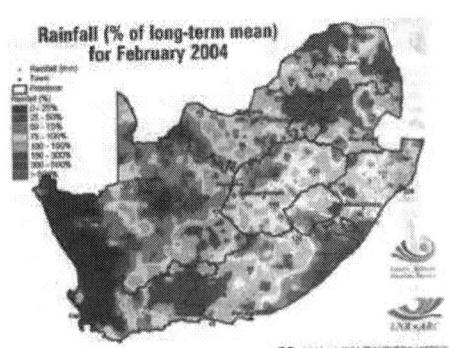

The darkest blue on this map is 150-300% of long-term mean, the darkest brown 0-25%

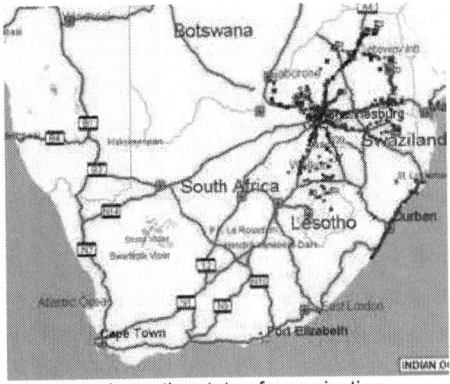

This map shows the state of orgonisation in mid-January 2004

Since our intensive busting of the eastern Free State in mid-February may have influenced the statistics, I am showing the status after the placement of 2 more CBs in the area and the busting of the Welkom-Bloemfontein-Ladybrand-Ficksburg area in mid-February.

The coincidence in the northern parts of the country is pretty much 95%. I shall pay more attention to such maps in the future and target the areas shown as below average.

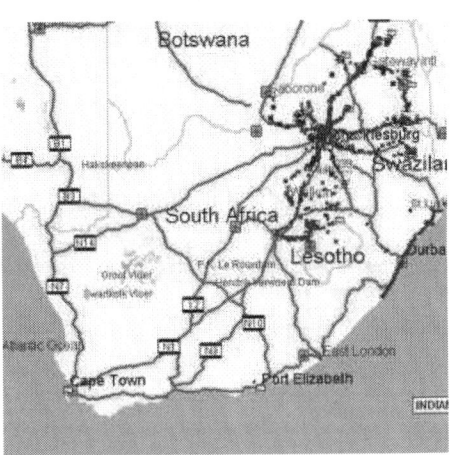

Status after busting the Free State the second time

Followed by sylphs – the trip to the Eastern Cape

From here, I wanted to do a busting trip to the Eastern Cape, which had still not received much rain and had so far not been reached by our efforts. Unfortunately James, who originally wanted to accompany me, had to stay home due to some urgent work on the farm. It looked as though I would have to do it alone. Luckily, my elder daughter Katharina (whom I would call Bustagirrl on this trip) volunteered to accompany me. Friederike and my younger daughter Isabella stayed on the farm.

Lately there has been a lot of talk on the forums about the nature spirits, especially the ones of the air, also known as sylphs.

I am not able to say if these beautiful cloud formations are "beings" in a conscious sense, or just swirls and vortices of energy.

I had been told by friends in our network that I would see them more often now, and that is exactly what is happening.

Sylph over JCM's farm on day of departure for the Eastern Cape

Looking at them regularly makes me smile. While the scientific question of what these things are may still be open, I will henceforth refer to them as sylphs.

On the day we started off, Thursday 15 April, we were greeted by a whole bunch of them, as if they had known that we would be ready to go on that day. (The days before we did not see a single one.)

It felt as though a celestial escort had arrived, waiting for us to get moving.

As we went along, we soon noticed that the sylphs were following us. They formed rapidly over us and stayed at those places we had already passed.

Some vortex is coming alive with happy nature spirits

Our busting tours are often a really 4-dimensional experience, as changes happen dynamically and are connected to our own movement and activity. It is very hard to convey that experience.

It is hard not to think of them as etheric beings

111

However, I sincerely hope that my reports allow you to imagine at least some of it.

As quantum physics has postulated: there is no independent observer, only participators. That is as true for the orgone dynamics on a planetary level, as it is for the subatomic level.

This display of sylph-like cloud formations was to become the real hallmark of this trip. I had not seen them in such quantities ever before. Careful observation confirmed that they were not present ahead of us or far to the left or right of our path.

It was an amazing feeling.

It took us more than 2 hours to get to this mountaintop array, but ...

More sylphs as we go along ...

... and more

... we were allowed to cross beautiful mountainscapes like this!

Sylphlike sky over Xhosa settlement – some dissipating HAARP ripples still visible

Eastern Cape 2004

The cloudbuster we had brought went to Rob and Serena in Bathurst, a small historical settler town 50 km south of Grahamstown. The choice of destination was spontaneous, as we had only just met them at James's farm in the Free State, and the originally intended recipient in East London was still away on a trip out of the country. The Grahamstown area had not even originally been on our itinerary.

Serena, Rob, their children and BUSTAGIRL with the new CB in Bathurst

They make herbal ointments from beeswax and organic sunflower oil (from James's farm). It turned out that Rob is a well-versed expert in the history of the Eastern Cape, especially in the history of the wars between the Xhosa and the encroaching settlers (with great sympathy for the side of the Xhosa), and a special emphasis on the role played by Freemasons and other secret societies in creating the present-day situation. Even though time was short, we had the most interesting conversation. Coincidentally, it turned out that Port Alfred, a small port nearby, and Grahamstown, the long-time unofficial capital of the Eastern Cape, were Masonic hotspots of note. Coincidence? Who or what had led us here?

Prince Michael Duke of Kent, Grand Master of the Grand Lodge of Mark Master Masons and Provincial Grand Lodge of Middlesex.

Port Alfred even sports a Masonic Street, where the local lodge is fittingly situated.

One should not underestimate the significance of this little town for the satanic network of the Freemasons.

Prince Michael, Duke of Kent, is coming there personally to initiate the new Grand Master ...

We have earlier elaborated that orgonite does not work only on the physical but also on the spiritual plane. (See report of Uganda trip in November 2003.) Gifting Masonic Lodges, places of human sacrifice and blood ritual – meant to spiritually enforce the age-old spell

The body of evidence

of covert control and bondage of humanity under the yoke of these self-proclaimed "masters of the dark and occult arts" – has become an increasingly important part of the bigger perspective of our work.

So we gifted the lodge well, as well as all the towers and other places of bad energy generation.

Rob then showed us the Masonic layout of Grahamstown on a tourist map, indicating the old lodge, as well as the new (active) one.

As we were busy hiding our Easter eggs there, we saw some cars pulling up and members entering. To describe one older man (adorned with a golden medallion and other ceremonial garb) as an old reptile is not an exaggeration. His head resembled that of an old turtle.

We usually feel the stale and negative atmosphere around these places.

No wonder Freemasonry is (at least in its visible outward circles) on the decline. It just looks so outdated. I imagine a lot of the occult power is nowadays withdrawn from old-fashioned Freemasonry and invested in the various flourishing New Age cults. This bizarre organisation has, however, been a major controlling force (in competition with the Afrikaans Broederbond that had different membership and ritual, but of course obeyed the same controlling force) in South Africa, more than in many other places.

I have heard many accounts of how people were approached to join, and how it was considered absolutely futile to start out on a professional career without being a member ...

And also here the sky turned sylphlike after the deed was done

The Anglican Cathedral in Grahamstown is situated on a triangular space at the intersection of the 2 main roads (one road entirely commercial, the other entirely religious, if you want to call the Masonic cult a religion).

It has a crypt that is not mentioned in any of the leaflets available for tourists. This crypt has historically also been used for Masonic ritual, so the place was gifted well.

After driving 2500km in 3 days and gifting about 230 spots, we were quite exhausted when we returned to James's farm. It had rained all night in the Eastern Cape, on the second day and into the morning of the third day. Some scattered thunderstorms had been forecast by the weather bureau, but certainly not a constant downpour over a large area, accompanied by a strong wind coming from the north.

Coming home and assessment

We drove home after only 5 hours' sleep, to find that it had not rained much in Johanesburg in our absence, much to my anxiety.

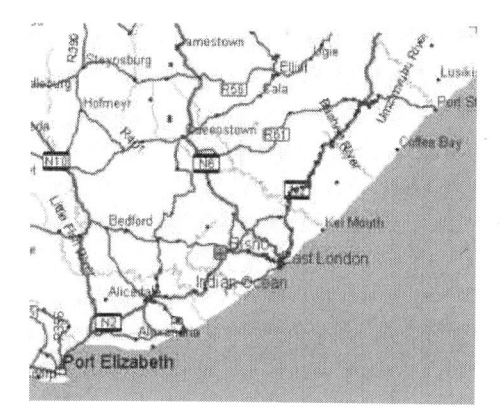

The newly gifted area – blue dots are gifted spots, the flag symbol represents a cloudbuster

The night of Monday 19th to the morning of the 20th surprised us. In the middle of the night there was a heavy downpour, accompanied by very impressive thunder and lightning, which continued until 8 in the morning.

This developed very rapidly almost out of nowhere (there was a bit of cloud build-up in the evening, but nothing to suggest this deluge), producing a respectable 26 mm of rainfall. We had by now received the full annual rainfall with 5 – albeit traditionally dry – months to go.

Since the above maps only show the gifts that I have personally recorded with my GPS, the actual situation is better than it looks here. Trevor has done some gifting in KwaZulu-Natal and Cape Town, and Andy has done large parts of Botswana.

The new state of affairs in South Africa

Three days in Cape Town
June 2004

An older and more experienced rain making colleague

Peter von Maltitz is a distant relative of Eddie von Maltitz, the well-known Free State farmer (see earlier reports). The split in the family tree seems to go back some five generations and the two could not be more different in personality.

Peter von Maltitz has (apart from studies in agriculture, plant pathology, anthroposophist farming and homeopathy), undergone training as a spiritual healer (sangoma) in the Xhosa tradition and practises under the name Zanemvula, which means "he comes with the rain". Some time ago, I had come across him on the Internet while looking for his relative Eddie, and we had corresponded about Credo Mutwa, whom Peter also happens to know and admire. I thus luckily landed on his email list.

You can read more about Zanemvula and his work on his website www.zanemvula.co.za.

A few days before, I had received notification that he would be holding a rain-calling ceremony on the Paarl mountain near Cape Town. Spontaneously, I decided to participate and take a cloudbuster for permanent deployment in the Cape.

Since I was somewhat late in arriving at the meeting place (I had underestimated the distance from Cape Town, where I was staying), I had to climb up to the top alone. After a somewhat sweat-drenched power hike with the 20kg cloudbuster in my backpack, I approached the summit. On the last few hundred metres I was guided to by the sound of African drums. I was soon to find that nobody had actually brought drums. The sound, although clearly audible, had only been in my head, yet it led me to where I needed to go. (No, I am obviously not writing my warrant for internment in a mental institution.)

I had expected a huge crowd of more than 100 people from all over the country and was a bit disappointed when I found only a small group of people gathered on the rounded rock.

The participants sat grouped in a rough circle, including Zanemvula who was busy stirring a greenish liquid in an iron pot with a forked twig.

Zanemvula was later to remark that the eleven people present was exactly the right number for what we intended to ask.

Zanemvula addressing the circle

Nobody said much and I got down to unpacking and assembling my cloudbuster, under the curious glances of the other participants. I did not want to impose myself too much, and therefore placed it outside the circle.

Peter (Zanemvula) then asked all the participants what rain meant for them. Themes of fertility, relaxation or relief were mentioned. At first I did not know what to say because I wanted to avoid uttering platitudes. Then I burst out with, "Rain is the opposite of desert forming, desiccation and drought." Since I have made it my mission to restore natural rainfall everywhere in Africa, this was the most essential thing for me. "For this reason, I have brought this strange contraption, of which nobody need be afraid as it is absolutely compatible with the endeavour of this group," I continued.

I will not try to relay the whole ceremony in all detail. I can only say that it was serene and beautiful and there was a great simplicity and therefore real spirituality.

Peter manages to present the spiritual and rational realms in total harmony, an ability that I have also noticed in Credo Mutwa.

This is, of course, in stark contrast to widely held prejudices about shamanism, animism and the like.

While we were busy with the ceremony, some great cloud formations showed up, of the kind that we had already earlier identified as "air spirits", "sylphs" or, more precisely, their physical manifestation.

Originally, I had planned to hand over the CB to Zanemvula. Unfortunately, it turned out that he had only a small flat in Cape Town.

This one really looks like an angelic being

I was therefore happy when Alfriede and her daughter Kathie, who live on a farm not far from the Paarl Rock, volunteered to host the CB.

The following photos were shot in quick succession, just after descending the mountain. They are indicative of the great revitalising force we all felt.

Sylphs over Paarl

More...

The body of evidence

... and more

I did a little extra round to orgonise the city of Paarl, and then went to their farm for a nice afternoon chat with coffee on the veranda, where we were joined by Alfriede's husband Neill.

They had already assembled the CB and found a nice place for it.

Alfriede and family with CB

We later had a nice dinner together and I am sure that the CB is in good hands with them.

Neill is a farmer and entrepreneur who has his feet firmly on the ground, but maintains a sceptical open mindedness towards biological farming and spiritual and natural healing issues – a good basis for meaningful observations.

I went back to Cape Town that night, but not before leaving a few orgone gifts on my way through Stellenbosch, Khayelitsha and Mitchell's Plain.

The Lonesome Buster...

(Here I ask you please to imagine Ennio Morricone's soundtrack from "Once Upon A Time In The West" ...)

I spent the next day busting the Cape Peninsula, in the widest sense, in my rented tin can, a Toyota Tazz.

This was mostly unspectacular legwork (on the accelerator and brakes mostly), apart from two highlights.

The Rhodes Memorial

I have had my sights set for quite some time on the Arch-Illuminatus Cecil John Rhodes, destroyer of the traditional Africa and power-wielding manipulator (see earlier report from Zimbabwe).

It is said that his body lies buried in the Matopos Hills in Zimbabwe, but his heart is kept in the Rhodes Memorial at the Groote Schuur Estate, which had been his residence for a long time.

The Matopos Hills were holy to the Matabele and their predecessors and were known as the centre of a "rain cult" of great influence and fame (a typical misunderstanding by the missionaries, as this was not a different religion, but an aspect of the universal African traditional religion) that is still alive in the region with the rain sanctuary of Ingelele Rock a bit further south.

Rhodes, who won the trust of the Matabele and gleaned a lot of knowledge from their sangomas, only to betray them terribly not much later, had this area declared a National Park. This meant, in effect, the expulsion of the original inhabitants, as he wanted to take possession of this magical piece of earth for his own dark magical purposes.

We had of course already orgonised his grave there earlier (and that of his notorious "lieutenant" Leander Starr Jameson), and now it was the turn of the other mortal remains of this restless spirit – a plan that had been on my agenda for a long time.

Rhodes Memorial at Groote Schuur Estate
This is where his heart is buried. His body lies in the Matopos Hills

Further orgonite gifts were distributed in the city bowl and in the Victoria and Alfred Waterfront, a refurbished docklands area, with new upmarket housing and commercial ventures – very popular with tourists. I could see lovely sylphs in the sky all the time.

Sylphs over V+A Waterfront and harbour

The air pollution in Cape Town, mostly from the unregulated burning for heating and cooking as well as all kinds of trash in the growing slums, is substantial and it competed heavily with the more positive phenomena in the sky.

The Koeberg nuclear power station

Towards the end of the day, I drove north via Milnerton and Bloubergstrand, where I had seen air pollution of the worst kind from the distance. This area had already been treated by Trevor, not long before, so I concentrated mostly on gifting the water bodies with my etheric stick hand grenades.

A few gifts were also left near Ysterplaat Airforce Base, though (you never know about these places ...) and a few other points on the way.

Koeberg should now become the adventure of the day.

The body of evidence

Pondering the motto "alone against the nuke", I approached the monster that was built out into the sea from the beach.

Air pollution over west coast (Bloubergstrand). Koeberg is not far from here.

Some very HAARPy antennas at Ysterplaat Air Force Base

It was already dark, and the route from the nearest accessible parking was some 3-4 km long. The power station had an eerie presence by night, lit up with yellow lights and the backdrop of the dark and raging sea. As I got closer I felt tense and anxious. What would happen if I was detected? It was almost full moon and I had the impression of seeing a large lenticular cloud, said by many of our compadres to be a sure indication of a cloaked (mostly friendly Lemurian) UFO.

That thought gave me courage.

I had to climb over slippery surf breaker rocks in order to get closer and also had to negotiate a huge and grimy discharge pipe from which a tree-sized jet of hot foul-smelling water was constantly splattered on to the beach. Still clambering over the slippery rocks, I rounded a corner and then understood the whole layout of the plant. The cooling water was being taken directly from the sea, in vast amounts, and pumped back at high pressure and volume through a wide channel, separated from the intake by a quay of surf breakers that extended out into the sea for a few hundred metres, thus preventing the mingling of the cold intake water with the somewhat warmer exhaust water. The whole thing is pretty gigantic.

I could unfortunately only reach the outlet side, where the water shot out into the sea like a river 15-20m wide. The orgonite gifts (three etheric stick hand grenades) will probably not last very long under these conditions and will have to be replaced soon.

I felt so much lighter when I got away from the influence of this monster machine and the torchlight beams of the (luckily) somewhat sleepy guards and, singing and whistling nonchalantly, I made my way back towards the car.

It was only on my way back that I noticed the "No Entry" signs that forbid access, even to the unfenced periphery of the plant. Well....

The intake is unfortunately fenced

off in such a wide area that I had to abandon for this night every dream of crowning this little adventure by gifting that side as well.

I think this task could best be accomplished from one of the many seagoing yachts that can be hired for sports fishing tours, et cetera.

At last: A mountain hike

For some time I had been in contact with Cristo Louw from the UFO research group Saufor.[33] He had told me that the area known as the Old Silvermine Reserve had been reported in many UFO experiences as a place of peculiarly intense activity; very well worth treating.

I thought: "Why not spend the few hours before my flight back to Johannesburg on a nice mountain stroll?"

Off I went, paid the 10 rand entry fee (nature is surely not for free in Cape Town), and drove up to the Silvermine water reservoir through the Silvermine river valley, throwing the usual gifts out of the car window approximately every 250m. (They are all green so they do not spoil the landscape.)

Silent mountain lake in Old Silvermine Nature Reserve, a place with many UFO sightings. The sending mast is hardly visible in the picture, but is situated on the dark mountaintop at the back.

I left two of my special water gifts there, and behold, a giant transmission tower on the peak in the distance caught my attention. Whoops! Would I have a chance to make it up there in the short period of time remaining before my flight back to Johannesburg?

"Well, I can try at least," I thought.

So I trotted off in the general direction.

It was a gorgeous day and everything smelled of aromatic herbs.

It was about 9.30 am and the flight was scheduled for 3 pm.

The view over the Cape Flats was fantastic although it was difficult to distinguish between fogbanks and the sea.

Lonesome hut

Further up, I passed by a hut, perched dramatically on a mountaintop. Who would not want to spend a week there in meditation, provided someone else carried up all the food provisions?

The path led to a cave that showed some surprising green fern growth in the interior.

The whole thing looked somewhat unreal. I left 2 orgonite gifts, in case I did not make it up to the top.

The body of evidence

Fern growth in interior of cave

I should have turned back at the cave if I wanted to be sure to catch my plane. But now my ambition was fully aroused and I thought, "Well, I could continue until 11 am."

Finally, almost there...

... and arrived! (Please note the small globe in the background: weather radar, a source of DOR par excellence.)

When I finally reached the top and had laid out my gifts around the base of the tower, it was almost 12pm.

I tried to call Friederike to ask her to try to reschedule my flight, but in mid-sentence the battery of my cellphone went flat.

Dammit!

I started running downhill, taking a risky short cut by galloping straight down the steep slope, cursing and yelling through the thick knee-high shrubs. I did indeed make it back to the car within 45 minutes and was at my friends' apartment in Fish Hoek, where I had been staying, at 12.45pm. I only had to get the bed linen from the laundry, make the bed, clean the kitchen surfaces, wash hand basin, bath and toilet, stuff everything in my big bag, put a new T-shirt over my soaking wet body, and then I was off to the airport. I almost forgot to leave the key with the caretaker.

At 14.35, I was at the check-in

counter of Kulula Air and they would still have allowed me to board, had I not needed to dump the rental car first.

Luckily, there was no problem and they booked me on the next flight an hour later without any extra charge.

Throughout the flight I observed a low foggy cloud cover with a clearly defined upper limit. A lot of moisture was already there.

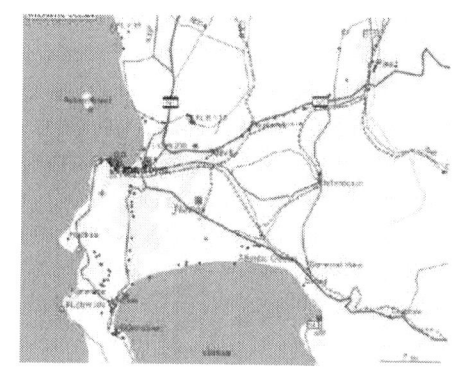

Blue dots indicate orgonite gifts. Flags are cloudbusters

Résumé

We would only see in the next days and weeks whether the effort was worth it. Apart from the many sylphs, dramatic confirmations, in the form of downpours, did not occur. I think it was because this was just the beginning – the western part of the country had so far benefited the least from our efforts.

Consequently, while the drought could be almost completely stopped, and even partly reversed in the eastern parts of the country, the western part, especially the Atlantic coast, was still suffering below average rainfalls. This is where we will have to concentrate in the next few months, in order to prevent the development of drought in the next planting season.

We therefore planned finally to pull off our long-planned trip to Namibia and the Northern Cape that had been postponed the previous year for lack of funding.

For this trip we would need at least five cloudbuster sponsorships.

Addendum 04 June 2004

In the meantime rain clouds formed over the Cape Peninsula as shown in the radar weather map below.

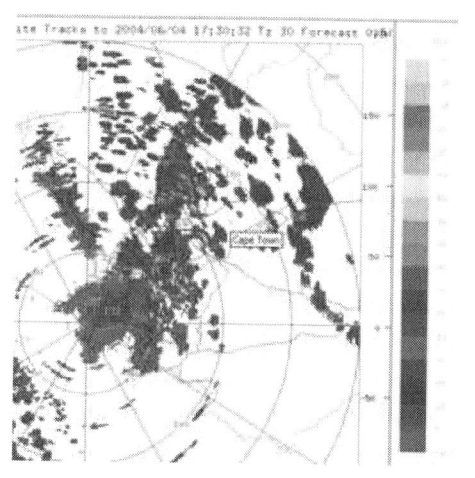

The yellow and red areas show the highest cloud density and are most likely the spots where it has already started to drizzle.

The weather forecasts predicted solid 100% rain for at least the next 3 days, starting that night in Cape Town, Paarl and Hermanus.

Mama Mbeki's zapper and cloud buster

07 July 2004

Since the end of the previous year I had been in contact with Dr Kizito, a Ugandan medical doctor who lives and works in South Africa's Eastern Cape province. I met him through Drs Batiibwe and Kayiwa with whom we had been working in Uganda for some time.

When I showed him the zapper at our first meeting, he said, to my great joy and surprise, that this was nothing new to him.

He had received his medical training in the then Soviet Union. According to Dr Kizito, the basic principle of therapy by weak electric current has been known there since the beginning of the 20th century and is being used on a wide variety of ailments. The name given to this therapy in Russia and the other countries of the former Soviet Union is ELECTROPHORESIS.

Since Dr Kizito's emphasis was on sports medicine, he had mostly seen applications in the healing of sports injuries and wounds.

He is an internationally recognised expert in natural healing methods, especially in the field of African healing plants.

Apart from many other diseases, he has had mind-boggling success with AIDS patients.

A special role is played by the products of the *Moringa tree*, which is indigenous to many Equatorial African countries, among them Uganda. Moringa contains a remarkably complete palette of micro nutrients and vitamins. Further antiviral effects have been noticed.

Many AIDS patients who were suffering from extreme weight loss, were bedridden and plagued by all kinds of secondary diseases, have been restored to full vitality.

Indicators hailed by orthodox AIDS medicine as significant, such as the "CD4 count", regularly show visible improvement. (I reserve the right to have my doubts about virtually any dogmata of conventional "AIDS science").

At Dr Kizito's suggestion, I sent his presently most prominent patient, Mama Mbeki, the 88-year-old mother of South African president Thabo Mbeki, a zapper. (Of course it was an EL SILVERDO.)

She was suffering from bad arthritis, with joint pain and reduced mobility.

A few weeks later, Dr Kizito called me to tell me how enthusiastic Mama Mbeki was about her zapper and that she would like to meet me. She also asked if I could bring one of my cloudbusters as well.

I did not hesitate, and an appointment was scheduled for 2 July. Of course I also wanted to see Dr Kizito's work with AIDS patients.

The visit with Mama Mbeki went beyond expectations. She is a wonderful, elegant and charming lady who is far from appearing old or even frail. Mama Mbeki lives in Idutiyva in the former Xhosa homeland of Transkei, now part of the Eastern Cape province. Apart from a little cabin for the presidential guard, her house does not show any signs of an elevated social status; in fact, it spoke of very modest circumstances.

She chose this lifestyle as she wishes to be close to the community of her origin.

Mama Mbeki was very happy about our visit and volunteered much positive comment about the zapper. Her general vitality and agility were the best proof that she felt well and was no longer suffering from debilitating pain.

She has dedicated her former more stately home, in which she shared the last years of her husband's (the late Gowan Mbeki, a paramount leader of the ANC) life to be utilised by Dr Kizito as a hospice and clinic.

Dr Kizito was to establish a community care facility there, which was urgently needed in the generally impoverished area, which is plagued by diseases of poverty (not only AIDS).

Originally the idea was to place the cloudbuster at this future hospice. But on inspection it became clear that it would not be well guarded there before the clinic was opened.

It was thus decided to place the CB in Mama Mbeki's yard. The sky had been overcast with ugly chemcrud for a while. Soon after the erection of the CB, we saw a few blue openings and the beginning of cumulus clouds.

Later we would see a vortex forming around the location of MM's CB that was visible from afar. And later that evening, we got further confirmation in the form of a weather forecast showing a rain front moving through at this unlikely time of the year. We were to witness this front moving in on our departure, though not yet the rain itself.

Mama Mbeki showed delight over the CB, especially over the aspect of its possibly contributing to breaking the vicious cycle of rural impoverishment, overpopulation, biodegradation, erosion, and destruction of cultural traditions and consequent depression and lack of initiative.

We parted in a heightened mood after some animated conversation.

During the following one and a half days, we visited several of Dr Kizito's patient groups. Most of them were diagnosed HIV+ and AIDS sufferers.

The majority of these groups were in the care of church organisations run by volunteers, most of whom had themselves been diagnosed HIV+ or were confirmed to have AIDS. The successes through improved nutrition and the application of Dr Kizito's immune-boosters were reported by all.

Nevertheless, I felt that both the patients and helpers had been programmed by fear.

From all sides, it is hammered into their brains that they are suffering from an incurable disease that will inevitably lead to an early death, after a protracted phase of sickness under the influence of the side effects of antiretrovirals (as if they had any proven beneficial effects).

Even those who had been

emaciated skeletons and had subsequently fully recovered with Dr Kizito's immune boosters were still psychologically transfixed by this imaginary predicament.

The programming is reinforced by remote-controlled AIDS activist groups, especially the TAC (Treatment Action Campaign), and also increasingly by government health agencies.

This is the more regrettable as President Mbeki and the Health Minister Dr Manto Tshabalala Msimang, who has just been reaffirmed for her second term, have voiced serious and well-founded doubts about the comical vodoo beliefs of the deadly AIDS orthodoxy.

The pressure exerted by the interest groups behind these voodoo beliefs still seems to be overwhelming, steamrollering mercilessly over all legitimate doubts and any questions.[IV]

In view of the social and economic factors that come together here, it is difficult not to believe in a deliberate effort to reduce the black rural population, who have been unofficially declared "superfluous eaters" by the protagonists of the New World Order (corporate fascism).

The cynical consequences of this plan bring tears to one's eyes, especially after meeting the brave victims fighting for their lives and those of others, while being fed with false information from all sides.

This is even more tragic when one considers that AIDS victims can easily be restored to full health by detoxification, nutrition therapy, good food and a zapper.

Some patients had already had some positive experiences with the zapper, but not many. Of the five zappers I had sold to Dr Kizito, most were given to individual private patients.

For this reason I gave three zappers to trustworthy (HIV+) caregivers in order for them to use them on themselves and interested patients in their care.

The advantage of this arrangement is that all three have access to testing (HIV Antibody, CD4 and Viral Load) which may help to widen our body of evidence.

Ethically, I am asking you to understand this in view of our multiple experiences of strong improvement in HIV patients. We have received reports about use of the zapper increasing the total sero-conversion and its complete harmlessness in terms of side effects, based on the experience of thousands of users over many years.

All three volunteers we are working with are strong and charismatic personalities, who have not allowed themselves to be held

---

[IV] Now, 2 years later the situation has not improved. Minister Manto Tshabalala Msimang has been subjected to merciless mobbing by the media which has driven her to a point of near exhaustion. She has apparently now given up most of her resistance against the mass administration of antiretovirals.

back by the illness and the accompanying propaganda. The perspective that the disease could possibly not only be held back, but conquered completely in a relatively short time, has given them new enthusiasm.

I am looking forward to the negative results of this little experiment, as well as getting to meet these impressive women again.

Mozambique – another African country de-HAARP-ed

Days 1 and 2: Getting there and busting Maputo

When we approached the Mozambican border on 8 July, a wall of negative energy seemed to tower in front of us. The cloud formations looked gooey and held in place by electromagnetic fields, which we shall further refer to as HAARP, for simplicity's sake.

My heart was sinking down to about knee height; would we able to make a difference here, with our modest arsenal of 200TBs, a few water busters and 2 cloudbusters?

We passed Maputo on our way to the first overnight stop, a camping ground 40km to the north. Naturally, all the death ray emitters along the way (of which there were many) were treated in the usual way.

In the evening we erected one of our CBs to stay in place for the duration of our stay. Even this little "foreplay" resulted in an unseasonal drizzle, which lasted the whole night (not nice for camping, but ...)

Next morning Katharina (my 9-year-old daughter) and I went to bust Maputo and its surroundings, while the others (Friederike and Bella, our 7-year-old daughter, and neighbour's son Dylan, 9) stayed at the camping ground.

Despite the initial cleaning effect of our approach, Maputo's sky was covered with poisonous chemcrud, HAARPed into a rippled carpet.

Luckily this was to change significantly in the course of the day, into visible results and confirmation of our work. To witness something like this always creates a euphoric mood which is however difficult to document. It would need an experienced filmmaker to reproduce the 4-dimensional space-time experience of such a gradual transformation. He would also have to have an idea of what to expect, in order to get the right camera angles in advance and so on.

I hope that the following pictures and comments will give an idea of the process.

Dense HAARP-Chemsoup, here above a transmitter mast

The body of evidence

Typical HAARP cloud, already somewhat dissolved. The original rippled structure from the HAARP is still visible. We see this happening all the time

Hotel Costa Do Sol, a landmark situated at the end of the Maputo beach road serves tasty seafood dishes. We had a nice lunch break there.

The HAARP clouds in the foreground are already in dissolution, still behind the dense carpet as initially found everywhere. One should make a movie of this.

Transformation of clouds in full swing: In the background, luminescent cumulus clouds, in the fore, dissolution of HAARP carpet and beginning of vortex formation.

HAARP carpet dissolving

Looking back at Maputo, we saw healthy cumulus cloud and some remnants of the HAARP carpet.

Mozambique 2004

"Energy flares" dissolve DOR-based "false" clouds.

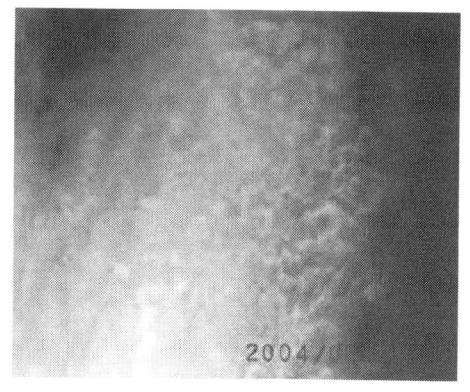

A telling picture, showing how the "false" HAARP cloud dissolves under impact of orgone energy.

Transformation of "flat" chemcrud into cumulus

Peri-urban settlement north of Maputo

An etheric battle rages: healthy cumulus and dissolving chemcrud.

Soviet era kitsch still rampant in Maputo cityscape. After all, Mozambique was a client state of the Soviet Union during the cold war and socialist monuments still abound all over the country.

The body of evidence

HAARP array in Maputo

Postcard sunset on the way to Mozal plant

Transformation: Both types of clouds to be seen at the same time.

Still somewhat HAARPy but getting better by the time

HAARP installation II did not escape our scanning eyes for long either

Mozal aluminium smelter by night

Driving through the poorer suburbs of Maputo, we found that the people live in relative paradise compared to many South African slums.

I am surely a hopeless romantic saying something like this ...

Every family lives in their vegetable orchard and sells their produce right on their doorstep. Neatly trimmed thorn bush hedges surround the simple homesteads.

A rather well preserved Soviet star on a large roundabout near the airport reminds one of the recent past of Mozambique as a "client state" of the Eastern Bloc. One sees many other touching leftovers of those times, with Soviet and East German kitsch elements of all kinds all over the country ...

After that, we went on to the "MOZAL" aluminium smelter, hailed as the pride of Mozambique's recent economic boom. Coincidentally, it was a major DOR emitter, like all plants or installations that use or produce large quantities of electricity, not to mention the poisoning of the small river it uses for cooling. This, together with the related electrical relay station, was our last major target for the day as it was already dark.

One can still spot a lot of HAARP influence in the sky, but I view the wonderful luminescence in the atmosphere as a sign of increasing orgonisation.

Next morning, we decided to leave the CB with the very nice owner of the camping ground, who had shown keen interest in the device. She promised to let us have the results of her observations (she has recorded rainfall over the years). I would have preferred to have it stationed in Maputo, but the contact person we had planned to ask to host it was unreachable.

Days 3-12: Vilanculos, Inhambane and back

Driving north we found a layer of HAARPed cloud, always receding in front of us. Towers were at first spaced at about 10 km intervals, always grouped in pairs on both sides of the road. These intervals widened as we drove further north.

Receding HAARP carpet near Xai-Xai

The HAARP carpet was consistent along the whole road

We entered Vilanculos at night. Again, it was a feeling of hitting a solid wall of negativity. The air was filled with acrid smoke from numerous coal-burning fires, hurting the eyes as we drove in.

Since the local HAARP array was easily spotted in the centre of town, we hit it right on arrival with one of our last TBs. Interestingly, I never noticed the same level of pollution again during our five-day stay.

The extreme negativity of Vilanculos, despite its appearance of paradise, was later confirmed by a long-term resident, who told us that all people who stayed there longer than three months typically developed depression at some point. She said that Vilanculos was sitting on a negative ley-line.

While Mozambicans are normally a mellow and friendly bunch, the atmosphere between the mostly white tourists and the local population in Vilanculos was rather tense, with an undercurrent of aggression. I am sure there are complex reasons for that ...

We hope to have infused some positivity into that conduit.

Tourist image 1: The kiddos on traditional fishing dhow

Near our campsite, we found a sign saying "medico tradicional", meaning traditional doctor, and off we went in search of a suitable custodian for our CB.

While verbal communication was difficult, the atmosphere was relaxed as we waited outside and watched the family pounding sorghum in a traditional pestle and mortar.

We received the full treatment from Alexander, the traditional healer, including a cleansing wash in wonderfully smelling herbs. Unfortunately, all predictions and advice that resulted from the traditional practice of "throwing the bones" were lost on us, but the combination of prayer, herbal treatment and ritual were surely not in vain.

Medico traditional Alexander in his treatment room

We felt very elated afterwards despite many misunderstandings because of the language barrier.

We finally found someone to translate from English to

Mozambique 2004

Portuguese. Thus Alexander, besides receiving an appropriate fee for the treatment, became the custodian of the Vilanculos CB.

Alexander, his wife and the CB

Some travellers on their way to Malawi took the three remaining water busters (also known as the etheric stick hand grenade) to plant in the important Save and Zambezi rivers and Lake Malawi.

On our way back, we spent five more days near Inhambane, in another postcard setting of coconut palm lined beach. We had rain every day, which was totally unseasonal, but were able to enjoy some swimming and some intermittent warm hours as well.

How this fits into the general effort:

In December 2003 and January 2004, we had unlocked the rainfall by following the idea of unblocking the coastline. This had proven extremely successful, as we managed to stop a terrible drought and unleash rain over most parts of Southern Africa. We had done the South African coastline from Port Shepstone to Saint Lucia, a 600 km stretch, and the whole area along the Kruger National Park.

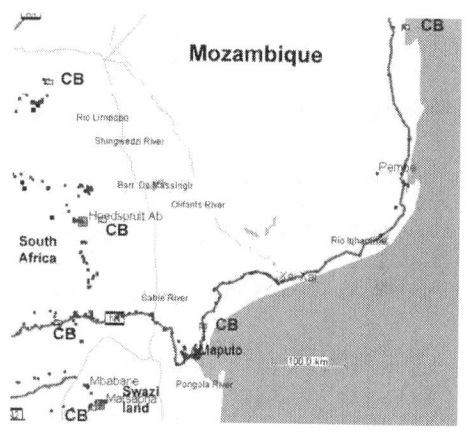

Map showing the state of orgonisation in the area under review here. Blue dots are recorded orgonite gifts by Orgonise Africa. The other areas include those gifted by activists known to us.

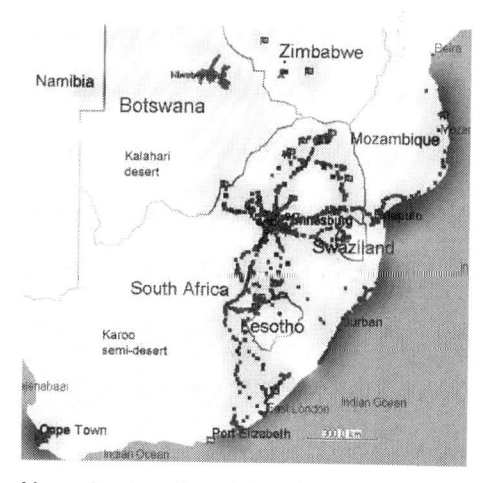

Map showing the state of orgonisation in Southern Africa as of 27.07.2004. The yellow (land) and dark blue (water) areas indicate areas well treated with orgonite.

133

The coast of Mozambique was therefore the only remaining place where major HAARP influence could remain. Of course it was to be assumed that most of the electromagnetic interference would be concentrated around the capital Maputo. Surely some bad spots may remain, especially as we did not get to the major port city of Beira in the north and there may be military bases, et cetera, in otherwise unpopulated areas.

Judging from the visual confirmations that we got in dissolving the visible HAARP carpet, we at least achieved "air superiority" for the time being. It was a good beginning.

A lot remains to be done, especially in the western part of the country, and naturally past successes need to be consolidated by more CBs and orgonite gifts.

I hope that a lot more activists will answer the call in the near future and help us fill in the gaps.

Operation Desert Rain, Namibia

September – October 2004

We had been planning this trip for a long time in order to connect our efforts on the eastern side of the subcontinent to the Atlantic coast!

Namibia is one of the driest countries in the world, despite its having a coastline (some 1600 km of Atlantic beach), in a somewhat moderate climate zone in the African context, as far as latitude is concerned.

It is a strange anomaly that is explained by the official weather guys with talk of the cold Benguela current.

Of course we do not believe a word of that, and see the reason for these fatal weather mechanics in one of the few coastal deserts in the blockage of orgone energy flow. Causes and exact location of this blockage are as yet unknown, but we have heard rumours from esoteric circles that the blockage was installed by "dark side" forces some 10 000 years ago. (That makes it the late period of Atlantis, right?)

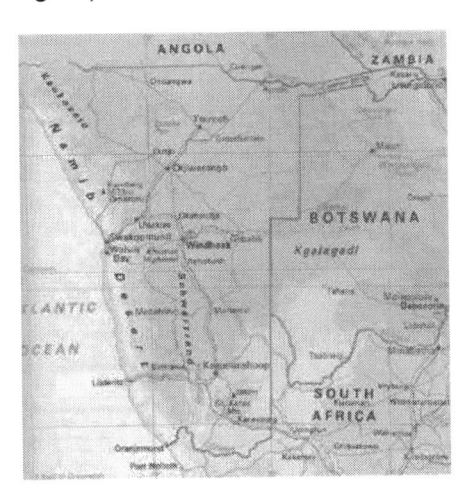

Map of Namibia

Namibia was a German colony until 1918 (Deutsch Südwestafrika), and still has a German feel about it in many respects. A large proportion of the white population is of German extraction and still speaks German as a mother tongue. I felt strangely touched by this "Germanness" and could not help but delve a bit deeper into the German colonial past.

In post WWII Germany we were systematically educated in self-hate, which included the automatic presumption that Germany must have had an especially gruesome colonial past, leading to the atrocities of the Nazi period.

That this is not really the truth, I learned in Uganda during talks with our very learned friend Bishop B, a Tutsi who knows much about the shenanigans of all colonial powers in Eastern and Central Africa.

Apart from the arrogance – shared by all Europeans of that period – with which colonial powers felt entitled to endow their "culture and civilisation" (and extract labour and raw materials in return from those lands), upon peoples with inferior weapons technology the world over, the Germans invested much more into the future of their colonies than others. Others who were out for fast gain include Belgium under notorious "butcher of the Congo" King Leopold, the British under Rhodes, and the French who depopulated and deforested large tracts of Africa with great gusto.

Today, the German influence in Namibia is still tangible, in the form of an unobtrusive functioning of things and a widely shared love of neatness and cleanliness. That cannot be so bad.

Day 1: (25 September)
Johannesburg to Gaborone

We drove from Johannesburg to Gaborone, the capital of Botswana. There we stayed at our friend and buster companero Andy's house.

We spent a nice evening being pampered by his wife Marrieth. Another friend of Andy's was there too, the former editor of a well-known South African business and economics magazine. He was astonishingly interested in and open-minded about our work.

The route to Gaborone had been thoroughly busted long ago, so we could leave late and travel at ease.

Day 2 (26 September)
The Transkalahari Highway

The road through the Kalahari was rather boring. One does not see many wild animals any more, since extensive breeding of cattle, sheep and goats has taken over the grazing and left no space for the original game. Instead, there were plenty of death force transmitters (some still call them cell phone towers) to bust. Andy had done the larger part of that route already, but I thought: "Safe is safe".

Transmitters along Transkalahari Highway

Crossing the Namibian border with 400kg of orgonite proceeded without problems. I had done some atmospheric improvement work with the PW first by strongly visualising friendly, waving customs officers, who would take no interest in our cargo.

That night, we were the guests of our dear cloudbuster client Georg in Gobabis, or rather of his wife Sabine, because Georg had to be in Windhoek and we would only meet him there next morning.

Both were very concerned that Namibia might experience a situation similar to that in Zimbabwe with farm occupations.

Georg's CB from Orgonise-Africa

But Georg felt that the relationship with his farm workers had improved a lot, and threatening political campaigning had abated somewhat after putting up a CB next to his house in town and on his farm 70km away. He had also distributed some more orgonite gifts, including some at the local SWAPO (the ruling party) headquarters.

It had also rained more on his farm and on that of his neighbour Ingo, also CB-owner of the surrounding farms.

I do hope, however, that the mental effects of orgonite will also help Georg to develop a more friendly and long-term, sustainable attitude towards his fellow black Namibians.

Gobabis is the centre of cattle ranching in the east of the country (Omaheke Province), and because of the relatively lavish rainfalls, (400mm/year is lush for Namibian circumstances), it is sought after for grazing. It is probably the only part of the country where some real pressure is felt from the Hereros (who are very numerous despite the alleged genocide by the colonial Germans), towards taking over the white-owned farms.

The increase in rain that we seek to achieve with our initiative will obviously relieve some tension in such a situation, as it would suddenly increase the carrying capacity of the existing grazing lands. This is apart from the mental effects (reported over and over again), which so often allow parties gridlocked in unproductive strife to find new possibilities of amicable cooperation.

Day 3 (27 September)
From Gobabis to Windhoek

On the way to Windhoek, we had put out a TB every 10km, in order to complete an "orgone corridor" from the Indian Ocean to the Atlantic. There were relatively few death force transmitters (or cellphone towers), but there was a high tension power line.

Near Witvlei we found a German military cemetery and gifted it with an HHG.

high security. It goes without saying that the bombastic complex was properly pre-inaugurated.

Masonic coven in Windhoek

Georg gave us the phone number of his friend Ingo, and we agreed on a meeting that night. Ingo and his wife Bärbel have already built a CB and are fully clued up on orgonite.

Who would have expected to meet such wonderful people!

I was really very excited to see that an independent group of CBers had sprung up here. It was touching to see a life-size CB in a strange country, made by strangers (at least up to that point).

Uncle Sam (Nujoma's) new palace

We were given a lot of useful hints that night, as well as the phone number of Bärbel's equally CB-owning sister in Walvis Bay. The death force transmitters in Windhoek, as well as the main Masonic coven and various governmental targets, were hit that day. President Sam Nujoma is having a somewhat oversized bunker-like state house built by some flown-in North Koreans under

Windhoek township

Day 4 (28 September): From Windhoek to Sossusvlei

After that, it was into the desert, as we headed in the direction of the Namib Naukluft Park.

En route to the desert

The vegetation was becoming increasingly sparse and vistas of grand emptiness opened up in front of us.

Since there were no death force transmitters on the way, we decided to bust the dry riverbeds, of which there are many. They mostly have some underground water veins that could be used to energise, than larger areas.

This was the method we would utilise during the whole trip.

It was a somewhat new situation for me, as in almost all previous expeditions death force transmitters were found in such density that busting all of them and a few outstanding or obvious targets would provide sufficient coverage for an area.

The fact that we received very little visual confirmation for what we were doing did not make things easier. I often had the feeling of "shooting in the dark"; not knowing if our efforts would result in any success.

This hill looked like a giant reptile

This made it even more important to stick to the plan and systematically bust the whole country, as far as possible. I had dowsed the positions for our 5 CBs before departure. Now that we had found a functioning CB in Windhoek, we had a spare one to deploy in Ovamboland, a welcome addition to our target list.

Vortex over Sossusvlei

A nice cloud vortex formed over Sossusvlei, southwest of our camping ground, after I temporarily deployed one of our CBs.

Day 5 (29 September) Sossusvlei

We went from the camping ground (Sesriem) to Sossusvlei. A "vlei" in Afrikaans is a marsh-pan, which may become marshland or a shallow lake in the rainy season, but may dry out completely in the dry winter months. Generally, almost all rivers in Namibia only carry water in the short rainy season.

Exceptions are the Kunene on the Angolan border, and the Fish and Orange Rivers on the border with South Africa.

Oryx in the shadow of a tree

You can see that the dry riverbed of the Sesriem and the dry pan of Sossusvlei do carry life-giving underground water.

One finds an astonishing multitude of trees, shrubs and quite a few animals in this green strip through the desert.

We were told that the drying-up process is still intensifying.

Day 6 (30 September)
From Sossusvlei to Walvis Bay

On the 30th we left Sossusvlei. In the morning we went to have a quick look at the Sesriem Canyon and to leave some gifts there.

Dune landscape near Sossusvlei

Here we walked up and dug in an HHG

Sesriem Canyon

Water hole in Sesriem Canon

There we found an open water hole.

Recording the meagre rain falls at Solitaire

In the late afternoon, we arrived at Walvis Bay, where we found hospitable accommodation at Ingo's sister Heida's place. She kindly allowed us to stay in her house, although she was away. In Heida's garden we saw another well-crafted CB of her own making. Again, the Masonic dungeon in town attracted our attention right at the beginning with its particularly stale aura (or rather, the absence of any positive energy). Three judiciously placed gifts should put an end to that – sorry, no more Baphomet...

Harbour of Walvis Bay

As usual, we distributed some orgonite in and around town and did not fail to drop some in the water as well.

Day 7 (01 October) Walvis Bay to Lüderitz and back by air

We noticed through Internet access in Walvis Bay that we had received some good orders in our absence, so our financial situation looked a bit better than anticipated. The thought came up to rent an air plane and bust the otherwise difficult to access (only with permit and very hard and slow to drive), desert strip between Walvis Bay and Lüderitz (approximately 400km south), from the air.

We systematically dropped one TB every 10km over land. On the way back, we flew over water, hugging the shoreline and did the same with our etheric sticks. I just couldn't accept that there should be a desert directly bordering the sea.

Operation Desert Rain – Namibia 2004

The plane

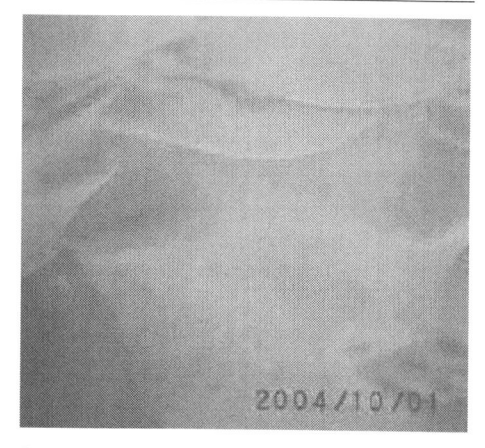

Dunes and sea waves astonishingly similar

The team in the plane

Sesriem/Sossusvlei from the air

Tracks of "4x4 enthusiasts" destroy the sparse vegetation cover around Walvis Bay

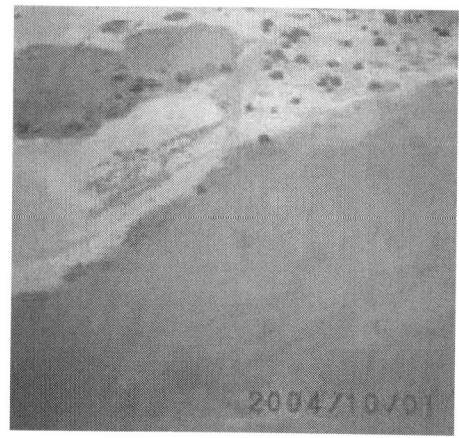

Life in the desert – the occasional and sparse rains run off quickly

The body of evidence

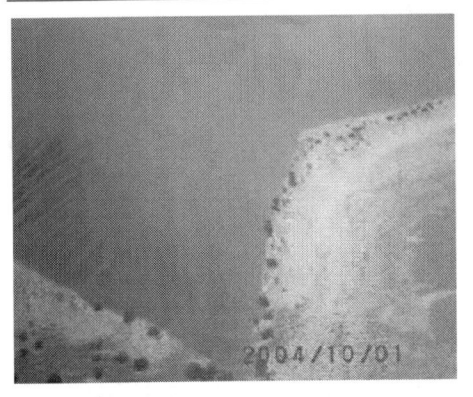

Dune encroaching on Savannah

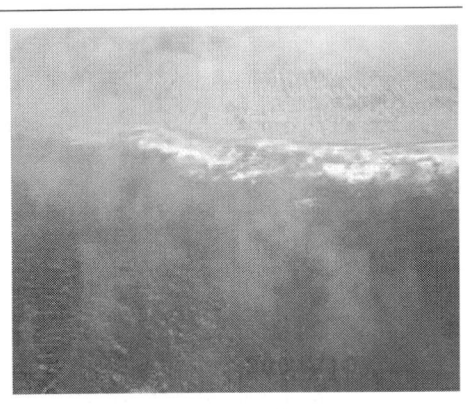

Cloud banks just up to shoreline.

Desert near Lüderitz

Coastal fog

Lüderitz under "aerial attack"

Coastal fog

we made contact with a friend of Heida's sister Ute, called Achim, who lives in Swakopmund.

Bombarding the coast - 1 piece of orgonite every 10 km

Astonishingly clean and neat streets also in the black Townships – is that still the German Influence? (I have not seen that anywhere else in Africa and I have been to quite a few places by now.)

We visited him in the evening and had a lively chat. Later, after having something to eat, we put up the CB. Achim was very well clued-up on the sinister dealings of all aspects of the dark forces, yet somewhat disheartened by some terrible blows fate had dealt him, and was not without fear for the future.

Desert border

I would have loved also to bombard the "Sperrgebiet" (blocked area) from the air, but that was not possible because of cost and fuel range considerations. The "Sperrgebiet" is even more secretive than the Namib-Naukluft Park. It is almost entirely under the control of De Beers (in a joint venture with the Namibian state), and who knows what the "illumined brothers" are using it for, apart from scraping for diamonds ...

After we had found a functioning CB in Walvis Bay (another of our premeditated deployment spots),

Achim, Friederike and Arjen with Achim's new CB

I got the impression that our visit

and the perspective that it is possible to fight back and win, built him up a bit. Achim also advised us where to find the local Masons' den, which was earmarked for extinction on our way to the Brandberg the next morning.

Day 8 (2 October) From Walvis Bay to the Brandberg

HAARPy sky over the Brandberg

Our next goal was the Brandberg, venerated as a holy mountain by the various indigenous peoples of the region for millennia. In the area of the Brandberg, which rises so dramatically out of the flatlands, more than 40 000 rock paintings, engravings and drawings have been identified. Falsely, they have been attributed solely to the Bushmen (Khoi-San) and their close relatives, the Damara.

The most famous of these drawings is the "White Lady". According to Credo Mutwa, it is a depiction of a Phoenician prince hunting. Some 2000 years ago, according to oral tradition, there existed a Phoenician empire, founded there by a small troop of Carthaginians after their mother city was destroyed by Rome. This empire was overthrown, after a few hundred years by an uprising of the enslaved Bantu people of the region and its capital, situated in a now dried-out lake, was razed to the ground. Some of the hewn stones are said to have been collected by the legendary Monomotapa to build the magnificent walls of great Zimbabwe.

A brief hike to the "White Lady"

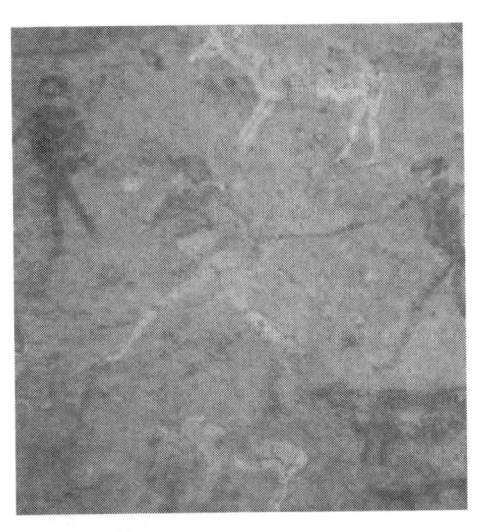

The "White Lady" of the Brandberg

It was surely a bust-worthy place.

Day 9 (03 October) From the Brandberg to Windhoek

On 3 October, we had to drop Friederike at the airport in Windhoek. She could not participate in the whole trip because of the kids. On our way, we passed through Omaruru, where we witnessed a colourful parade of Herero in traditional uniforms and dresses, commemorating events of the war between the Herero and the German colonial "kaiserliche Schutztruppe" soldiers of 100 years ago.

The Herero women wear impressive formal gowns, inspired by the European fashion of around 1900. Especially noteworthy are the headdresses made from a silky cloth that resembles a helmet with cow horns.

These people have a much better memory for tradition than we Germans and not only still use the German words for their military ranks, which are only very slightly Africanised, but also their parade uniforms are styled after the Imperial German ones.

Now (5 HHG later) the sky already looks much better here

Luminescence is regularly a confirmation

I forgot to mention a chance target that we stumbled upon. As usual, magically attracted by a "NO ENTRY", sign we came across a Chinese military base some 50km north of Swakopmund. It was quite eerie and out of this world in the middle of Africa with its distinctly Asian roots and slick shiny newness.

It got hammered with some TBs, but we made a very rapid about turn at the entrance, when we saw the "no jokes" faces of the Chinese guards with their MPs. I later learnt that this is a listening post with advanced "signal interception" capacity, and who knows what else.

Traditional Herero women in festive gowns

The body of evidence

Herero women on parade

Such "Power Spots" do get some orgonite of course ...

Herero on parade in military dress

Day 10 (04 September)
From Windhoek to Omihana

Arjen orgonising Von Bach Dam near Okandja

The next station was to be Chief Mateus's place at Omihana, where we planned to deploy another CB. Mateus is a Herero spiritual healer and seer of some reputation. We got the contact from Ingo, who had consulted him in the past when cattle thieves raided his farm repeatedly. Not only did Mateus identify the thieves clearly, but he also asked if Ingo wanted him to kill them right away (by remote spiritual means of course), which Ingo refused gratefully, as long as the perpetrators would be prevented from repeating their transgressions.

We met Mateus on the way to his place, a collection of somewhat derelict huts in the dried out bush.

His oldest son spoke English very well, which made communication easy.

Immediately the council of elders of the village (extended family) was convened, in order to examine the strange gift. The setting and manners were very formal and had a strange dignity.

Mateus had apparently expected an "apparatus" in the Western sense, and seemed disappointed at

Operation Desert Rain – Namibia 2004

first when no loud or visible effects emanated from the contraption.

He uses a rusty nail and a mirror shard as his instrument of divination and by those means our CB was checked and passed as "OK" and its remaining at Omihana was approved.

All this was done without any emotional displays of gratitude or curiosity. Everything seemed to be perfectly normal to Mateus.

After a symbolic offering of food as a present, we were granted permission to pitch our tent.

Formal reception by the village notables

Sunset at Omihana

Later that night some of the younger inhabitants found their way to our campfire, where a lively exchange took place over some beers. However, the respected elders kept a courteous distance.

That Omihana could surely use some rain had already become obvious to us on arrival, when some youngsters asked us for drinking water, as they had only some muddy, stale water from an almost dry water hole in the village.

Day 11 (05 October) From Omihana to Opuwo

From Omihana, we went on to Opuwo, the commercial and administrative centre of the Himba people (Kaokoveld).

The Himba are a group of people who split off from the Herero some 100 years ago, avoiding close contact with the colonialists.

Opuwo was one of our pre-selected deployment points for another CB. Luckily we found a very open and interested custodian in Bernhard Kuyuu. He would also guide us the next morning to visit an authentic Himba village.

Opuwo CB

147

Because the Kaokoveld is very remote, they have been able to preserve their traditional pastoral way of life up until today. Increasingly now the area is opening up to tourism and the traditional dress with the characteristic full body paint of ochre and fat are becoming a popular subject for photographers.

The Himba are becoming increasingly aware of the economic value of their cultural otherness, which is not without corrupting consequences for their cultural integrity.

Day 12 (06 October) From Opuwo to the Kunene river

It became apparent in the village that the chief had recently passed away. The HHG that I presented as a gift was intuitively perceived as a spiritual offering and was connected to the commemoration of the deceased chief.

Village elder with HHG

The "First Lady" of the village, shown here, who is the senior wife of the deceased chief, spontaneously fell into a wailing trance in memory of the chief.

Again, this demonstrates the close connection of orgone energy to the spiritual realm.

Boy cooking

More elders were summoned and I was asked to place the HHG on to the grave of the deceased, which I saw as a great honour and show of trust.

Cattle skulls as a sign of the wealth and importance of the deceased

After this visit in the morning, we went on to the Kunene River, the perennial border river with Angola. Beholding the thunderous Epupa Falls and feeling the freshness of the gushing waters was spectacular, especially after all the sand and dust of previous days.

Epupa Falls

We spent the night some 100km east of the Epupa Falls, on the banks of the Kunene River.

Day 13 (07 October)
From the Kunene River to Ovamboland

In juxtaposition to the rugged and varying Kaokoveld, Ovamboland is a boring flat plateau. The Ovambos are largely Westernised and the area has been developed by costly infrastructure projects.

Indicative of the stark contrast with other areas are the hundreds of kilometres of straight irrigation channels with regular outlets for cattle watering ponds, and brand new tar roads with street lights every 10-15m in the population centres of Oshakati and Ondangwa. The fact that President Nujoma is an Ovambo is seen by many as the reason why Ovamboland is getting such a large allocation of development funds.

Here again we noticed the cleanliness that is untypical in most parts of Africa.

Sylphs over Ovamboland

Day 14 (08 October)
From Ondangwa to the Etosha National Park

Arjen, our first "Orgonise-Africa Safari guest", should now finally get some well-deserved rest and be privy to a real African wilderness experience.

First, we had to find a suitable custodian for our next CB that was earmarked for Ondangwa. A girl who had shown great interest the evening before, let us down completely. Maybe the parents talked her out of her initial enthusiasm.

We made three attempts in total,

riddled with substantial communication problems. (Most people speak Afrikaans as the only "white" language, but it's not exactly my strong point.) Luckily, on the third attempt, we found Mr Mbinga who spontaneously warmed up to the idea.

His 2 sons were fluent in English, so we managed to explain the basic concept satisfactorily. Also, Mr Mbinga felt a tickle from the energy above the pipes.

He lives in a large traditional kraal, consisting of a fenced enclosure with some 20 or so reed huts within, all connected by an intricate system of reed-walled walkways, in which his apparently numerous women and their various offspring are accommodated. These traditional lifestyles and dwellings are unfortunately disappearing fast.

Mr Mbinga, his 2 sons and Arjen

Day 15 (09 October) Finally: Proper "Africa Tourism"

Decades ago, Namibia was renowned for its abundant wildlife. The first white settlers found vast herds of elephant, rhinoceros, zebra, giraffe and all sorts of antelopes. Like everywhere else in Africa, the "civilised" white man managed within a short period of time to decimate these unbelievable riches. (They were aided by the culturally uprooted brown and black peoples, who had also been introduced to firearms, among other destabilising factors.) In the process the landscape was also ruined, after relying on fertilisation by the great herds of African animals for millennia.

The Etosha National Park, around the seasonal water body of the Etosha Pan, is the only continuous great habitat where a glimpse of that now vanished splendour can still be had.

Managed with little inspiration, it unfortunately only caters for the self-driven tourist, who wheels up and down the long dust roads to view the animals from the safe environment of his car. Fortunately the animals are easy to spot, especially in winter when they congregate at the few water holes, some of them artificially maintained by pumping borehole water.

How much more exciting it would be to offer guided walks, or even horse trails, in the area.

Elephants at the water hole

It was, nevertheless, a good experience and a welcome break.

Day 16 (10 October) From Etosha to Waterberg

On 10 October, we went via the small mining towns of Tsumeb and Grootfontein and neighbouring areas to the Waterberg.

The Waterberg was the place where the battles for their land between the Hereros and the German "Schutztruppe" took place.

The rendering of these events as a genocidal war is mainly the result of British propaganda, designed to justify the illegal annexation of the German colonies after WWI. Although the facts tell it differently, the story has gained a life of its own, like so much propaganda does, even after the original authors have long refuted it.

The fact is that it was a colonial war of conquest and resistance, fought with great fury on both sides and with little reference to such luxuries as the Geneva Convention.

The Herero were far from being unarmed or "innocent" victims, but fought with great tactical skill and superior knowledge of the topography, winning many battles.

They were also equipped with some 6000 mostly quite modern British rifles (who would see the "ordering hand" of our dear brothers from the lodge here?), and opposed by only 1500 soldiers on the German side. They had 10 machine guns and a few cannons.

After the so-called "Battle of the Waterberg", in reality a series of fierce skirmishes, that was by no means decisively won by the Germans, the Hereros used the cover of the night to escape the intended capture. Completely unnoticed by the German troops, the main body of the Herero set out east into the Omaheke, where many of them would later perish from thirst.

There can be no talk of a deadly blockade by the Germans, who were so exhausted and without food supplies, that they could only attempt a half-hearted pursuit 6 weeks later. Omaheke is also not at all a desert, but normally good grazing land which was only known by the Herero.

Tragically, the area through which the fleeing groups travelled had not seen any rain that season, which was a total surprise for the Hereros as other parts of the country had received normal rainfall.

The Herero suffered harsh losses, but were far from eradicated, as witnessed by their numerous presence today, more numerous than at any time in their warlike history.

If you want to know more about this and are able to read German, I recommend the well-researched book by Claus Nordbruch: *Völkermord an den Herero in Deutsch Südwestafrika – Widerlegung einer Lüge*.[34]

Apart from such controversial perspectives, to me this seemed an important place to bust.

To my great surprise the energy on the plateau, where most of the fighting had taken place, was astonishingly positive. Could this be the result of numerous peaceful joint commemoration ceremonies of former Schutztrupppen soldiers with the Hereros?

Day 17 (11 October) From the Waterberg back to Windhoek

German military cemetery at the Waterberg

As the Herero had evacuated themselves overnight, leaving behind their dead, wounded, sick and anybody else who was not able to undertake the excruciating march, their dead had to buried anonymously by the German soldiers. We were told by one of the rangers where the graves were, and so were able leave some gifts there as well.

Board to commemorate fallen Herero warriors. Endowed by the "confederation of former Schutztrupppen soldiers"

Contrary to the legend of the genocide, the sick and wounded Herero were treated in the makeshift field hospital of the German troops, and the weak and old people who had been left behind were given some of the meagre food and water still available.

View over Waterberg plateau

Former imperial German police station Waterberg, now a stylish restaurant

Day 18 (12 October)

Because our drawdown on ammunition had been considerable and we had also overestimated the initial number of TBs we had brought (it was closer to 750 than 1000), we had to make a halt in

Windhoek in order to produce some additional ammo.

Bärbel at the pouring party

Ingo and Bärbel offered us their garage and Bärbel participated with gusto in the happy pouring party. We bought 2 x 25kg resin, six muffin pans and a bag full of aluminium shavings. For crystals we used simple breakage of milky to opaque quartz that we had earlier collected in the field.

For both of them (Ingo joined us later), it was a good inspiration and a demonstration of how easy mass production really is.

The muffin pans and the leftover resin were kept by them for future projects.

Day 19 (13 October) Next Station: "Brukkaros Crater"

Now we were on our way south. The main artery of the country in terms of traffic is the B1, from Windhoek to Keetmanshoop. We had one CB left that was originally destined for Lüderitz.

Chemtrails at the southern periphery of Windhoek

Since we had already exceeded all estimates regarding distances and costs and Lüderitz had already been hit from the air, we asked the pendulum (Bärbel's one hand dowsing rod that she was using in a sovereign way, in this case), if we could skip Lüderitz and put the CB near Mt Brukkaros instead. Friederike had found this imploded volcano in an official travel guide and intuitively identified it as an energy point of sorts.

Chemtrails further on in dissolution already

The body of evidence

Now already transforming into lively loose clouds

On our way we paid a visit to the North Korean Stalinist built monument, with which Sam Nujoma wants to celebrate his "liberation war". In reality the process took place mostly on the negotiating table.

A somewhat dominant transmitting array towering over the southern exit from the city also had to be neutralised on the way. It was locked away in a gated and fenced private housing estate.

Korean-Stalinist Heroes' Kitsch

Obviously, they were government guesthouses, or those of very wealthy individuals, because the quite expensively built houses were embedded in almost untouched wilderness of great scenic beauty. Luckily, the security guard at the gate let us pass without too many questions.

The biggest mountain top death ray transmitter does not escape unbusted...

Close-up

Day 20 (14 October) From Mt Brukkaros to the border

More chemsoup

Sylph or soul snatcher?

Sunset over Namaland

Solomon with the CB

We were the only guests at the campground and the tent was almost blown away by the wind. In the morning, I presented the CB to Solomon, who had accompanied us from the little town of Beersheba in order to open up the communal campground for us.

Miss Bitchi stood up well for all 11 400 km

The body of evidence

The interior of the crater

Cloud armada moving in

mining town under full security surveillance, that belongs to the state-owned company Alexkor. It is situated in the north-west corner of South Africa and forms the only access to the Namibian mining town of Oranjemund. A special permit is required to visit Oranjemund. Even in order to visit Alexander Bay, we had to register, identify ourselves and expect to be searched on departure.

Since we had not treated the Sperrgebiet between Lüderitz and Oranjemund from the air, I wanted at least to bust the mouth of the Orange River thoroughly so that the (already mentioned) Benguela current would bring charged water to the coast of the Sperrgebiet.

View of Orange River mouth

Coast near Alexander Bay

He accepted the CB as a gift to the whole community.

We hiked into the centre of the crater and when we came back after some 2 hours, an impressive armada of very healthy cumulus cloud had already moved in from the north.

Day 21 (15 October) From the border via Alexander Bay to Springbok

Alexander Bay is a small diamond

Operation Desert Rain – Namibia 2004

Coastal road to Alexander Bay

The sky becoming more alive

As we drove through the mountains south of Springbok, we saw some more clearing up of chemtrails.
See the pictures below for a typical sequence:

Cloud sequence: Dissolution of chemtrails south of Alexander Bay and Springbok

Day 22 (16 October) From Springbok to Upington

In Springbok we found, to our great amazement, a "Masonic Hotel". The receptionist just laughed when I asked if it was operated by the Masons.

Original chemsoup south of Springbok

Signs of energy radiance already showing

Masonic Hotel in Springbok

Transmitting towers on Gamsberg

Augrabies Falls

I had kept one etheric stick hand grenade for Augrabies Falls. They are rather a series of rapids and smaller falls.

In summer, when the Orange River carries more water, the main fall is very impressive. There, in a cavity washed out over millennia by the plunging waters, it is said that an otherwise extinct species of catfish lives, devouring every living thing that is unlucky enough to be washed down the falls. Nobody has ever seen them, but they have allegedly been identified on sonar.

That is exactly where the orgonite went.

Day 23 (17 October) From Upington to Johannesburg

On our last day we spotted a military radar installation near Olifantshoek. We were only able to treat it preliminarily with an HHG at a 2-3 km distance, as we had taken the wrong gravel road and getting closer would have been another 100km detour on gravel.

Radar station north of Olifantshoek

Our ammo was finished shortly after Kuruman and it was clear that we would have to revisit this region soon in a separate expedition that would include Kimberley, the capital of the Northern Cape.

Lenticular cloud

Operation Desert Rain – Namibia 2004

Rain clouds near Kuruman

In the end, we had travelled 11,400 km on roads of various descriptions and some 900km by air; quite a tiring schedule for three weeks, given the road conditions and regular detours for distant mountaintop arrays accessible only on arduous 4x4 tracks. A week later, I was still completely exhausted.

Results

As our expedition took place at the end of the regular dry season, we did not see a drop of rain during the more than 3 weeks we spent in Namibia. (Only in Upington, on our last day, did we see rain.)

I was therefore very delighted, when Bärbel told me on the Monday after the trip that Windhoek had gotten 40mm of rain and that there had been rains countrywide. She said the rain was atypically abundant for the time of year and very positive for the vegetation, as it came down in a slow drizzle rather than violent thunderstorms, as is often the case in Namibia.

The two maps below are from the website of the US-Navy weather service and show the distribution of rain in the last week and the previous 24 hours (from time of writing).

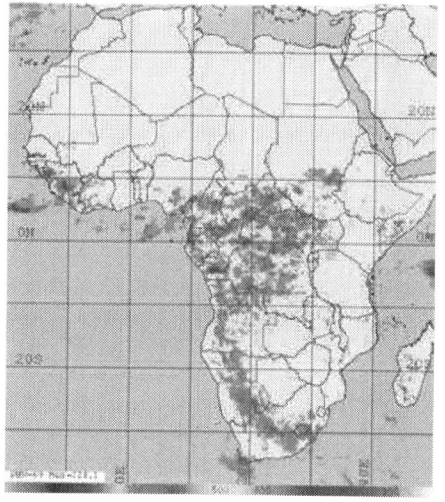

Accumulated rainfall in the week up to 21 October

The map below is especially telling, as – contrary to the week before – rain can be seen in the coastal desert zone as well.

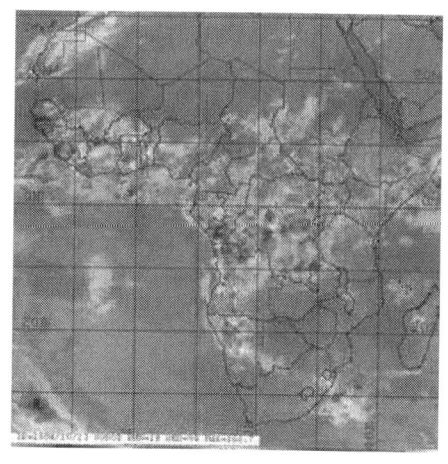

Rainfall of the last 24 hours (23 Oct, 12.00 GMT)

159

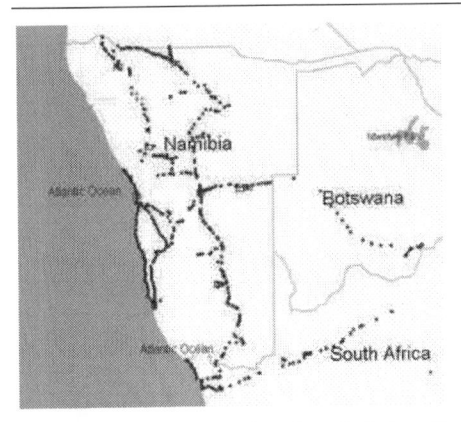

Map of all orgonite gifts placed during the expedition

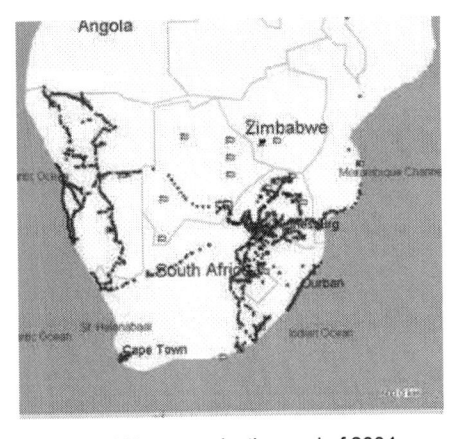

Southern Africa orgonisation end of 2004

it will now be impossible for the other side to stage all-out "El Nino" drought scenarios. (I prefer to call them "El HAARPy" anyway).

The true picture is a bit better than shown here, as some areas such as parts of KwaZulu-Natal and Botswana, have been busted by others.

Update 17 November 2004

I've just had email from our friends in Walvis Bay. Even there, in that harbour town in the Namib Desert, it is raining, and that holds for the whole country.

Only G. from Gobabis reports that it is raining everywhere but over his cloudbuster ... Strange that. I told him it may be that the universe is punishing him a bit for his antagonistic view of his black fellow Namibians.

We shall have to wait and see. The last word has surely not yet been spoken.

Otherwise it looks like an overall success.

See also the report "All that rain" on page 229, for the longer-term results of our trip.

The overall picture of Southern Africa still shows frightening gaps in orgonisation. But something has been achieved in two years. I hope

The Big Hole: Filling a gap in Kimberley

January 2005

The Northern Cape, of which Kimberley is the capital, contains some of the driest country in South Africa. In the north it is the Kalahari dry savannah or semidesert, in the south it is the Karoo, another semidesert.

On our way back from Namibia, we were able to lay at least a thin trail of orgonite in an east-westerly direction from the Atlantic, near Alexander Bay to Vryburg, where we finally ran out of ammunition.

Thus this whole area, including the capital Kimberley, had to be earmarked for revisiting.

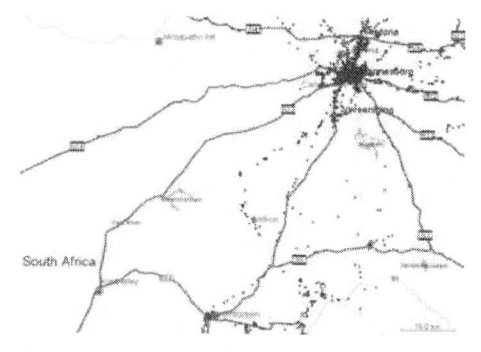

Status quo before the Kimberley expedition.

Potchefstroom was one of the stations on the way to Kimberley

The gap is obvious and intolerable. (Blue dots are orgonite gifts; flags are CBs.)

We left Johannesburg early on the Saturday (4am), because we had little time and much work to do.

First we paid a visit to some large mining operations near Klerksdorp, operated by Anglogold.

Tossing it out in the morning

An ugly tower in Potch ...

More gruesome stuff on the road (date stamp is wrong)

We did another HAARP array on the way, which I have included in my "proof" pictures, because the change was so immediate and drastic.(See page 44 ff)

High tower outside Klerksdorp

Despite above average rainfalls in most parts of the country, the drought-related propaganda continues up to the present date. We were therefore travelling with eyes open for any signs of drought, but only the opposite was the case. All the way to Kimberley we found the grass unusually green and saw water puddles everywhere.

Somewhat run down Masonic lodge in Klerksdorp. They often look like that, stale and negative! GOTCHA! This one is busted.

"The drought was so bad, we saw lush green and water puddles everywhere..."

Kimberley, being part of the Kalahari dry savannah zone, surprised us with its fresh greenery and lushness, not only in town, where this might be attributed to watered lawns, but also in the wider surroundings.

I think the friendly agencies that planned and engineered the drought scenario for Southern Africa have a problem realising that their plans did not pan out as expected. Only very small patches of drought remained to be sorted out in the next 12 months. One of them is the west coast of the Western Cape, where we would hopefully create some change over Easter.

Still, there was talk of low filling levels in dams, despite the good rains, but hey, there is a Masonic coven in every town, and what would prevent them from asking their buddies at the water works to let some water run off at night to keep up at least a semblance of scarcity and the fear that these shadowy figures so thrive on?

Another one busted

Vortex forming towards the evening: the sky is coming alive

Busting the Big Hole in Kimberley has been a longtime plan for me, since the occult power, as well as the sheer financial wealth of the Oppenheimer family and the history of Cecil John Rhodes, the other big Illuminati operator in Southern Africa, is so closely linked with it.

Busters reward: cumulus everywhere!

Did you know that this famous hole used to be a mountain before the combined greed of hundreds, if not thousands, of adventurous diamond diggers sank it straight down a few hundred metres? (Then it was bought out by the Oppenheimers, when the diggers ran out of steam and the capital to go deeper.)

In fact it was a holy mountain and certainly a natural energy point.

The Big Hole of Kimberley

The big hole is now a tourist spot as there are no more mining operations going on there. As far as I know it still belongs to De Beers.

Historic headgear

Sarel hitting the hole wide and far

Luckily we met Lorraine at the gem shop, and she turned out to be not only a very gentle person, but also quite energy-sensitive.

Lorraine and Liz with their new CB

It is quite logical that she became the host of our cloudbuster destined for Kimberley. Her friend Liz, visiting from London, is a physiotherapist and natural healer with even more developed energy sensitivity.

It was great to connect with the two of them, and they greatly appreciated the gift to the city and the environment.

Lorraine also pointed out the location of the local Masonic lodge to me.

The Mason's den in Kimberley got well covered.

Kimberley 2005

After this we did some orgone sightseeing in Kimberley.

Big microwave tower in Kimberley

Parliament of the Northern Cape

Sky in transformation

A stimulating fresh architecture, but something was being radiated from underground

The muck dissolves

Sky in transformation over Parliament buildings after the treatment

High tower outside Kimberley

And look how nice the sky looks now! This is one of the regular rewards we receive on our busting expeditions

Back in town: healing vortices everywhere

On our way back, we took a different route. In Jan Kempsdorp, we were alerted by the sight of an unusual number of fresh graves outside the small town (rather village).

We found a grieving father, who had just buried his young daughter. (I think she was 23 years old.) He told us that young people die in the coloured and black location every day and there are 3-4 burials every weekend.

Jan Kempsdorp: culling the rural poor?

The obvious contention is that this is AIDS or whatever the real genocidal cause of this massive dying of the rural poor may be.

We gave him some TBs to distribute in his neighbourhood, and gifted the local water works and laid out some extra TBs along the road as we passed through the town.

Very sad!

We also passed through Taung, the place where some of the oldest human fossils worldwide, notably the famous Taung child, were found but we could not find the actual archaeological site.

The place was peppered far and

wide, though, including of course the ubiquitous death towers.

Further stations on the way back were in Schweizer Reinecke, a town of particularly stale and bad energy, which got thoroughly gifted.

When we finally got home, it was 4 in the morning on Monday, and we had spent 2 x 17 hours "in the saddle", so to speak. It was quite a tiring job and I needed almost the whole week thereafter to regenerate, including the already familiar "after gifting blues".

Apart from the obvious cloud changes (see picture above), we had no immediate confirmation in the form of torrential downpours and the like, but it rained twice in the week after we gifted Kimberley – so I was told by Lorraine.

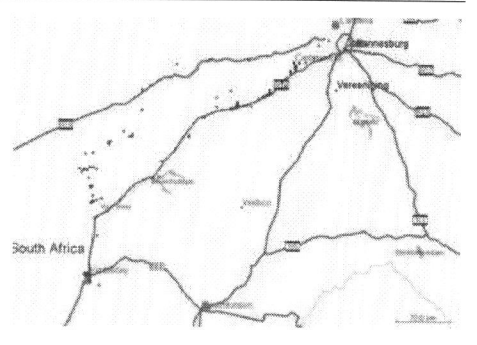

That was the trip

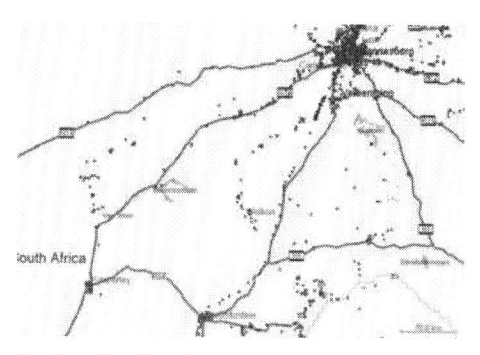

Region after the trip

Obstacle run to the Western Cape,

22 - 31 March 2005

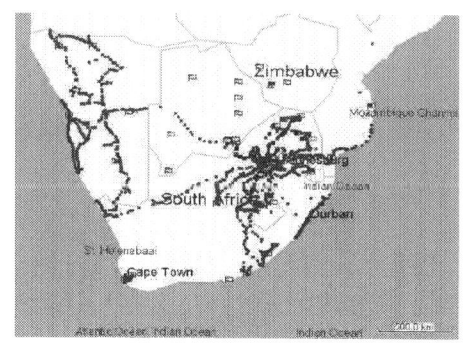

Situation before the Western Cape expedition (blue dots are orgonite gifts, flags are CBs)

Large areas of the Western Cape province have been a drought disaster zone for at least the last 2 years.

We had only been able to place a few hundred TBs and a CB in Cape Town and surrounds.

Those were obviously not yet sufficient to turn around the climate situation in the region.

The map to the left shows the great gap.

Thus a somewhat more in-depth treatment of the Western Cape and the establishment of an orgone connection between Cape Town and Johannesburg were on the agenda.

Getting there

I went by car with my oldest daughter Kika – in order to orgonise the whole road down to the Cape – while Friederike flew down to Cape Town with her parents, who were visiting, and Isabella, the youngest.

We started off with a little car accident just before Bloemfontein. After encountering damage to the rear wheel bearings on my brand new cheapie car, I hit a car port pole in a petrol station parking lot.

It appeared to me as if I had clear vision and nothing was in my path! It was as though "something" had blanked out my perception, or even fed a wrong picture into my cortex.

Smack-Bang! Ugly wound to the head, but not dangerous. Kika screamed for half an hour in shock and I bled into the car like a freshly slaughtered pig.

Bustagirrrl Kika already smiling again...

Orgone warrior with head wound, slightly dazed...

Luminescence above Bloemfontein the same night – a sky full of guardian angels?

Somehow I was reminded of the incident on the Makgaben trip almost 2 years before, when I hit a cow which I had not seen, despite clear sight and not excessive speed.

Of course it's purely speculative to speak of attacks by the dark forces when extreme stupidity would suffice as an explanation.

But it was interesting that a member of our forum told me in an Internet chat that same evening, that she had seen the accident before it happened and tried to warn me or otherwise prevent it. Maybe I owe my life to her vigilance.

We got a rented car through my insurance (faster and better) and continued the journey with a bandaged head. We spent the night in Trompsburg, approx. 90 km from Bloemfontein.

Everything from Jo'burg up to and including the city of Bloemfontein had already been done in the past, so we only started putting out TBs now, as soon as we spotted bustworthy targets.

Of these, there were many on this most important highway in South Africa. (N1, Jo'burg to Cape Town)

Western Cape 2005

Gariep Dam

After doing the Gariep Dam we crossed the Orange River that was gifted again from the bridge. Several transmitter sites on the way were inaccessible on high mountain peaks. In these cases we laid out strings of 15 TBs over 5 km to neutralise them.

This touch of green is quite unusual for the season (autumn) in the Karoo

After the first 200km of busting some cumulus clouds showed up, until finally we saw a huge cloud circle with blue hole inside over Mooifontein. The diameter was approximately 30km.

All the way there was a high density of transmitter sites in the empty landscape, approximately every 2-3 km. Is this all really needed to keep the drivers on the N1 in touch? Using a cell phone while driving is allowed only with a hands-free kit anyway as I was reminded by two unmarked police patrols, who had been stalking me.

I was stopped twice for alleged use of my cellphone on this trip and served with fines, although I seldom use the phone in the car. Both times they were unmarked vehicles with plainclothes policemen. I can't avoid the feeling that these molestations are systematic since I have frequently been stopped by police cars in the last few weeks for petty issues like not wearing a seat belt or not stopping completely at a stop sign etc.

Both plainclothes policemen appeared to have above average intelligence and the second one said they'd been lying in wait for me. (Did he really say that?) I felt they were some kind of agents as normal traffic police officers are rather down-to-earth and not that smart.

Rain clouds at the coast near Hermanus

The next few days we spent in Greyton at the home of our friend Frans from where we made various excursions into the neighbourhood, especially the coastline from Strand to Cape Agulhas. Greyton is a sleepy little town in the mountains, an ideal place to retire, where children can play on the roads without fear of being run over (very nice).

Greyton's water supply was energetically improved

A fat transmitter in Kleinmond

Clouds freshening up with beautiful luminescence after busting

Transmitter near Stanford

Western Cape 2005

Fog coming up

Friederike in mountains above Greyton

Two eagles (in picture) and one falcon showed up above us after we had placed our gifts in the mountains. They were suddenly just there!

Georg on mountain above Greyton

Coast line near Betty's Bay

The body of evidence

View of Gordon's Bay and Strand

Bye-Bye, Greyton: Frans, Friederike's parents and 4 Ritschls

After these beautiful days we went on along the coast, via Mossel Bay, an ugly industrial town with lots of petrochemical industry and offshore gas fields, then George and Knysna to the Tsitsikamma Forest, a nature reserve on the coast where we were to spend 2 nights.

Transmitter in Strand

Sylphs above water reservoir in Riviersondereind

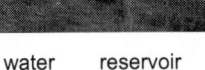

3 Ritschl-girls at southernmost point of Africa (Cape Agulhas)

Mossel Bay

Masonic lodge in Mossel Bay (busted!)

Interlude: Dissolving HAARP over George in less than 30 minutes

Above the small city of George we saw a spectacular HAARP sky such as I haven't seen in a long time.

(I call any kind of electromagnetic weather manipulation HAARP after the well-publicised installation in Alaska (High Altitude Auroral Research Program)).

It was even nicer to see the whole slime dissolve after a dedicated attack on the 6 or 7 HAARP transmitters (with civil "dual use" as cellphone towers). A great example of the potency of the small Tower Busters (TBs) of which we only used about 15 here.

The "David and Goliath Principle" in action. (Pictures see page 45 ff)

This tower was the culprit

Late at night, after some wild detours through the townships above Knysna and after gifting the lagoon there, we finally arrived at Tsitsikamma.

Tsitsikamma Forest, Port Elizabeth and Graaff-Reinet

On a hike (with gifts) to a waterfall some 5 km from the camp on the next day, we saw 3 dolphins jumping out of the water just outside the surf line. Unfortunately I wasn't fast enough with the camera, but I got the impression that they liked our work.

Water fall in Tsitsikamma Forest

Coastline at Tsitsikamma

Friederike entering a boat

Storms River Mouth canyon

We went on via Port Elizabeth (one of the 5 biggest cities in South Africa) to the Addo Elephant Park. All these places were, of course, abundantly gifted.

We spent about 4 hours on Port Elizabeth and gifted the most important suburbs, downtown and the harbour front.

It is clear that a major population centre would warrant much more thorough attention than what can be accomplished in 4 hours but, again, my strategy is to cover as wide as possible an area with at least a preliminary orgone blanket, before going more into detail. I can only hope that South Africans will finally pick up the baton and start taking responsibility for their own neighbourhoods.

Sylphs over PE

Sylphs over PE

Other than in North America and some European countries local activism has so far been disappointing and sporadic.

I wonder if that has to do with the peculiar history of South Africa, where it is still difficult for the various racial groupings to feel something like responsibility for the whole. Is it not funny, that the most active busters in Southern Africa, apart from ourselves, are all foreigners? Andy in Botswana is British, Robert in Cape Town is Dutch, although he grew up mostly in South Africa.

On the way back I made sure to include Graaff-Reinet, original seat of the Rupert family, the most influential money family in South Africa after the Oppenheimers, and probably a main shareholder of the South African Reserve Bank, our terrorist "National" Bank (charging interest on non-existent money, the favourite Illuminati game) similar to the FED in the USA.

After thorough busting of the city we were rewarded with a most magnificent spectacle in the sky, in stark contrast to the previously "dead" or "cardboard-like" sky.

It appeared like an aerial battle with a final triumphant victory of the angelic forces.

All this is an effluent of my over-active imagination, of course, and not scientific observation. OK?

I do not know if the following picture will convey the excitement.

See for yourself:

UFO clouds over Graaff-Reinet

Untreated evening sky over Graaff-Reinet: slightly smeared with chemtrails

Pure Illuminati romance in Graaff-Reinet: Pyramid, microwave tower and palm tree

Etheric aerial battle?

The body of evidence

Victory! Radiating luminescence over dam at Graaff-Reinet (after 20 minutes)

Results of the trip

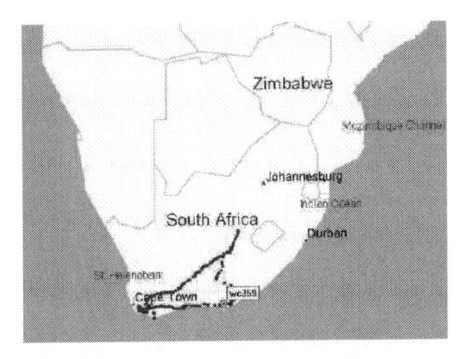

The trip

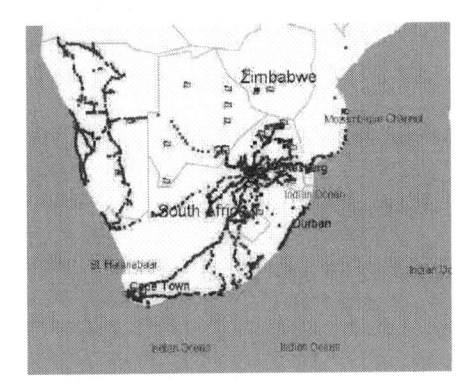

The overall situation after the trip

Hefty rainfalls after the trip (eureka!) led to rapid swelling of rivers and some road damage in consequence, which was overemphasised by the press. I get the notion that press reports are deliberately biased in order to induce negative feelings towards rain.

In general, the rain was beneficial in most areas of the Western Cape and without damage to crops and infrastructure, according to reports in Farmer's Weekly.

The damage to major roads occurred only in the Caledon area, where most of the natural fynbos vegetation has been destroyed and replaced with ploughed stone fields (a sight to behold, but obviously they harvest crops from these acres of ploughed gravel, just minerals, sun and rain needed) so there's no water retention capacity left in the river catchment areas and the water gushes right down the rivers, taking bridges, topsoil and all with it to the sea ... In Johannesburg we also had above average rainfall during the whole of April. It was obviously significant that we had now created an uninterrupted orgone line from Cape Town up to Johannesburg and beyond.

Here is a small selection of press reactions:

Stormy relief for Western Cape

THE UNEXPECTED storm and hard rain that lashed the Western Cape recently should buffer farmers against the impact of the drought in the province. Swartland farmers reported good rain with Malmesbury and Moorreesburg receiving between 35mm – 60mm and the Sandveld receiving around 22mm.

Moorreesburg farmer Alwyn Dippenaar said the rain had broken the despondency of farmers in the region and had enabled them to plant new grazing. He added that the rain bodes well for farmers preparing to sow wheat next month.

In fruit producing areas in the Boland, as well as in the Breederivervalley, good rains have been reported with no damage to harvests. Daan Louw, Agricultural Economist of the University of Free State, pointed out, however, that most of the rain was absorbed by the soil resulting in very little impact on dams in the Breede River Valley. Unfortunately little or no rain was reported in the northern parts of the province and in the Karoo area. The Olifantsriver region also did not receive any rain, but the weather conditions are promising. – *Glenneis Gleason*

Article in *Farmer's Weekly* 22 April 2005

Western Cape 2005

From drought catastrophe to flood emergency? *The Star* 14 April

A somewhat reflective article in *Farmer's Weekly* of 22 April 2005 about the damage caused by 2 years of drought and how far the recent rains can remedy that

Mr Tata's Isandlwana

August 2005

The purpose of this trip was gifting the Zulu heartland and particularly all those historical battlefields that hold so much symbolic meaning for the formation of what is now the modern post-apartheid nation of South Africa.

The main roads defining the perimeter of this large area had been done before.

Of course we would do all the entropy transmitters on the way, but the main idea was to pacify the lingering spirits left over after those decisive battles between Zulus, Englishmen and Boers — like Isandlwana, Majuba, Rorke's Drift, Spioenkop, Ulundi etc ...

Majuba power station (gifted)

Beautiful floral decoration of huts near Majuba

Death force tower in Standerton

High tower above Newcastle

Hilltop array above Dundee

The Battle of Majuba

The battle of Majuba in 1881 was the first battle of the First Anglo-Boer War, known to the Boers as the "Eerste Vryheidsoorlog" (First Liberation War).

In this battle a numerically inferior Boer militia defeated a British contingent. The British Commander, a dashing and somewhat arrogant young lieutenant, directly from Sandhurst, fell in battle.

This was the first of a series of pitched battles that finally led to the crushing of the independent Dutch/Afrikaans speaking Boer republics (Zuid-Afrikaansche Republiek and Oranje Vrystaat) and incorporation of the goldfields of the Transvaal into the greedy British Empire. But this was only after a policy of scorched earth with burning of farms, and the incarceration of women and children in the first ever concentration camps, where tens of thousands died under unspeakable conditions. These goldfields at times produced 70% of the world's newly mined gold.

The Boers are really a somewhat tragic people, since right after they had snatched the land from the blacks (of course never acknowledging that it ever belonged to them in the first place), the English came along and snatched it from them. And, not surprisingly, they did so after the gold finds on the Witwatersrand had proven substantial.

The battle site was bought by the Ossewa Brandwag, a popular right-wing nationalist Afrikaner movement that strongly sympathised with Nazi Germany in World War II.

Surely a place at which to leave some gifts ...

Almost no event in South African history divides the nation more

The body of evidence

deeply than the Battle of Ncome or Blood River. A party of Boer Voortrekkers under Andries Pretorius repulsed a superior force of Zulus, killing about 3000 without suffering any casualties other than 3 wounded. This battle took place after a party of Boers who had visited the royal kraal of Zulu King Dingane for negotiations were slain by the Zulus, an act that was seen by the Boers as the ultimate treachery.

Battle of Ncome (Blood River)

So the astounding victory over a large Zulu army, won from the defensive position of the "laager", a ring of ox wagons tied together with the gaps filled with "fighting fences", was hitherto celebrated as something like the mystical founding day of Boer nationhood.

No wonder that the same event that meant "deliverance" for the Boers, was a national catastrophe for the Zulus.

Zulu elder Credo Mutwa told me some of the things he knows about the background to these events:

According to the oral history handed down to him, the slaying of the Piet Retief party at the royal kraal was the result of a British intrigue in which a missionary resident at the kraal sneaked into the royal harem, a serious crime that could only be answered with death under Zulu law, and made it appear that the Boers were the perpetrators. Thus they were killed as "sorcerers" who had violated important taboos in Zulu society.

Whether this is true or not is beyond my scope of research, but wouldn't it fit nicely into the British strategy of "divide and rule" that was so successfully employed to subjugate much larger peoples in the rest of the world over, skilfully setting them against each other in order to finally rake in the winnings, when all other combatants were exhausted ...

According to Credo, the Zulus sacrificed themselves at the Battle of Ncome by endlessly storming the cannons and rifles with their spears, with practically no hope of entering the laager alive. This must have been out of a feeling of guilt for the murder of the Retief party which was, of course, a sacrilege under Zulu law and custom.

Laager Monument: Overall view

The "New South Africa" has built a new museum on the other side of the Ncome River to represent the

Zulu side of the story, but it lacks the monumental kitsch and grandeur of the gigantic 1:1 reproduction of the laager on the Boer side and the marble replica of an ox wagon in front of the museum.

Kitsch marble ox wagon monument glorifying the land grab

More of the Laager Monument

The day of this battle was one of the most important days of commemoration of apartheid South Africa, a day on which blacks had not much to laugh at. It is now still commemorated, but as "reconciliation day" in an attempt to build the "rainbow nation"...

When I last checked, however, Afrikaners were still celebrating around the laager in traditional Boer costumes, waving placards reading "apartheid is heiligheid" (apartheid is holiness), while the Zulus were celebrating on the other side in a rather hostile and unreconciled fashion.

You would agree that some massive gifting of the place was appropriate, wouldn't you?

The Battle of Isandlwana – first defeat of a major fighting formation of the British Empire by an "indigenous army" (Go Zulus go!)

The Battle of Isandlwana in 1879 was the first defeat of a regular unit of the British colonial army at the hands of colonised "indigenous" people.

The Zulus completely annihilated a whole regiment, leaving more than 1100 British soldiers dead on the battlefield. This had never happened to them in Arabia or India or wherever else they chose to expand their empire.

My heart goes out to those brave Zulu warriors who overwhelmed the supreme firepower of an arrogant occupational force! There are no graves to honour their fallen heroes.

The battle site is full of Masonic symbolism. No fewer than 5 obelisks, etc ...

We went on via the battle site of Rorke's Drift from where we wanted

The body of evidence

to continue to Ladysmith and later to Ulundi, the "Great Place" of King Cetshwayo where the Zulus suffered their final defeat in the Anglo Zulu war and still a centre of traditional Zulu power today…

Unfortunately that was not to be, as we had a terrible car accident on the way.

Was somebody trying to stop our advance?

Before we could reach the royal kraal of Ulundi, Mr Tata met his very own Isandlwana

We felt like a defeated army – Napoleon in Russia or something like that

This is, of course, highly speculative, but isn't it strange that I had 3 almost fatal accidents within a timespan of a little more than 2 years and all on these busting expeditions? In 26 years of daily driving before that, I had only minor bumps and never caused a severe accident.

In all three cases there was a moment of blanketing, a missing time of fractions of a second.

This accident was completely unnecessary. With no other vehicles involved, I suddenly found myself getting carried out of a sharp bend and rolled sideways twice after a misguided attempt to correct the steering.

Luckily there were no trees or large rocks, so after the frightening tumbling stopped we stepped out and realised we were unharmed. Our luggage, a CB and a few hundred TBs were strewn about. The whole population of a nearby village gathered and helped us collect our stuff and generally cheered us up while we waited for the police and tow truck.

The CB we had brought for Ulundi was left with our hosts in Dundee, the owners of a little B&B where we had spent the night before and now had to spend the next night as well …

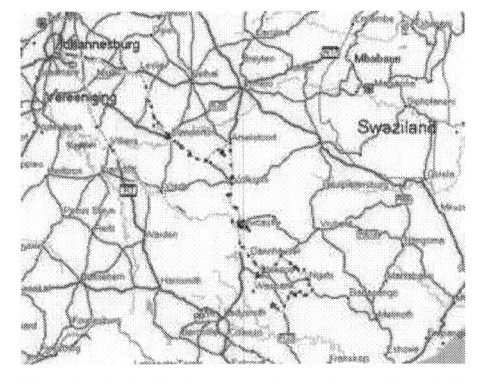

The aborted mission, petering out near Dundee

182

Western Cape 2005

They proved unexpectedly open to the whole idea and were very grateful for the gift. I think the CB is in good hands there.

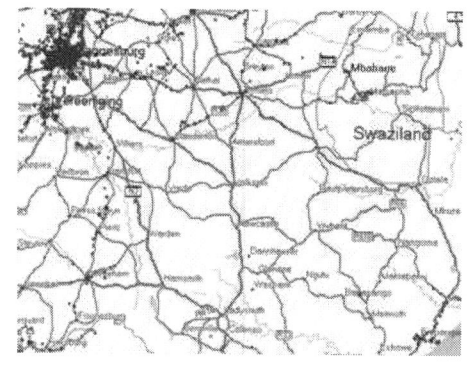

Situation before our trip

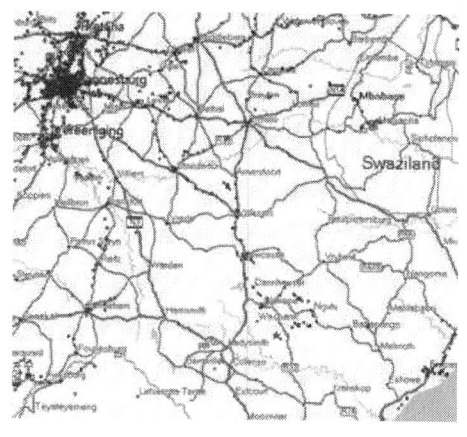

The new situation

We will come back another day to gift the Zulu heartland properly.

The Sky above Germany

(and Switzerland and Austria)
September 2005

After a long time it had come to pass: A visit to Germany, Austria and Switzerland.

A combination of family events and an invitation to speak at a symposium on free energy in Bregenz (Austria) brought us all back to the old continent. It was to be the first time since the commencement of our orgone activities, and an especially thrilling aspect was the expectation of finally meeting a lot of our new Internet friends "face to face". We equally looked forward to meeting with old friends and family members.

After landing in Zürich, I was met at the airport by Urs. We visited the Rhine Falls at Schaffhausen and then went to the home that he shares with his girlfriend and her mother.

We had a very animated conversation and took an extended evening walk through the adjacent fields and forests.

I really liked the nice Orgone tools that Urs is making.

I noted with some astonishment that 2 serious busters such as Urs and Andrea have never met, even though they live only one hour's drive apart.

Is this typical of the alpine republic of Switzerland that everyone lives in his valley and never or seldom ventures out? Of course it's great when everybody at least starts taking responsibility for his or her valley. But since our orgone network is still a bit thin, this

183

is not enough at this stage and I recommend a somewhat more strategic and large-scale approach.

What can prevent a person from grabbing 3-500 TBs and quickly busting everything along the Swiss highway network? Since transmitters are placed at 2-3 km intervals along these arteries, this would quickly create a skeleton structure of positive orgone transmitters that could later be fleshed out by other individuals.

Urs with girlfriend and her mother

The symposium "New hope for earth and mankind" was organised by Adolf and Inge Schneider, two very dedicated journalists, who publish among other things the **NET-Journal** (Neue Energie Technologien) and books on "border science" themes through their "Jupiter Verlag" publishing house.

A broad spectrum of speakers was represented. Backyard mechanics, engineers, astrophysicists and philosophers: Everybody was there!

Chemtrails on the way to Bregenz

Chemtrails on the way to Bregenz

The symposium went very well even though I was quite anxious before my lecture.

The general atmosphere was very "heavy" and marked by "scientific seriousness" before my little speech. So I was hoping to break this up a little bit.

I was still afraid, though, that I would hit a "wall of silence" because of calling the parasitic occult New World Order by its proper name in this address.

"NWO-no thanks".

But it was well received and changed the atmosphere of the whole gathering considerably. Everything was suddenly bubbling with interest and sparkling with energy.

Prof. Bernd Senf, who has participated in some expeditions with James DeMeo, not completely unexpectedly brought up the same concerns that DeMeo has voiced vis-à-vis Don some time ago.

The classical "orgonomists" are afraid that an "Oranur-Effect" could result from overcharging with orgone. Strangely, nobody in our extensive network has ever observed such effects when working with orgonite. This must be due to the completely different principles of functioning between orgonite and the classical Reichian technology.

I do have to get hold of the original report on the Oranur experiment by Wilhelm Reich, though, and find out what it really was that he did to achieve this sickening effect.

Bernd Senf is a lot more open to spiritual issues and other alternative healing modalities than DeMeo seems to be, and is a true scholar of Wilhelm Reich's work. The videos of the Namibia Expedition with DeMeo are very impressive and absolutely demonstrate the effectiveness of classical Reichian "Cloud-Busting".

We had a private talk that lasted more than an hour and found that we agreed on more things than either of us would have imagined in the beginning.

Terms like "Holy Hand Grenade" etc. frighten him however, since he does not share our "conspiratorial world view" and studiously ignores the phenomenon of chemtrails and other means of weather warfare. (Or maybe he is forced to?)

On the whole, the symposium did a lot to elucidate the "new scientific paradigm" in which a lot of different streams of thought flow together and suddenly gave us a first glance of how the "new physics" could look. A universe based on spinning energy vortices in the vacuum out of which all known energies and matter manifest.

Wilhelm Reich already described this in the 1940s in visionary fashion in his book Cosmic Superimposition.

The visit of some of our friends from the German Forum was really good and resulted in many satisfying talks and the birth of new projects.

I had sent a large box of orgonite to Andrea in Switzerland which she brought with her. So I was able to sell interested participants some orgonite in "hectic boot sale style" and improve my "petrol kitty" for the trip considerably in the process. Plus I had some "ammo for the road" as well. (Never leave home without it, heh?)

Via Stuttgart, Heidelberg, Frankfurt and Leipzig to Berlin

In Stuttgart we paid a short visit to Karin and Stefan Bamberg and Mark Thompson who greeted us affectionately, treated us to a sumptuous meal and we also had a vivid exchange about our work. They also gave us some fantastic orgone creations for special purposes, 2 books and a very special crystal that will find its destined place at the southern tip of Africa. (Cape Agulhas)

Some other interested friends of theirs also popped in so that we had a very stimulating afternoon. It was a pity that we had to move on.

We spent the night with Tobias (von Grauenstein) in Heidelberg and also met Josef (Hunting Veggie) there. This was also a very interesting evening and morning the next day, with lots of good talking.

Chemtrails over Frankfurt

Massive chemtrails over Frankfurt and along the whole route reminded us that the impression of harmony and wealth that a visitor from a third world country like South Africa, full of social and racial tensions, might receive is very treacherous ...

The next station was Leipzig, where we stayed with Kerstin and Hans Jürgen. Both are very energy-sensitive and do a lot of good work.

Chemtrails over Thüringen

They live close to an old Nazi underground base that had been in continuous use by the Soviets and their clientele East German Army. And today? Well, IN DUBIO BUSTO! ("If in doubt, I bust") Since their location is in a western suburb of Leipzig, one can see the city a distance. It was covered with a thick fog of HAARPed up chemtrails.

Humans are orgone generators

We did a spontaneous experiment by positioning ourselves (the four of us) on a small hill, directing the open palms of our hands towards the city as sending antennas and concentrating on dissolving the CTs.

You wouldn't believe it: It worked! As we were standing on that hill, concentrating, a marked vitalisation was happening in the sky. The oppressive, amorphous slime started to reform into shapely cumulus clouds.

This vitalisation was enduring and

persistent. When we later left Leipzig for Berlin, the positive transformation was still in full swing and spreading.

Berlin

In Berlin (another rather large box of orgonite was waiting there for us) we first did a trip to the inner city on the good old S-Bahn (Berlin has 2 subway systems, of which the S-Bahn is mostly above ground) with a backpack of TBs and STHs to create some orgone enhancement there.

Symbolic buildings like the new seat of the Federal Chancellor (Bundeskanzleramt), the remodelled Reichstag, but also the museum island and the Berlin Cathedral (with the burial crypt of the Hohenzollern dynasty and an overall symbol of their "God-given right to rule") had to be treated.

Some STHs went into the Spree River at various places. We climbed the high cupola of the cathedral and hid gifts in appropriate places. This proved to be a good move as we were rewarded with a blue hole in the previously slimy "2-dimensional" sky, centred right above the Cathedral, and the general vitalisation and forming of more articulate lively clouds.

That night we stayed in the city to have dinner with some very good old friends from our old times in Berlin. We were happy to find them all well and especially happy that they took our new occupation with these "weird phenomena" with great interest and curiosity.

New Bundeskanzleramt

Berlin Cathedral (Internet-Archive Photo)

Reichstag with new cupola (Internet-Archive Photo)

Over the weekend of 17 and 18 September Robert and Karin (the Tapiers) from Eastern Friesia and Andrea (Bajor) from Switzerland came over. We did a few little forays into the surrounding areas together.

Andrea (Bajor) and Karin in Summt

Since all were lodged at the inn my brother owns in Summt, just north of Berlin, a quick visit to the town of Oranienburg and to the Sachsenhausen concentration camp came in handy.

Oranienburg was an SS garrison during the Nazi period and Sachsenhausen, the first large-scale concentration camp in Germany, was the organisational hub of Germany's "Gulag Archipelago" during WWII. The treatment of concentration camps is very close to my heart for 2 reasons: Firstly, because of the sheer negativity of these places as a result of the cruelties and murders that were committed there.

Secondly, because of the hypnotic abuse that these places have been subjected to by the NWO cabal in order to eliminate Germany as a cultural and political power via trauma-based mind control.

Of course we have all noticed by now that orgonite not only works on the physical plane but even more in the etheric/spiritual realm. Places of mass murder (human sacrifice), mass slaughter of animals (think of what the mass slaughter of the bison did to the American Indian, apart from depriving him of his traditional food and economy base) and the like have always been used by the dark side to create and maintain negative energy fields.

Tapier and I on the way to Sachsenhausen memorial site

Entrance to the concentration camp

The Soviets continued to use the camp as an internment camp for what they regarded as fascists, including many elements they were pleased to eliminate. So their obelisk is even more pathetic, when one considers this recent history. Of course, its shallow symbolism only commemorates communist inmates

The sky above Germany 2005

of the camp, hence the red triangles.

Soviet obelisk - a convex mirror of negativity

Wow: Energy explosion after some thorough "orgone gardening" on the concentration camp's grounds (that means digging with a small shovel)

The Tapiers and Bajor, who are rather sensitive to these things, strongly felt the presence of the people who were tortured and maimed here.

The energy eruption shown above (in total stillness without any wind as is usual with these etheric changes) was felt by us as the ascent of the unhappy undead souls trapped in this place. I was reminded of our experiences in Uganda when we treated Budhagali Falls and the souls of those mass murdered by Idi Amin's minions escaped in the form of gigantic swarms of bats in the middle of the day. (Normally bats come out only at night.)

The forests around the concentration camp are one single mass grave and whoever ventures there in search of mushrooms will most likely kick up a few human bones. We found a few places of specially concentrated misery that were adequately treated.

We also found a massive HAARP array and many regular transmitters in the surroundings of Oranienburg.

Still after the deed in Oranienburg: An eruption of positive energy

In the evening we had a nice garden party, hosted by my brother, where we were joined by both new and old friends.

Sitting in Summt with Bajor

The body of evidence

City-busting with digging tool – Long live the Berlin Alley Tree (not only for our four-legged friends)

Bustin' da City

After Berlin we went on to Salzburg (Austria) where Friederike's brother Henning was to celebrate his marriage to Monica from Italy with many friends and relatives. (Austria was of course chosen because it's between Italy and Germany.)

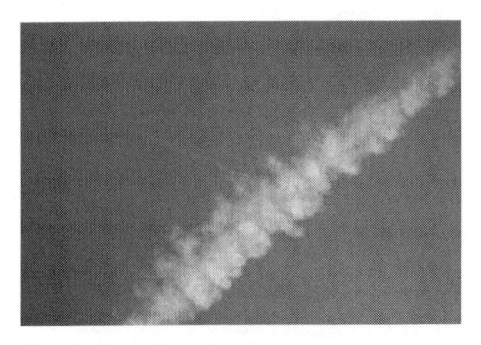

Chemtrails on 2 levels

Everywhere we saw active spray planes on a scale that I have never seen in South Africa. I swear to God that the sky didn't look anything like that when I left Germany 8 years ago.

Salzburg is a town that is permeated with occult symbolism and offers many rewarding targets for gifting with orgonite. How nice that after the wedding festivities Axel, Lisa and Klaus from Linz showed up and we could pay a visit to some prominent points around Salzburg together. (Friederike and I had already done the old town centre and the fortress with the kids in sightseeing mode.)

Again, a great opportunity to meet some of our Internet friends face to face!

Masonic and Templar symbolism galore at Salzburg's St. Peter cemetery (and elsewhere in town)

The sky above Germany 2005

never leave out an opportunity to enhance their power by latching onto the pre-existing natural power points.

Massive entropy transmitter station on the Geißberg

This also stands near the Kaiserbuche, now surrounded by TBs

Imperial crown near Kaiserbuche placed on Ley line

Axel pointed out that the Imperial crown was enshrined on top of a steep pyramid just on top of a very important Ley-line. These occultists

Untersberg Mountain – pilgrimage centre for occultists of all colours – now positively charged (Axel and Lisa)

The Untersberg is another powerful Spot, with many legends about strange beings living in caverns that crisscross the body of this rocky giant. The Dalai Lama and pretty much every occultist who has a name in the NOW hierarchy has already been there.

Surely some experienced alpinist should take care of all these clefts and caverns. We just took the cable car and left some 8 TBs near the summit. The reaction in the sky was nevertheless quite strong.

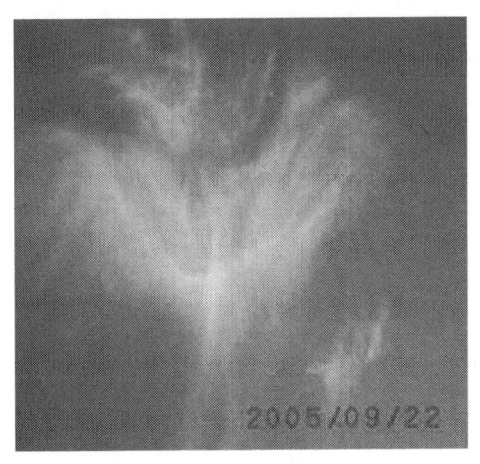

The dragon slayer motif in traditional woodcarvings – very popular in Bavaria

A sylph near Untersberg – thank you!

We spent a few days with friends in Munich, where we also met the 2 staunch Spain-busters Gerhard and Richard. That was another afternoon well spent.

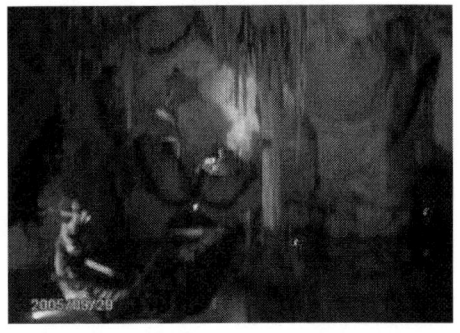

Lohengrin Grotto

A serenade on the way down – great remedy for vertigo

From Munich we left the highway shortly before Garmisch-Partenkirchen to get on to the "romantic castle road" alongside the fantasy castles of tragic King

Ludwig of Bavaria, who tried to maintain Bavarian independence against the Jesuits, the Pope and the Prussian hegemony under Bismarck and was driven to death, not before having been declared insane by his "advisers". (The Illuminati have always used the same methods, only then without the electronic gadgetry they have now.)

Temple of Diana, Linderhof castle

Courtyard Neuschwanstein

The "Kini" (bajuwarian for "King") is still very popular in Bavaria and his fantasy castles have long since recouped the extravagant expenditure, for which he was so heavily chastised, a thousand-fold for the Bavarian state in the form of endless streams of Japanese, American and all kinds of other tourists pushing through these beautiful figments of his imagination.

Could it be that the prevalence of dragonslayer motifs in the area has something to do with Ludwig's unsuccessful rebellion against the Illuminati machinations to deprive Bavaria of its independence?

By the way, we found another one inside the castle.

And is that possible? Another one! (And they all carry my first name, hehe)

We went on via Bregenz again, along Lake Constance to Basle, where we spent another 3 nights.

The body of evidence

The Goetheanum: rather darkish, I must say, despite all my love of organic forms

Apart from a visit to my uncle Dietrich and a meeting with my cousin Christian, we laid out a few more gifts in the area, especially around the "Goetheanum", the spiritual centre of Anthroposophy, designed by Rudolf Steiner, and at the Ryfenstein, a ruined medieval castle near my uncle's residence in Reigoldswil where I often played as a little boy.

We were joined by Andrea, who lives close by in Liestal, on this little trip.

Andrea on the Ryfenstein with her 2 dogs

Back in South Africa we are happy that we made this journey but also happy to be back in sunny Africa. I would need some time to get used to the relative darkness of northern and middle Europe if I ever chose to live there again. The amount and stark visibility of chemtrail spraying was shocking and in great contrast to the sky in 1997, when we left.

I cannot believe the amount of denial that someone has to muster in order to declare these as "natural" or "just contrails".

I live not far from the airport in Johannesburg and can see enough normal air traffic going overhead. If any of these checkered and striped patterns we saw all over Germany, Austria and Switzerland was a normal consequence of dense air traffic, we would observe it here as well.

I include this remark for those who are new to this theme, since those who have been in the orgonite network for a while would normally not argue about the reality of the secret spraying programmes.
In South Africa even in the heyday of chemtrail spraying it was never as omnipresent as we saw it in central Europe.

In the last 2 years I have seen less and less of it and it's really difficult to point out a real chemtrail to someone in South Africa nowadays. My most optimistic assumption would be that they have stopped the programme in South Africa because of all the orgonite.

It's just not sticking any more.

Really, we have 99.9% chemtrail free skies in South Africa.

If you cant believe it, come and visit me. I will show you around.

Counterattack in the Kalahari

15-17 October 2005

Another dry planting season was announced (planned)[V] by the Powers That Be for 2005/2006. We were feverishly thinking of how to counteract their plans this time ...

Luckily new, very concrete and precise information about secret military and alien underground bases in Southern Africa has become available to us recently and we are losing no time in acting on that information.

So, after coming back from Europe in early October we identified the area around Kuruman and Hotazel with several suspected underground bases as our priority target zone.

On this trip I was accompanied by our healer friend Karin Horn for whom this would be a very interesting experience because she was about to witness the conversion of DOR to POR on a large scale for the first time ...

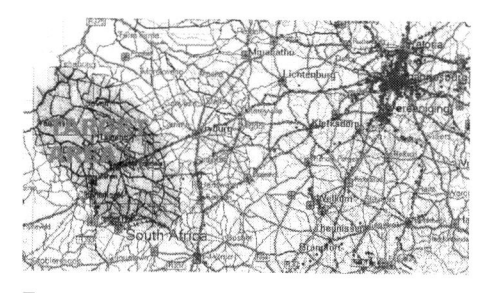

Target zone: Hotazel is also spelled Hot-As-Hell by some

Greetings from above

Karin is an accomplished herbal healer and has some psychic abilities too. She works mostly with a combination of reflexology and energy healing, called "reiflexology" (from Reiki and Reflexology). We have been working together for some time now.

[V] I recommend a simple mental exercise: When reading the orchestrated press or listening to TV from the "What To Think Network", generally replace the words "prognosticated", "forecast" or "anticipated" with the word "planned". You will see that the news suddenly makes sense. Actually reading a newspaper can become quite enlightening and entertaining that way. It is a sound scientific method to form a hypothesis and see if it matches the observed realities better than another hypothesis like the one forwarded by the WTT-network, for example (our ordained reality).

The body of evidence

Karin getting some refreshment: Kuruman is famous for its strong and very clear source of fresh water, called the Eye of Kuruman

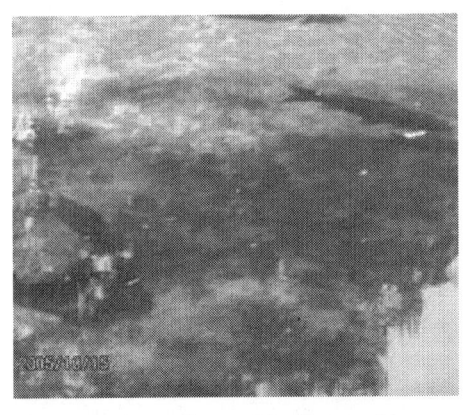

Mr Tata II, our expedition companion

The water is really crystal clear and seems energetically very much alive

Karin Horn, herbalist extraordinaire and psychic companion

We busted Kuruman and surroundings well before continuing to Hotazel. On the way we felt drawn into an extended valley by the sight of 2 distant microwave towers.

It turned out that the valley was a giant old manganese mine with the hills mostly formed of terraced mine tailings.

The whole valley felt eerie and was therefore stringed with TBs and an earth pipe inserted at a place that felt right.

Mine dumps in Hotazel

According to our information the ground under Hotazel is hollow and used for negative underground activity. So we peppered the area well and inserted a few earth pipes in the small town and the exhausted manganese mine areas just out of town.

Banging it in

Exhausted manganese mine in Hotazel

Planting a double pyramid near Hotazel

A sylph saying "Hi"

From there we went further north towards the Botswana border, via the small mining town of Black Rock that got its appropriate share of gifts. Our feeling was that the whole area, being one of the driest and hottest in Southern Africa, needed to be thoroughly gifted.

Small mining town of Black Rock

Cactus blossoming in Black Rock

The body of evidence

Manganese mine in Black Rock

Maximum DOR in northern direction

Tower in Black Rock

We went mostly parallel to the dry bed of the Kuruman River that we gifted at regular intervals

I found this funny ...

Chemtrails dissolving over Kuruman river bed

After leaving Black Rock and travelling further north, we felt as though we were driving against a solid wall of bad energy. DOR. The photo gives only an incomplete impression of this overall sensation that was strongly felt by both of us.

As we went along we could see how our constant gifting effort pushed back that wall of blackness and negativity and left behind a totally altered, enlivened atmosphere.

A most fascinating sight to behold was the formation of beautiful puffy cumulus clouds out of this deadly mist of concentrated DOR.

First cumulus cloud forming

And after: visible instant transformation after putting it down

Now there are 2 already

Leaving Severn 15 minutes later: Now we've got a whole flock of beautiful sheep-clouds

Some 50km further in Severn: An ugly sky before we put down our load

Cumulus forming everywhere

After Severn (a one-tower settlement, consisting of a road, a post office, a shop, petrol pump and an extended black shanty town) we went up to McCarthy's Rest, a

The body of evidence

border post to Botswana, and from there on for 200km along the border which is defined by the dry bed of the Molopo river on deeply rutted sand tracks. Everywhere we could see the same transformation happen as we went along, leaving our gifts at regular intervals.

And more...

And more...

... and a sylph finally!

The next night was spent in Kuruman again after this extended tour of sandy tracks had ended in some night gifting.

The first target next day was the radar base above Olifantsfontein. I had tried to gift that a year earlier on our way back from Namibia, but really never came near it.

This time we found the right access road and, ignoring a lot of "unauthorised access forbidden" signs, we got our gifts pretty close.

Fairly James Bond-ish, these huge radar dishes...

The revitalised vortex attracted an eagle

The next target was Lohatla army base. On top of being a normal training ground with shooting range, boot camp and all that, it has extended underground facilities with mind altering and weather modifying capacities.

Entrance (En-Trance) to Lohatla Army Base

Coats Of Arms: please note the snake entwined around a sword with the Maltese cross. I'm fairly sure that's our underground guys ...

Another lonely tower in the bush...

A one million rand investment for 3 subscribers and 5 **Pay-as-you-go** clients? Or does it have a different function after all ...

While it was fairly easy to approach the base from the main road along its western boundary, the back proved much more difficult. We soon got lost in a maze of endless farm tracks leading nowhere. The bad thing is that you mostly need an hour or more to discover that a track is not leading where you want to go. We finally decided that a certain stretch of farm road was as close as we would get and laid out a string of gifts along that stretch.

Looking towards Lohatla after the deed

Rock paintings at Wonderwerk Cave

Much pendulum dowsing and soul searching gave us the feeling that we had done enough for now.

The day ended at Wonderwerk Cave, an old Bushman (San) hideout that had been inhabited by a Boer family, aptly named Bosman (Bushman) for a few years during and after the Anglo-Boer war.

Finally: Some real rain clouds

Excavations going on at Wonderwerk Cave

We still had to drive all the way home to Johannesburg and do some busting on the way of course, so we arrived at something like 4 in the morning the next day because busting always takes longer than anticipated, but you know that already.

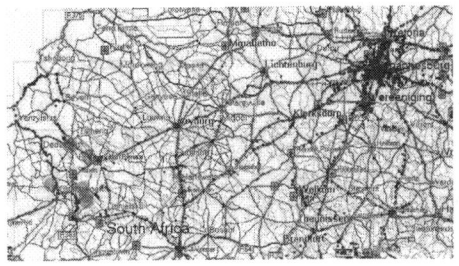

Our guide "Kleintje" (Small One) with Karin

The situation after the trip. Pink spots are the locations of anti-DOR treated military underground bases

What a survivor: Cactus growing out of cleft in the rock above the entrance to the cave.

So, yes, you guessed it right: you will hear more about deactivated secret military and alien tech belonging to the illegal one-world plotters in their various disguises. One thing we did find out about it is that the darksiders do retaliate harder after we disable their death-tech in earnest than when you just bust a few surface towers as we used to do most of the time.

But I guess it has to be done and

I'm sure the attacks will become less strong when we are closer to having all those bases disabled, one by one.

We definitely get a lot of spiritual protection from higher positive forces, otherwise this work would not be possible, and surely we have universal and constitutional law on our side since all these installations are in flagrant contravention of all the human rights, arms control treaties and national sovereignty rights that one can think of.

Matatiele – instant satisfaction as usual,

January 2006

I have just asked myself why I write these reports.

I'm going to show you a lot of pictures of landscapes, skies and people in Africa again. Not all of them are meant to prove a point. For me, gifting this beautiful continent of Africa is a constant **journey of discovery**, a **service of love** to the land and its people. I hope that some of this love and excitement is conveyed in these reports and may inspire you, the reader, to look at your part of planet Earth with equal compassion.

With love, dedication and orgonite we can turn this planet around. Apocalypse doesn't have to be our future. We have a choice.

Instant satisfaction as usual.

For a few months I've been in contact with a defected NWO insider with extensive first-hand knowledge of the secret military's infrastructure and inner workings.

Hence underground military bases have lately become my pastime, or call it my new frontier, if you wish.

His information has so far proved accurate, judging by the effects of treating the places pointed out by my contact.

After the Kuruman / Hotazel area and various bases around Johannesburg, the Matatiele / Quacha's Nek area in the southern Drakensberg, where the Eastern Cape Province borders KwaZulu-Natal and Lesotho was identified as an immediate priority to save this year's planting season, routinely predicted (read planned) to turn into a drought catastrophe by the NWO minions at the South African weather service.

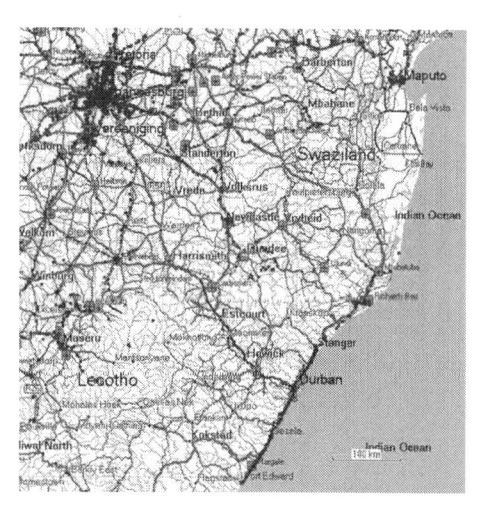

Situation before our trip. You can see the coast is well busted, but the "hinterland" leaves much to be desired.

The distance to Matatiele was

203

about 800 km without the busting detours and cost us about 100 TBs and some stick hand grenades for the watercourses crossed.

Towns busted on the way included Ladysmith, Estcourt, Howick and Underberg.

On the way we experienced a beautiful thunderstorm, but that stopped 20 km short of Matatiele. In Matatiele total drought persisted. For the whole of the rainy season, which normally starts in October, it had rained only once, on 1 January.

The area is infested with underground bases and microwave towers above ground.

HAARP cloud over Matatiele

We were accommodated in a very nice "traditional African guest house" that is run by the local communities as an initiative to develop tourism as a source of income for the underdeveloped rural areas of this former "black homeland".

They offer this guest house with an opportunity for riding and cultural village tours and expeditions and a hiking trail in the Drakensberg Mountains that includes 4 huts with full breakfast and dinner awaiting the hungry hiker.

Mr Tata II at Masakala guest house.

Putting up our CB produced an immediate reaction: An immediate build-up of cumulus clouds and a light drizzle gave reason for hope!

Next day (5th) we went out on horseback. This was of course part of the holiday programme. The kids need to have fun and we also loved it very much. Two towers got busted from horseback.

Big Sky - The mounted team

For the duration of our stay Robert Mnika was to be our guide. He turned out to be very knowledgeable, competent, and great company.

At the beginning of our outride we stopped under a rocky overhang where some San paintings were to be found. These paintings clearly have a magical purpose and were used as an interface for the San medicine men to communicate with the spirit world. It is not widely known, but the interactions between the black people (Bantu) and the San (Bushmen) was much more frequent, peaceful and mutually beneficial before the arrival of the white man. Credo Mutwa told me that all sangomas (spiritual healers and seers) in Bantu tradition have San blood in their veins. His name "Mutwa" actually means Bushman in Zulu.

When I was in Uganda, I learnt that in the language of the Baganda people the same word is used for the small pygmies who still live there in some tropical rain forests and who resemble the Southern African San in stature and feature, only their skin is much darker.

Robert explaining the San ("Bushman") paintings under a rocky overhang

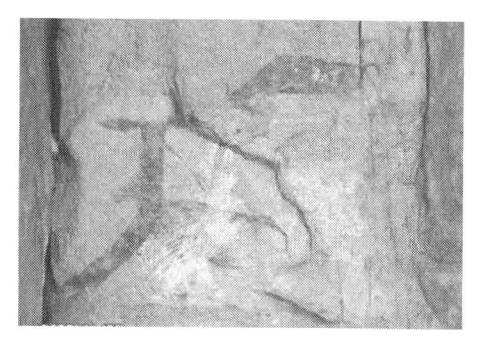

Detail of San painting

On our outride we could observe the formation of a giant blue hole, indicating a huge vortex formed by the CB, surrounded by a well-defined ring of towering cumulus clouds.

Beginning of blue hole

The boody of evidence

Segment of blue hole

From this perimeter rain cloud was forming in the late afternoon in different directions and this rain closed in on Matatiele in the evening.

There it starts raining

Target 1 – the blue hole was fully visible from here in all directions

In the evening I took off with Robert to bust most of the towers in the Matatiele area and 2 of the **underground bases** to which my informant had alerted me. Strange but true: The **ground does sound hollow at those spots**, even though not much else indicates extensive underground installations. But in both cases above ground military bases are not far and could provide the access points for the secret stuff.

Target 2 – weather already brewing

A rainbow seen from the foot of the biggest tower above town

We got back just ahead of a major downpour.

Robert was fairly impressed because the causality between putting up the CB, busting the towers and bases and the fantastic display in the sky was so obvious once you knew what you were looking at.

The next day (6th) the girls were happy to relax because the 6 hours of riding in the hot sun had been quite exhausting. So I took off with Robert to do the wider surroundings, especially the hollow mountain above the border post to Lesotho (Quacha's Nek) and another mean underground base near Ongeluksnek (Afrikaans for "Disaster Neck").

Every time we could clearly observe the changes in the sky.

The changes were particularly obvious when driving towards the base near Ongeluksnek.

Shortly thereafter: Fat thunder clouds, lightning, rain ...

Sheets of rain coming down while the sun is still lighting the mountains. A sense of freshness and joy in the air

Quacha's Nek – the UG base is under the flat-topped mountain

Before: HAARP ripples (slightly dissolved)

The 3 sangomas: Thondi, our host, and another lady who helped with the cooking

In the evening we were visited by 3 sangoma (spiritual healer) ladies who came to inspect the CB. They were given an orgone pyramid and some TBs to revitalise those holy spots that were used for prayer and ceremonies before the missionaries and westernisation messed it all up.

Reaction: great joy!

We were asked to their homestead afterwards, where they performed a dancing, singing and drumming ceremony for us, involving some 20 children as a background choir. This description is of course much too shallow, because the women went into a deep and intense trance in which they pleaded and communicated with the spirit world as a form of prayer to God (N'kulunkulu) using the spirits of the ancestors as intermediaries and witnesses.

The 3 sangomas performing their prayer ceremony

Although the encounter with the healers was originally part of the "cultural village tour" this was a deeply moving experience and tears run down my cheek as I write this. Even though I understood only a few words, it was clear that they prayed for us in a full intuitive grasp of what we're trying to do.

Dancing, singing and drumming create powerful vibrations. The word sangoma means "Person of the drum"

My goodness, what a stale event a normal Christian Sunday Service is in comparison with this. No wonder I always fell asleep in church as a child or became restless and wanted to get out. Too much DOR from the pulpit.

In the evening: light drizzle.

On the morning of the 7th we rode out once more to a nearby Xhosa village where another cultural dance performance was presented to us.

Here are some scenes from the Xhosa village:

Women dancing

Woman dancing inside House

Man dancing

Designer kitchen Xhosa style

Around noon it started raining again and that lasted the whole day and night and it was still raining the next day.

A complete success!

CB in the rain

Masakala drenched in rain

Dripping , dripping ...

Robert, who had been driving and busting with me for one and a half days, was by now well convinced that the "mulungu muti" (white medicine) was working. So he and the 3 ladies who were there to cook meals and look after the house were quite eager to look at my website with pictures from other expeditions.

Even the next day (8th) we had ongoing rainfall on our way down to the coast, approximately 250km from Matatiele. On the way we busted a lot of towers along the road and the towns of Kokstad and Izingolweni.

Oribi Gorge nature reserve

Sylph clouds near Oribi Gorge

Masonic lodge in Kokstad – busted

Mzimkulu river mouth

On our way back via Ixopo, Richmond, Greytown and Colenso we took intensive care of the town of Richmond, long known as a hotbed of violence in South Africa. Bloody and deadly fights between ANC and Inkatha supporters, originally fanned by so-called "third forces" continue to this day. One of the most feared groupings in the old South African Army, the "Koevoet Battalion" supposedly operated (or operates?) this base with a lot of secret Russian mind control and weather modifying tech. No wonder people kill each other with such abandon in Richmond.

Matatiele 2006

Struck by poverty: Graves near Richmond close to UG base

Top of the mountain

This mountain according to our information is hollow and houses an UG Base

Friederike banging it in

The stones on top look as though they once formed circles. A place of power

Sunset between Greytown and Colenso

The boody of evidence

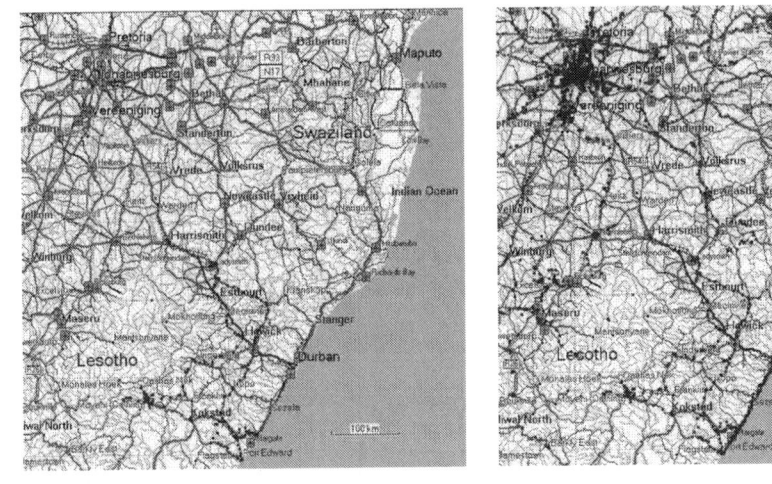

The gifts put out on this trip

Situation after the trip

Making rain – Does this look like a drought?

February 2006

Plenty of rain washed practically all of Southern Africa for the whole of January and well into February. Another drought that did not take place. The pictures below show the daily rainfall accumulated for each day. The light blue represents approx. 10-30 mm rainfall, the darker blue 40mm. I do not think this looks at all like a drought.

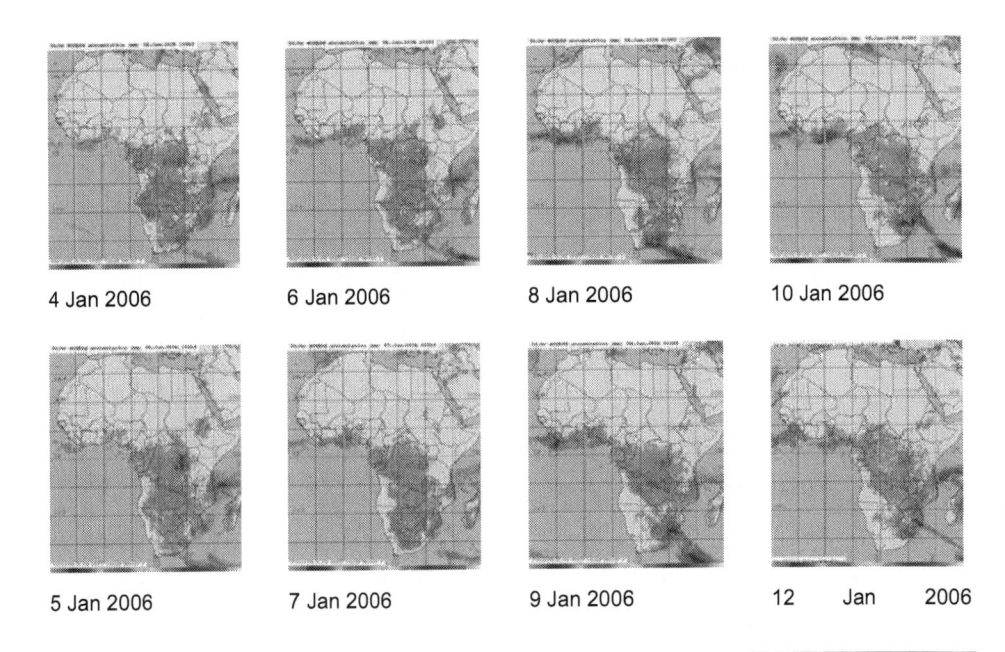

4 Jan 2006

6 Jan 2006

8 Jan 2006

10 Jan 2006

5 Jan 2006

7 Jan 2006

9 Jan 2006

12 Jan 2006

Making rain – does this look like a drought?

13 Jan 2006 18 Jan 2006 23 Jan 2006 28 Jan 2006

14 Jan 2006 19 Jan 2006 24 Jan 2006 29 Jan 2006

15 Jan 2006 20 Jan 2006 25 Jan 2006 30 Jan 2006

16 Jan 2006 21 Jan 2006 26 Jan 2006 **31 Jan 2006**

17 Jan 2006 22 Jan 2006 27 Jan 2006 01 February 2006

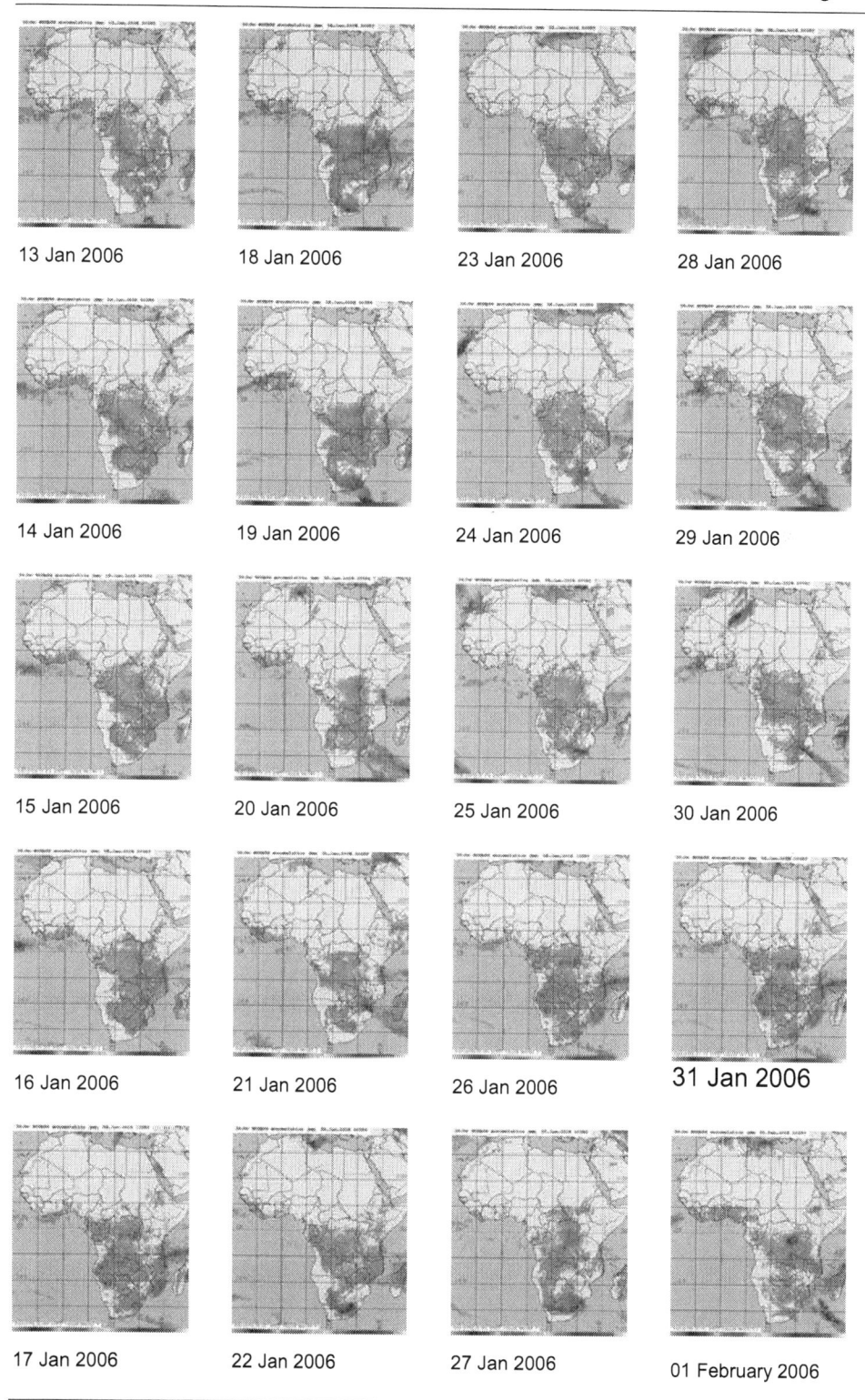

Of course the west coast is getting a bit less, but you can see that the rain covered the coastal desert strip of Namibia and the Northern Cape frequently. In fact we were told that parts of the desert that had not experienced something like that for ages, were blossoming!

Ocean Gifting – Part I

20-24 March 2006

Off to a slow start – delays and obstacles

About a year ago we received a generous gift from Steve Baron in Toronto: a few boxes of Dolphin Cups (orgonite gifts specially manufactured for ocean gifting). The idea was for us to distribute them along the coast of the Indian Ocean.

I sent almost half the cups to our friends in Walvis Bay in Namibia. They own a freighter that goes north along the Namibian and Angolan coast, and they pledged to distribute them along that stretch.

So far this seemed easy and straightforward.

I started investigating ways of getting on a boat and gifting the stretch from Durban to Dar es Salaam (Tanzania).

I checked with various freight shipping companies that service that route, but none of them take passengers.

I became a member of various "sailing crew wanted or offered" forums, etc. In the meantime my friends' boat in Walvis Bay had hit a mysterious underwater obstacle and sank within minutes. Luckily, all the crew got into the inflatable life raft in time. Was it torpedoed?

As all this had produced no result, I started looking at luxury cruises as possibly the only means of getting on a boat without too much hassle. And, bingo, that was to be the way.

A new cruise company was offering my preferred route from Durban to Dar es Salaam and Zanzibar. But before I could even come up with the money, the company was liquidated and the ship seized by the sheriff of the court.

It seemed like all hell was mounted in resistance to our endeavour. I reckoned that this ocean gifting project must be really important when so much was happening to prevent it from taking off ...

Luckily we were able at least to get started with a "Luxury Cruise" from Durban to Bazaruto, which is about halfway to Dar es Salaam.

Thanks again to Steve Baron for sponsoring the tickets for that cruise!

This first leg covered approximately 1150 km at sea.

The goal was to lay out a string of gifts spaced approximately 10km apart over the whole stretch.

Of course some of the distance

would be covered at night time. But looking at the cruising schedule, we figured that we would be able to cover those stretches on our way back during the daytime.

The itinerary of our cruise. Every blue dot is an ocean gift

Since I marked all the gifts with a small handheld GPS which also has a map function, it was not so difficult to insert those parts missed on our way back.

The GPS was also used to always determine the travelled distance from the last throw.

Since the average cruising speed was approx. 30 km/h we had to be ready to throw every 20 minutes.

I can tell you maintaining this for the whole day from 6 in the morning until after midnight without skipping a single one keeps one busy, even if it sounds very easy.

Please note the date imprint on the pictures is wrong. The first day of our cruise was 20 March.

When we left, the weather in Durban was overcast and rainy. The first night we busted until just after midnight. There was a constant drizzle and it was quite cold outside.

Cruise Ship Rhapsody waiting to be embarked

Leaving Durban harbour in the rain

Night watch

On the morning of the 21st (second day of our cruise) we saw large

The body of evidence

pods of dolphins accompanying the ship on 2 occasions for about half an hour each time.

They were diving under the ship, jumping out of the water and they were there in great numbers (50-100).

Unfortunately, I didn't manage to get a picture of them because the delay with a digital camera is too long. When it clicks, the dolphin is already gone ...

We overheard a conversation between crew members who said that this massive sighting of dolphins was very unusual for the season.

Find the dolphin

I was still suffering from a strange fever that I got after the vortex buster tour with Kelly. It lasted 2 weeks, with my temperature constantly 1-2 C° above normal. My left foot was swollen as if from some strange spider bite, and so the generally lazy atmosphere of the cruise was very welcome.

On the morning of the third day we approached the Mozambican island of Bazaruto in the early morning. This was the destination of our trip and the entire fun-seeking crowd of some 900 guests was to be ferried across in zodiacs for a day on the beach.

Bazaruto Island

Letting the zodiacs down

Rhapsody anchored near Bazaruto

Of course we dropped a few more gifts on the passage to Bazaruto but no more dolphins showed up. We spent a lazy day at the beach

216

with much swimming and snorkelling, looking at the abundance of colourful tropical fish on a nearby reef.

Passage to Bazaruto

Slightly sunburnt but generally energised and relaxed we returned to the ship in the late afternoon and left on the return leg of the voyage shortly thereafter.

We returned to Durban on the morning of Friday the 24th. We would still feel the swell of the seas under our feet for the next 3-4 days, a very strange sensation.

Back in Durban: Strange transmitter tower

The sea became very rough overnight and the next day vomiting bags were distributed all over the ship and many of the passengers were suddenly looking very pale. The typically high consumption of alcoholic beverages among most of the crowd may have been a contributing factor to the prevailing sea sickness ...

Africa's biggest harbour in action

Waterfront skyline

At the insistence of the kids we visited "uShaka Marine World" a theme park related to all types of marine life with aquaria and open pools and featuring sharks, tropical fish, dolphins, turtles and penguins. Here we had the dubious pleasure of watching some captive dolphins perform all kinds of tricks for a few sardines. Even though it's a fairly controlled environment we managed to slip a gift into the large dolphin show pool.

Captive dolphins

An hour later when we watched the feeding of the penguins, we saw one of the warders showing our gift to another, and looking very worried.

Obviously, they did not know what it was. One of the dolphins must have dived for it and proudly presented it to their warder.

Too bad for us, we had to settle for the second best option and place a gift near the inlet where the water for the whole system of aquaria and pools comes from.

Evaluation and outlook

If you don't have an ocean going craft yourself or choose to do ocean gifting from a small airplane, booking into fun cruises is probably the easiest option to get large stretches of ocean gifted. It tends automatically to become a family holiday because single passengers pay almost as much as 2 and the kids travel for free in off peak season. So I think this was not the last one even though I find the fun factor a bit disappointing, mostly due to the uninspired cooking on board and the huge crowd of loud, drunken and dumbed down fellow travellers that you can hardly escape in the confinement of a ship. But these are minor flaws in a great way to start covering the oceans, our new frontier, with orgonite.

In contrast to our usual tower busting tours, there were no immediate visual confirmations, although one wants to count the massive showing of dolphins, which could of course be coincidental.

A second leg is now lined up in the form of a sailing cruise starting from 07 April, that will cover the stretch from Durban to Cape Town. (approx 1500 km without the deviations due to tacking against the wind). This is a result of my research into "crewing" websites on the Internet.

The next leg of our ocean gifting effort I hoped was going to be on this beautiful boat...

Of course I'm very excited about this one, expecting much more personal encounters with our friends the dolphins from this much smaller boat.

In October another opportunity arises for a "luxury cruise" from Cape Town to Walvis Bay.

Then we would at least have the whole southern tip of Africa covered, and hopefully our friends in Walvis Bay will have a new boat by then to continue the work northward.

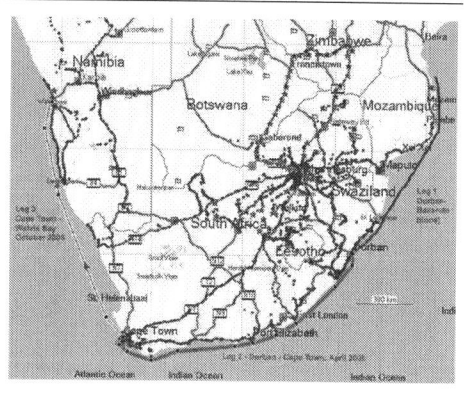

The picture above shows the accomplished and planned ocean gifting routes.

Vortex hunting with Laozu

March 2006

Laozu or Kelly McKennon from Palouse, Idaho, USA has developed a special gift for sensing qui which is, in his understanding, the Chinese word for orgone, quite accurately. A few years ago he started a systematic quest for revitalising energy vortices that had been compromised with negative energy. He observed that freeing these vortices was leading to the build-up of a continuous canopy of positive life energy. His quest has led him around the globe and he has written an ongoing account of his work on the ethericwarriors.com forum under the title "Heaven and Earth".

In March 2006 Laozu agreed to visit us in Johannesburg and to go on a tour with me, with the goal of opening the vortices of a large area in Southern Africa to create a positive energy canopy here.

I am quoting Laozu's own Report here. His text is set in italics; any comments from me are in straight text. I have also used some of my photos to illustrate the narrative. It is obvious from the context that **sheng qui** is very much the same state of the etheric energy that we refer to as positive orgone energy, or POR, while **sha qui** can be equated with what we call DOR.

It was now the latter part of November, and snow time was on the Palouse. Vortex opening would be on hold until February, when the weather would become milder again. Georg Ritschl, who has done so much gifting in Africa, had several years earlier invited me to visit his family in Johannesburg. It came to me that now was the time to take up his offer.

So in mid-February I set out for South

Africa. I had to change planes in Amsterdam, and the Amsterdam-Johannesburg flight passed over France and the Mediterranean Sea. I observed that that the European sheng canopy, which had been in the shape of a three petalled flower a half year earlier, now extended as far as Nice on the coast. Over North Africa the high qi of the sky was more negative than it had been in Europe before advent of the sheng canopy, but less negative than that of Japan had been.

Georg picked me up at the Jo'burg airport and we began work the next day. For about five days Georg drove me about the greater Johannesburg-Pretoria area and suburbs, opening latent vortices, and at the end of that period a sheng canopy was present over the region.

Now we began to travel a bit further away from town, and it was at this time we visited the most interesting vortex of the trip. Georg knew the owner of a rock and gem store northwest of the city, and he stopped to see what the man had on hand at the time. The owner told us a story about some Peruvian shamans, who had a school in Cape Town. They brought their students from time to time up to vortex in the area, because of the strong qi in the area. They had told him that it was even stronger than anything they had back in Peru. They had described to him where the vortex was located, and he drew a map for us.

We found what we thought was the place: a natural amphitheatre on a mountain in the Magaliesberg range. There was already a swirl of qi around the amphitheatre (clockwise looking down at it), but beneath the ground there was a feeling that was not entirely good.

Kelly digging in a TB or two

While resting from the climb up, a sheng being appeared and directed me to place TBs in appropriate places on the side. Georg remarked on the immediate increase of "energy" at the site.

There was, however, still quite a bunch of negative entities about. Another sheng being came to assist with their removal.

Typically, when a vortex is stimulated with TBs, a swirl of sheng qi rises into the air spiralling up. With this vortex, sheng qi poured out of the sky above into the ground near the centre of the amphitheatre – but not spiralling. The shape of the space in which the qi was pouring down was conical, but the sides were steeper than the cone of the up-spiralling qi of a normal vortex.

It was eventually time to leave, but we intended to return again, some time before the completion of my stay in Africa.

The extent of the sheng canopy was now such that we had to plan for a trip farther away from home. Three years previously Georg had been up to Zimbabwe, and his stories of the area captured my imagination. We decided to take a circular route: west to the southern boundary of Botswana, north through Botswana into Zimbabwe, east across Zimbabwe, and south again through to Pretoria and Johannesburg. It would take ten days or so, and we bought provisions for the trip, including corn meal for trade and gifts, and fuel cans for carrying extra diesel. Georg's pickup truck used this type of fuel, and he knew that these days diesel was unavailable in Zimbabwe. The latent vortices visited were too numerous to describe here, so I will just mention the more interesting ones.

Not too far west from Jo'burg we found a latent vortex situated on a high hill in the bush on private property. Georg stopped the truck just off the road. I had just climbed over a locked gate, when the owner of the farm and his wife drove up. Fortunately the farmer and his wife were very gracious, unlocked the gate so Georg could drive Tata II (Georg's pickup) on to his property and closer to the hill. He left the key to the gate with us, asking to lock the gate when we left later. This was somehow characteristic of the trip to come, in the kind treatment we were to receive throughout (with exception of the Zimbabwean borders). On this first leg of the trip, the vortices generally required more effort to reach, since the country was hilly and vortices tend to be on hills when such are present on the landscape. Georg however, perhaps from his many missions gifting towers, has a gift for getting his vehicle where he wants to go, and that saved us considerable time. One of the high points, from my point of view, was meeting with a kudu in the bush hiking in to one vortex. We crossed the South Africa/Botswana border near Lobatse about dark, and passed the first night in a motel on the Botswana side.

The people in Botswana were friendly, and seemed to be on the way up economically. The capital Gaborone was busy and growing. Somewhat north of that city there was a vortex on a hill not far from the road, but the place was gated and fenced. We drove in and found workers ready to go out into the fields. It was a government farm, and strictly speaking visitors were not allowed there, but Georg spoke with several of the workers about the vortex mission, and a couple of those who seemed to have more responsibility than the others told him that we could climb up the hill. It turned out that the vortex was not far up the hill, and upon return, a number of those still at the living quarters on the farm came out curious to see the pair. Georg explained about what the TBs do, gave one of the men a TB, and soon most of them wanted them. There were not enough for everyone, but quite a few got them.

Laozu in spontaneous healing session with the farmworkers in Botswana

In general we made good time throughout Botswana. The terrain was somewhat more level than it had been in South Africa, and it was often possible to find vortices closer to the highway. And when the pair had to leave the main road, there was often a farm road with an unlocked gate.

The last vortex we gifted in the evening was out in the bush, but there was a nice open flat space and we decided to use the good weather and camp out. It had been raining off and on since my arrival, and only that day had the weather been really fine. Georg cooked a good dinner over the cook stove and set up the tent. I tried to start a fire, but the wood was too wet so Georg poured on a little diesel, and the two enjoyed a campfire into the evening. Just before bedtime, the wind came up a bit, and a thunder and lightning storm blew up off to the south, where the opened vortices were strung out. After enjoying the spectacle for an hour or so, the two jumped into their sleeping bags and I (at least) fell asleep immediately. Some time later I was awakened by the tent blowing, and the sound of heavy rain drops. Gradually it turned into a downpour, and by morning, water was under and in the tent, and in the sleeping bags.

This wouldn't have happened in a Land Rover:: Pulling the truck out of the dirt

The dirt road outside was a mess, and Georg had to walk to the highway for help, and fortunately found a couple in a 4x4 who came to try to pull us out. But the 4x4 almost got stuck. After an amount of digging (with only a trowel), and various unsuccessful muddy expedients, more people showed up with a regular shovel. About five huskies (including Georg) lifted the left rear quarter of the pickup off the ground so that tree branches could be thrown under the wheel. We eventually got out and back to the road. The rest of the day it rained, but we managed to get several vortices opened (though in one cornfield I had to wade in up to my knees). The conclusion of the day was a three-hour border crossing into Zimbabwe. The Botswana side was no problem, but the Zimbabwe side was bad. One of the problems was the currency. Inflation was so bad that Georg had to pay 482 000 Zimbabwe dollars just to purchase obligatory highway insurance. And the exchange did not even issue actual currency – just cheques for the currency, cheques which had already expired formally at the end of 2005. Not far from the border we found a motel where we could stay the night, and try to dry a few clothes. In the morning we drove into the city of Bulawayo to make a few purchases, and then we headed into the Matopos Hills, which Cecil Rhodes had liked so much that he had his remains buried there.

Rhodes's grave in the rain

It was drizzling as Georg drove into the hills. The first lengthy stop was the huge rock formation which holds the graves of Rhodes and his henchman Leander Starr Jameson.

Several years before Georg had made friends with a noted Matabele rainmaker in the area, and we had with us in the pickup a CB which was intended as a gift for him. Luckily, one of the attendants at the grave-rock knew the man. He told us that he had died some time back, but agreed to take us to where his widow lived, later in the afternoon when he got off work.

The rain and wind had turned stormy, and the guide-gatekeepers were more than willing to let Georg and myself climb up to the graves ourselves, and indeed we had the place to ourselves. Georg had gifted the place when he had visited before with TBs, but this time, with no observers, we were able to secrete an HHG quite close to the grave.

The memorial plate indicating Cecil John Rhodes's grave

I noticed that there were two qi lines crossing over the rock. One, a sheng line, passed close by Jameson's grave. The other, a sha line, came from a sort of valley in the distance, but crossed the first some twenty metres or so from Rhodes's grave.

The hill on which the graves lie

I also observed that there was a latent vortex not too far away in the hills.

After descending the grave rock, we found an inconspicuous place on the sha line where there was sufficient soil to bury a ring of 6 TBs and so to change the character of the line to positive.

Laozu has found that to neutralise negative energy lines, a circle of 6 TBs does the best job.

After getting permission from the caretakers to roam in the hills, we headed off in the direction of the latent vortex. We found it on the top of a hill some distance away. The top of the hill was ringed by a circle of rocks, which made it look like a fortification, or a ceremonial place. And indeed after opening the vortex, we were visited by a high-level sheng being who assisted in doing some cleaning of the place.

Afterwards we slogged back to the pickup through the high wet vegetation. Georg decided he should go see about getting us a room for the night at the nearby Matopos Hills Lodge, since there was no similar place available for many miles. I decided not to go with him, but to go back up to the grave site to see whether our ministrations had effected any change. Sure enough, the sha line had changed into a sheng line.

When I arrived back at the caretakers' shelter, I found that they had left. While waiting for Georg to return, I noticed that there was a collection of photographs showing Cecil Rhodes at various times in his life, and photographs of Jameson, and of Alfred Beit. So I walked over and inspected them with considerable attention. The photos of Rhodes as a child, and even as a young man, show a hard, determined person, who feels some inner pain. In the photos of the mature and older man, the determination has changed to ferocity, and the pain has intensified.

Laozu in action

In the late afternoon, after Georg and our guide had returned, we drove off into the countryside where the rainmaker's widow lived. The road ran over a dam and, because of the recent unusually heavy rains, the reservoir behind the dam was overfull, and several inches of water were flowing over the road down the dam face. I was glad it was Georg at the wheel instead of myself (especially later on the return trip in the dark).

The woman was pleased to see us, but did not speak English, and the guide had to interpret. She invited us into her house, a 6-sided 1-room building of mud and poles, with a thatched roof. In the centre was a circle of stones for the fire. She took out some reddish powder and burned some of it, invoking several non-material beings in the building above us. She spoke as well during this process, but I did not understand what she was saying. There seemed to be no hole in the roof for the smoke to escape, and so the smoke became somewhat disconcerting – I understand this keeps the mosquitoes out however.

Later we took the CB out to the edge of the cornfield where the rainmaker's corpse was interred, and set it up. A number of the neighbours joined us, and the CB was ceremonially dedicated to the deceased. There were non-material entities also present during this time.

We were allowed to place the CB near the grave of the late Alexander Ndlovu

Typical Matabele homestead in the area

When we left, Georg gave the lady the greater part of the corn meal we had brought with us. She was very thankful. She said that she had had nothing to eat but field corn for about a month, and that with the corn meal they could have a real dinner that night.

We found this to be characteristic of Zimbabwe at the time. People could not afford enough to buy food, and many of the males with whom we spoke asked if we knew where they could find jobs in South Africa.

It was nearly dark by then, and so we drove back, and spent the night in the bungalow Georg had rented. There was water leaking in from outside on to the floors, and no running cold water, since the pipes leading from the dam had broken. But the electricity was working and so our wet clothes could be at least partly dried by a small electric heater in the place.

We often had to push through dense thicket, normally reserved for other animals like this formidable spider

Next day was the one day spent sightseeing on the trip, visiting cave paintings, a museum, and places of etheric interest.

Laozu looking at some paintings at Nanke Cave

After another night without running water, the pair headed east.

Some more mountaineering took place without Laozu finding it worth mentioning

Several years earlier Georg had given a CB to a man in rural Zimbabwe, and he was interested in driving to the man's home to visit him and inspect the CB. Due to the muddy road, we could not drive all the way, but had to walk the last half mile or so.

This is in fact the CB mentioned in our first report, see page 52. Unfortunately it seems that Kenny Ngwenya is not alive any more. Laozu found however that a happy entity was living there.

The body of evidence

When we got to the place, the man was not there, and the residence seemed abandoned. But the CB was still set up, was even protected by a small fence, and was working quite well.

With all the rain, the rivers through that part of Zimbabwe had water, and Georg made sure they (as well as whatever towers had not been gifted before) got TBs.

One of the latent vortices which was opened on our way east, was on a small mountain not far from the road. Here there was no way to drive off the road, and quite a few pedestrians were using the road. Since we could not afford to have anyone walk off with our diesel cans, Georg remained in the truck while I took off into the bush towards the mountain. After a short distance there appeared a couple of ragged looking individuals who approached me and asked me what I was doing. I told them I wanted to climb the mountain. One of them told me he would take me to a trail up the mountain, which he proceeded to do. When we came to it, he continued on up with me. He asked me if I were carrying a gun, to which I replied in the negative. Then he asked me why I was climbing the mountain. It took a little time, but I explained to him about opening vortices, and the sheng canopy and so forth. I don't know how much he really understood, but by the time we reached the summit, he was convinced I was sincere, and not a threat. At this point the second man, who had been following us out of sight the entire way, appeared. The two explained to me that they were gold miners, that gold mining was illegal, and that they were afraid I was a government inspector. They then asked me if I knew anything about mining, and showed me some of their nuggets. I opened the vortex, and we walked back down together, back to the pickup. I gave them a TB for their hut, and we parted friends.

For the rest of the day, progress was rapid and successful, and we reached the town of Masvingo by nightfall. In the morning we drove to the Great Ruins, and engaged a guide who told us about the history and former uses of these ruins. Their name "Zimbabwe" was adopted by the Shona as the new name for their country after they took over political control of Rhodesia. "Zi" means "great", "mbab" means "house", and "hwe" means "stone".

And there was a great stone house on top of a steep hill, the stones being granite blocks, partly hewn, and partly broken by heating and cracking. The ascent was quite interesting, designed so that any unwanted visitors could quite easily be disposed of by those above dropping rocks or shooting arrows. On the hill was a cave with acoustics such that words spoken there could be heard down on the plain below the hill. In that cave were two non-material beings, one quite happy and the other quite sad – the guide explained that the place had probably been used for ceremonial purposes.

From there we climbed up to the higher place on the hill, where public dances and ceremonies had been performed in front of the kings, in times past. As I recall, the place had been used for such purposes from the 12th to the early 16th century. There was a high concave rock, near to the king's seat, where a strong sheng being still lingered. It reminded me of the being in the old monastery ruins on Heiligenberg in Heidelberg which Cesco and I had seen the previous summer. In both cases the sheng being appeared and inspired me to do some work in locations. I suspect that the presence here of the sheng being was the reason that hill had been picked for the Great Zimbabwe.

Later we came to another part of the ruins down on the plain, surrounded by a great circular wall. Georg had told me that there was something special about the place, and indeed there was a latent vortex there. By that time, the guide had developed sufficient confidence in us that he permitted us to gift it. Georg told me that he would have been surprised if there had not been a vortex there. A photo of the enclosure containing the (now) open vortex:

Photo: Laozu

It was afternoon by the time we left the ruins, and we just managed to reach the South African border by nightfall. Again there was trouble "jumping through the hoops" on the Zimbabwe side, but it was not so bad as entering the country had been.

In Botswana and Zimbabwe, gates into rangeland had been mostly unlocked, and fences had been low enough to climb easily. This was not the case in South Africa. Especially difficult were the high game fences, often ten feet tall, with barbed wire and hog wire on one side, and sometimes electrified on the back. When confronted with these latter, I either looked for vortices elsewhere, or asked permission. On one occasion when permission was requested, it was refused on the grounds there was a tiger inside. We were fortunate in being given permission sufficiently often, and finding enough non-game fences, that vortices could be opened with the necessary frequency to successfully complete the circuit. Riding south I observed that the positive canopy had already spread along their previous route north through Botswana some three hundred kilometres to the west. Turning my attention to the far south, I became aware of a large swirl of sheng qi far to the southwest. I could feel that qi was dropping downward into the swirl, but rather than depleting the sheng qi above, the sheng qi seemed to be stronger there than elsewhere. Georg had a GPS device with the aid of which it was determined that direction of this positive swirl was quite close to that of the Magaliesberg vortex mentioned above. The closer the two travelled to Pretoria, the more we became convinced that it was that vortex. I was able to confirm this about a week later when I was once more in its vicinity.

Somewhere between 150 to 200 kilometres from the Pretoria/ Johannesburg area, we drove under the edge of the sheng canopy. I found it unusual that the canopy had spread so far north from the vortices originally opened, which were the source of that part of the canopy. I speculated that the special Magaliesberg vortex, visible from so far away, may have been some part of the reason.

After coming under the canopy, it was no longer necessary to gift vortices with such frequency as before, and we reached Georg's home not long after dark.

Georg was ill when we returned, and the severity of the illness seemed greater the next day. He in fact was suffering throughout the remainder of my stay, and when I returned to my home, I came down with apparently the same thing. At first I suspected malaria, but later it seemed more likely it had been tick fever, for I did get quite a few tick bites ranging about through the bush. At any event, due to his illness and the many duties which had piled up for him during our trip north, Georg decided to stay home for a few days.

For the last part of my stay in South Africa, I borrowed Georg's TATA II pickup and set off to the south, intending to extend the positive canopy parallelogram further. It now covers an area approximately 300 km by 1250 km. The corners of the parallelogram are roughly Bulawayo (Zimbabwe) in the NW, Masvingo (Zimbabwe) in the NE, Bloemfontein (South Africa) in the SE, and Kimberley (South Africa) in the SW. I say "roughly" because the canopy actually extends a bit further. Here is a map, provided by Georg, with the vortices we opened indicated by stars:

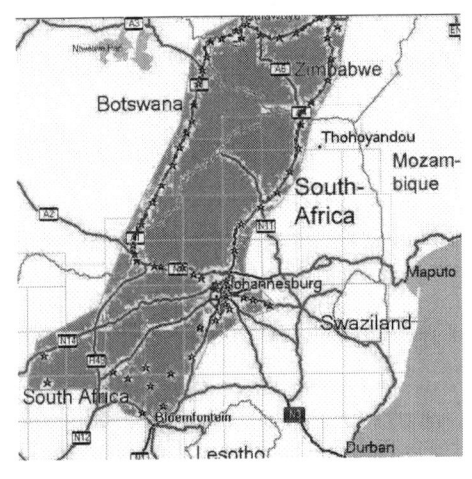

Map: Laozu

The area on the map coloured orange is my estimate of the extent of the sheng canopy when I left South Africa.

The only place I was accosted by authority during the trip was by a couple of private patrolmen on the Harmony Gold Mine (owned by the Oppenheimers, I believe), not far from the town of Welkom. The soil there was toxic and pretty bad. I had to scrub my trowel hard the next day to clean it. When they learned I was on the way out, they lost interest and drove on. About a hundred kilometres south of Kuruman, I found another unusual vortex. It was almost as if a number of vortices were together, for, instead of there being only one place to gift, there was an extensive area, and after I gifted one place, the resultant expansion of the canopy covered about 80 kilometres in the period of one night. Later I was to find more examples: one in Poland, and one in Ireland. On the way back to Johannesburg I drove through the town of Magaliesburg, not far from where we had opened that special vortex several weeks before. It was still the case that qi was pouring down straight into the vortex, but rather than sucking all of the sheng qi out of the area, paradoxically, the area was much more positive than usual. It had actually spread south to the town of Kuruman before I came upon it driving north.

Coming back to Georg's house after my circuit, I drove through a district of Johannesburg in which a minor riot was taking place. Strangely, many of the participants, as well as the police, seemed to be having a good time.

It was now nearly time to return home. I looked at the tree tops to see if sheng qi had begun to enter them yet from above. In Germany in August of the preceding year, the process had begun in less than two weeks; in Japan in September/October of that year it had begun in a similar period of time; and in Taiwan in November it had actually begun more rapidly. But here in South Africa, after nearly three weeks, it had begun only slightly, or not at all. I have wondered if the sheng qi pouring into the Magaliesberg vortex may have had something to do with this.

I owe Georg and his family much thanks, for providing the TBs and all they did for me during the trip.

On the return journey, due to a missed connection, I had a flight from Amsterdam direct to Seattle, which passed over north-eastern Canada. About the middle of Hudson's Bay, to my surprise, I observed the edge of a sheng canopy. As the route of the plane turned south over the provinces of Manitoba and Saskatchewan, the canopy receded from view. I only observed it again when entering southern British Columbia.

All that Rain!

April 2006

Since we started busting the secret underground bases in South Africa where the illegal electronic weather warfare was conducted, leading to widespread drought in Southern Africa, unprecedented rains have swept the subcontinent.

The planting season, which is normally from October to April/May was again predicted (read: planned) to be a drought season, albeit not in the same hysterical fashion as 3 years before. The perpetrators must have learned to cover their bets since the previous planned droughts were all broken by our massive orgonite gifting efforts. Of course it's difficult for them to change the song sheet in the middle of such a large-scale operation, so we continue reading "scientific" background articles about global warming etc. That's intended to prepare the mood for a few catastrophic droughts of course.

Someone very smart has now invented the term "global dimming" as a hedge theory, in case the "global warming" scenario doesn't happen. In this dimming scenario, pollution (of course no mention of the ubiquitous chemtrails) counteracts the effects of "greenhouse gases" and leads to a decrease in temperatures, unfortunately with much sickness and other side effects because of the toxic brew. (Again no mention of the worldwide illegal spraying programme.) I first heard of this interesting propaganda twist a few months ago in a BBC documentary.

Be all that as it may, the healing continues in a visible way that cannot be ignored by the mainstream much longer.

The rains started a bit late and in fact only got unlocked after we turned our attention towards those underground bases in earnest, which was in December 2005 and January 2006.

Since then average rainfalls as measured over many years have been massively exceeded.

This is what we measured at our place (Johannesburg):

October 2005 (Kalahari Expedition)

Rainfall(mm)	long-term average	Diff	Diff %
80.5	56	24.5	43.75%

The body of evidence

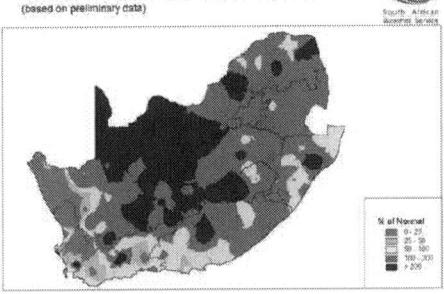

November 2005 (beginning of busting UG bases around Johannesburg)

Rainfall(mm)	long-term average	Diff	Diff %
135.5	107	28.5	26.64%

December 2005 (continued busting of UG bases)

Rainfall(mm)	long-term average	Diff	Diff %
115	125	-10	-8.00%

January 2006 (Matatiele Expedition)

Rainfall(mm)	long-term average	Diff	Diff %
147	114	33	28.95%

February 2006 (vortex busting with Kelly)

Rainfall(mm)	long-term average	Diff	Diff %
234	109	125	114.68%

March 2006 (vortex busting with Kelly and 1st Marine busting expedition to Bazaruto)

Rainfall(mm)	long-term average	Diff	Diff %
103.5	89	14.5	16.29%

Total planting season 2005/2006

Rainfall(mm)	long-term average	Diff	Diff %
815.5	600	215.5	35.92%

Rainfall in per cent of normal February 2006 (South African Weather Service)

The rains were well distributed over the whole region, and Namibia especially experienced rainfall such as had never been observed throughout the 20th and 21st centuries.

The map to the left shows the rainfalls in South Africa in February:

As you can see, the rainfall almost everywhere is between 100% and above 200% of normal.

An exception is the Western Cape, and the West Coast in general, which is still experiencing dry conditions. The Western Cape is for most part a winter rainfall region, however, and therefore the dry condition in summer is less significant, in my opinion. But of course the South African West Coast needs additional busting.

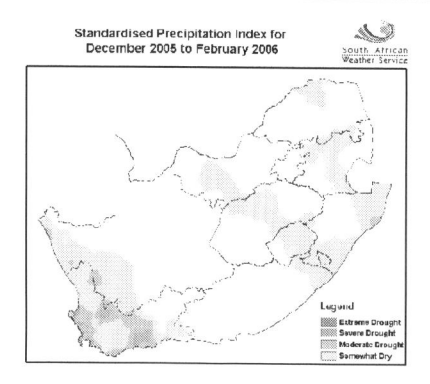

All that rain! (2006)

Standardised Precipitation Index for December 2005 to February 2006 — South African Weather Service

Legend: Extreme Drought / Severe Drought / Moderate Drought / Somewhat Dry

The map above shows that only small areas outside the Western Cape were "somewhat dry" in the period December 2005 – February 2006

Extra rains a blessing to some, a curse to others

Citizen, 4.4.2006

As usual, isolated cases where "too much rain" is causing problems, such as plant rot or flooding, are overemphasised

Rain in neighbouring countries

On our trip through Botswana and Zimbabwe we found both countries green and lush like I've never before seen them.

But the most exciting news reached us from Namibia which we had busted in our **"Desert Rain"** in September 2004.

My friends there tell me that the **desert is covered with a beautiful carpet of blossoming greenery** and nobody can recall anything like that, even back to 1900 or earlier.

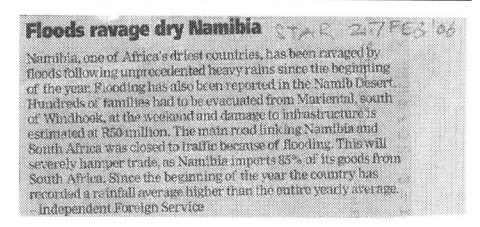

Floods ravage dry Namibia

Namibia, one of Africa's driest countries, has been ravaged by floods following unprecedented heavy rains since the beginning of the year. Flooding has also been reported in the Namib Desert. Hundreds of families had to be evacuated from Mariental, south of Windhoek, at the weekend and damage to infrastructure is estimated at R50 million. The main road linking Namibia and South Africa was closed to traffic because of flooding. This will severely hamper trade, as Namibia imports 85% of its goods from South Africa. Since the beginning of the year the country has recorded a rainfall average higher than the entire yearly average. – Independent Foreign Service

The Star, Johannesburg, 27 Feb 2006

Sossusvlei in the Namib Desert: Flooded! (Photo: AZ Windhoek)

You may want to look back at page 139 for comparison with what the Sossusvlei normally looks like.

Namibia green as never before, near Von Bach Dam (Photo: AZ Windhoek)

Flooding in Mariental (Photo: AZ Windhoek)

The body of evidence

Rain-soaked roads in southern Namibia (Photo: AZ Windhoek)

Overflowing Swakoppforte Dam (Photo: AZ Windhoek)

Let's hear some voices from the press:

The Namibian, Tuesday, January 24
2006 Farmers' unions optimistic after the rains *ABSALOM SHIGWEDHA

THE Namibia Agricultural Union (NAU) and the Namibian National Farmers' Union (NNFU) are hopeful that farmers will get a bumper harvest this year because of the good rains that have fallen since the beginning of the year.

NNFU President Manfred Rukoro told The Namibian on Friday that although the rain came a bit late, the good showers that are falling countrywide at the moment have brought smiles to the faces of many communal farmers.

"We are very, very happy. This looks like a promising year," said Rukoro.

He said towards the end of last year, many regions were on the verge of starvation, but the good rain that started at the beginning of this month raised hopes for a good harvest this year, especially if it could continue until April.

The Executive Manager of the NAU, Isak Coetzee, shares the same views.

He said the NAU was very glad about the good rains and expects good prospects for crop and livestock farming.

He said although there were still some areas in south-eastern Namibia that had received little rain, it was still early in the season and more rain had been predicted to be on the way.

The good rains have also raised the levels of the country's main storage dams higher than they were at the same time last year.

According to NamWater's latest dam bulletin, the Von Bach Dam is 67,8 per cent full compared to 37,7 per cent last year.

The Goreangab Dam is overflowing at 102,8 per cent of full capacity, while the Hardap Dam at Mariental is 61,4 per cent full compared to last season's figure of 38,4 per cent.

Clipped wings – the prisoners of orgone

July – August 2006

Great expectations

It was supposed to have been the trip of all trips, the expedition of all expeditions. For at least 2 years I had wanted to do this and preparations were extensive. Many people had helped us to make this great trip possible with donations and moral support.

XL from Austria had joined me to share the experience.

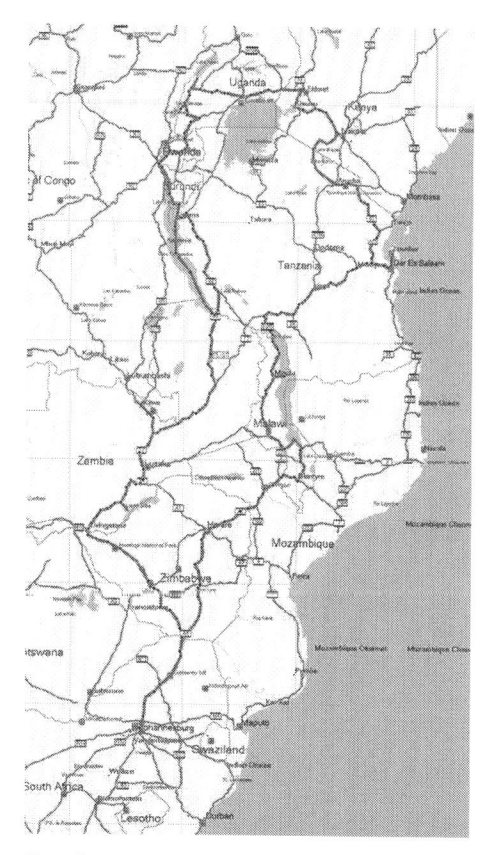

The trip as originally planned

We had 7 full size CBs, 2000 TBs, plenty of HHGs, many Dolphin busters, earth pipes and etheric sticks on board. XL had also brought some very special gifts for special places.

But it was going to be a very different trip from what we expected. Read here what happened:

The arsenal of orgonite for the trip

Zimbabwe – a country falling apart

The trip started with some strange confusion when we lost our way in South Africa on the main road to the Zimbabwean border, which I had travelled many times in the past.

For those who are not familiar with regional events in Southern Africa, I want to give a short introduction to the situation in Zimbabwe.

Zimbabwe has been spiralling to economic destruction after the

Mugabe government started evicting the white farmers from their land a few years ago.

Since then the country has not only lost most of its agricultural production and export earnings, but hyperinflation and an increasingly draconian neo-Stalinist approach have crippled all business in the country.

Essentially 5 million out of 17 million Zimbabweans are now "over the border", which means that they are making a living by working illegally in South Africa. Interestingly, that is about the same proportion East Germany reached after 40 years of communism, only in Zimbabwe it took a mere 6 years to achieve the same result.

No ordinary economic activity is possible any more in Zimbabwe and people are generally desperate, while the government prosecutes the poor fellows who try to find fire wood in the forests as "fire wood poachers" and puts them in prison, while high officials corruptly organise big game hunting safaris for rich foreigners with impunity.

Sick people are taken to hospital on handcarts, and many die on the way. In the morgues corpses are rotting because of the lack of refrigeration.

The EU and the Commonwealth (and I think the US as well) have put some 150 members of Mugabe's "inner circle" under sanctions, which contributes to the meltdown of course.

They also make it easy for Mugabe to blame the whole calamity publicly on Tony Blair and MI6, or what he calls neo-colonialist forces.

Of course the history is complex and nothing is what it seems. Mugabe uses a shrill anti-colonial rhetoric which still buys him a lot of support all over Africa.

But the irony is that he is in fact working for the New World Order takeover of his country.

It is necessary to know that he was put in his position by Lord Carrington, the "British Kissinger", in the Lancaster House negotiations in the 1970s that led to the present majority government in Zimbabwe. The renegade settler republic Rhodesia with its white minority government broke away from England and was finally overcome by a plethora of liberation movements with lots of Western secret service support. Mugabe's movement was only one of them, and not the most popular one either.

One of his first acts in stabilising his rule was a well-publicised massacre of more than 20 000 people in Matabeleland who were deemed to be loyal to the competing and possibly more attractive rebel leader Joshua Nkomo.

In the Lancaster House talks a 20-year moratorium for land reform was agreed to, after which large sums of money were promised by Great Britain for implementing a peaceful and lawful land redistribution programme. Of course this was because the white land grab by Cecil John Rhodes and his cronies in the 1880s was a historical injustice of magnificent proportions.

This promised aid did not materialise. So in a sense there is some truth in Mugabe's public argument, only that, sad but true, he works for exactly the forces of destruction that he so eloquently lambasts in his hateful public speeches.

Be that as it may, the country is a shambles and ready for the big corporate takeover after the elimination of any middle class, be it black or white.

In that sense, Zimbabwe is an advanced model of what's basically planned worldwide by the ruling elite, namely the elimination of any economically independent group, the creation of a state where a small functional elite is required to "keep things going" and a mass of economically enslaved serfs with no rights, as many as needed to keep up comfort levels of the elite. The majority of "useless eaters" (NWO parlance, not mine) is to be eliminated by biological warfare like AIDS, vaccination programmes, starvation, wars of attrition, weather manipulation and other forms of genocide.

So look at Zimbabwe: It's a testing ground for certain policies, just like Rwanda, Burundi and the Congo. (I forgot to mention Cambodia, of course ...)

And my feeling is that that's exactly the job that Mugabe is paid to do.

Your Bank Manager (I'm not talking about your branch manager, who is probably a nice person and has no clue of what's going on) is also working for the same goal and vision, hoping that he will be part of those chosen few who are allowed to survive the great population control drive.

Never forget that!

Of course that will only happen if we're not able to stop these plans in their tracks and create an atmosphere in which self-organisation and self-reliant prosperity are encouraged to grow worldwide, replacing the fraudulent international money system (wealth extraction scheme). Massive saturation with orgonite holds the promise of turning things around apart from its immediate positive effects on the weather and the fertility of farmland, securing abundant crops and stopping attempts at mass starvation through weather warfare.

You can imagine that the atmosphere in the country is pretty tense, can't you?

President Mugabe of Zimbabwe – MI6's best asset in the country?

Whenever I put forward my theory that Mugabe is actually doing MI6's bidding in destroying his own country, I get a lot of approval and mostly a lot of additional information from intelligent and aware black Zimbabweans (of whom there are many).

For example, what I just heard in conversation during this turbulent visit was that the **great mining houses**, especially LONHRO under Tiny Rowlands, shifted their allegiance from the white minority government to support the rebel movements, just as the Western secret services did.

Nothing is what it seems to be in this world of deceptive layers of smoke and mirrors ...

Rock formation near Ngundu. An underground base is not far from here.

We were going via Masvingo, the town near the ruins of Great Zimbabwe.

The first night we stayed in a lodge in Ngundu, about 100 km before Masvingo. Like everything in Zimbabwe, the lodge was on the verge of disintegration.

No warm water, but of course the prices were the same as in better days and had to be paid in foreign currency.

I had received very interesting information from an anonymous source, who claimed to have been a former operative in the secret "One World Army" that messes up Africa with all its senseless wars.

In fact, there is no war in Africa that is not run by outside secret services, who create the various 3-letter "liberation movements" that murder and create mayhem. All these insurgent movements are equipped and supported by the "One World Army" of the "New World Order".

This monster has many names – call it UN, French Foreign Legion, South African Mercenaries, CIA, MI6.

Its activities are supported by a network of underground bases with weather warfare and mind control capacities, secret and forbidden territories for training and assembling armies etc. Most rebel insurgencies originate from the vast "game reserves" in Africa that are mostly already under the control of NWO cover organisations like the WWF (run by Prince Charles of Great Britain).

Nowhere but in Africa is the NEW WORLD ORDER so obvious and so murderous at this present moment in history.

The information I received consists of a map with the location of hundreds of different places that are allegedly some kind of underground bases, some of them military, some of them alien in nature.

We had already started acting on this information on a tentative basis in South Africa and had received very good results. There were great changes in atmospheric energy after treating these places.

Also, we found clues at some of the places that indeed indicated some underground activity.

The prisoners of orgone 2006

What I'm trying to say here is that I am not able to judge the authenticity of the information we received and therefore treat it as unverified for the time being, but events on this trip, as well as our previous experiences, tend to lend a lot of plausibility to this information.

The first of these underground bases was near Runde. The place is marked as some kind of memorial on the map. Interestingly, we found a network of construction roads to indicate that there had been some kind of activity going on, and they (the roads) were demolished only close to the main road so that a casual passer-by would not notice anything unusual happening in the bush.

Bingo! The map was spot on again!

For the fine-tuning work of placing the gifts at the right spot one still needs some intuitive guidance, but luckily my travelling companion XL was quite good with that.

We normally place <u>1 or 2 earth pipes</u> over an underground base and possibly an HHG or some TBs for support.

Returning to the area of the famous ruins of Great Zimbabwe, which had already been gifted twice, was a revelation.

It felt like paradise!

Even though we were at the end of the dry winter season, the place looked surprisingly lush and a peaceful, very positive atmosphere prevailed.

The last time I had been there was with Kelly, also known as Laozu, when we gifted a vortex nearby and left some general gifts in the area.

This time we actually gifted the lake itself for the first time and found another hilltop array that had escaped my loving attention the last 2 times.

Ceremonial place in Hill Complex, Great Zimbabwe: The seat of an entity that Kelly noticed on our last visit. Having been there already 4 times now, the ruins of Great Zimbabwe feel very familiar to me. It is a powerful place, by all means

Lake Kyle near Great Zimbabwe

The body of evidence

The hill complex of Great Zimbabwe

The conical tower in the great enclosure

The great enclosure seen from the hill complex

The CB at the orphanage

Arriving in Harare, the capital of Zimbabwe, we checked into a derelict motel that nevertheless charged the proud amount of 50 USD. The next day was reserved for Harare and surrounds. Generally, the energy around Harare felt very bad. Also, we were stopped by a corrupt policeman who was fishing for a bribe by threatening to search our car thoroughly, and by several road blocks with traffic cops trying to collect speeding fines. The brand new radar guns seem to be the only functioning equipment in Zimbabwe.

We did 2 underground bases outside town and another one near the airport.

The one at the airport was obvious as it had various vent shafts showing above ground. The other ones were invisible but felt very nasty energetically.

We also did the town centre and the residential suburbs.

In the evening we found the place of Sheik Yusuf in Chitungwidza. He runs an orphanage with a school and feeds, clothes and teaches about 60 children who would otherwise live on the street.

His orphanage receives minimal or no support from the government and everything is very basic, including his own living quarters. But the place is neat and clean and the children seem to be happy there.

Sheik Yusuf and associates in Chitungwidza near Harare

Students' bedrooms

We left a CB in his yard and observed some immediate changes in the sky. As happens so often, an indistinct grey soup immediately changed into articulate cumulus clouds even looking more like rain clouds.

Rain cloud forming over Chitungwidza after placing the CB

From Chitungwidza we left in the direction of Mozambique, leaving gifts on the way as we went along. Generally, we had felt miserable throughout our stay in Zimbabwe with the exception of meeting the gentle and modest Sheik Yusuf. The atmosphere in the country is generally aggressive and negative. One feels one is being ripped off at every bend and corner because everyone is so desperate to make a living. So we were looking forward to leaving Zimbabwe quickly.

Involuntary Guests of "His Excellency" Comrade President Robert Gabriel Mugabe.

Shortly before the border post at Nyamapanda, we tossed out a last TB at a bridge. There were people around and XL actually warned me not to do it. But I had never encountered any difficulties with people watching us toss orgonite and ignored the warning.

How I was to regret that moment of stupidity!

I had not been aware how close we were to the border and also that all the seemingly inconspicuous people were police agents in civilian clothes.

Dammit!

At first we proceeded normally to the immigration and customs counters at the border, where our passports were stamped as usual. But as we got back to our car and were ready to leave, the civilian police agents started questioning us and asked for some documents that I had never heard of. I got angry with the officer, another mistake it seems. I had actually taken the bunch of guys for the usual parasitic money changers and "Madobadobas". (That's guys who attach themselves to every foreigner crossing an African border, offering "in an irresistible way" to help expedite the process.) The last thing that would have occurred to me, would have been that they were all police agents.

They then told us that we had been observed throwing an object from the bridge and somebody actually came up with the TB.

We were asked to follow them with the car to the nearby police station for further investigation.

We saw no other way but full disclosure of what we were doing. The car was completely searched and of course they were amazed at the amount of orgonite we had on board.

Any hope of a speedy clearance and continuation was soon frustrated when we were told we had to wait for the commanding officer.

In the meantime a lot of the guys were chatting to us in a friendly manner and we had the impression that we could win them over. Apart from the officer with whom I had had an altercation at the border, the others were rather curious and friendly rather than hostile. Soon we had a lot of budding friendships forming and a lot of orgone pamphlets, TBs and HHGs were distributed.

But little did we anticipate what was to come!

The commanding officer arrived late that night and didn't even want to talk to us much, so we were asked to sleep on the concrete floor in the charge office with people coming and going all the time and the radio crackling the whole night.

We were allowed access to our car under the supervision of an officer and we were allowed to get food, but they took the car keys and our passports.

The next day we were interrogated by the commanding officer and the CIO (Criminal Intelligence Officer). The latter turned out to be a sympathetic guy. Interestingly, his father had been a sangoma (traditional healer). He would have let us go if it had been his decision.

But it was not in his power.

In fact, wave after wave of ever higher ranking officers was brought in, asking basically the same questions all over again. Obviously they wanted to see if we would contradict ourselves in our story. I showed them my registration as a traditional healer with the International Traditional Healers Council of Malawi, which impressed the CIO but did not lead to our release either.

I told them I was doing my job as a rainmaker, protected by international agreements between the countries of Southern Africa regarding the work of traditional healers.

Then they decided to take samples of our stuff to Harare for forensic examination.

That would cost us at least another day we thought ...

If it had been only another day!

After 2 more days (we were allowed to pitch our tent on the police station grounds for the following nights) with many more interviews and getting to know all the guys at the station, befriending most of them in the process, it was decided we had to be transferred to another station where higher ranking officers wanted to have a look at us.

I was taken in my car, accompanied by 3 officers, using the last of our diesel, while XL was taken in a police van. Interestingly, one of the officers made a remark, disguised as a question, that showed that they were aware of outside interference in their weather, meaning HAARP-based weather warfare. The question insinuated that our tools might contribute to this foreign-sponsored drought creation effort.

XL's journey turned out to be the much more eventful one. The officers used the vehicle to conduct a brisk business on the side, like transporting chickens and goats, taking passengers for payment and buying boxes of soap which they then tried to sell at a profit in another village.

Hence he was not to be seen at our first destination, the police station in Murewa. As soon as we arrived there, new orders from above arrived, and we had to continue to Marondera, the central police station for the province of Mashonaland East. XL arrived about 3 hours later as a result of the business detours of "his" police officers.

Arriving at Marondera, we found groups of very high ranking officers (judging by their clothing and demeanour) waiting for us.

The car was completely offloaded and searched again.

A new series of interviews began. We still had the feeling that we could win them over with our natural charm and obvious unevil intentions.

I learnt from one of the junior officers, who was a bit sympathetic towards us, that we were now talking to the top charges of the Zimbabwean secret service (nobody ever introduced themselves to us, by the way) and that President Mugabe was involved in this.

Quite a confirmation of the importance of our work to get such top level attention, I think.

Unluckily the top secret service man in charge found the markings of underground bases in my map and that apparently really sent him into a real spin! My computer was searched and they were very disappointed that there was nothing really suspicious on it.

I told them that the markings on the map were bad energy spots that I had dowsed with a pendulum.

But Mister Secret Police was not very convinced ...

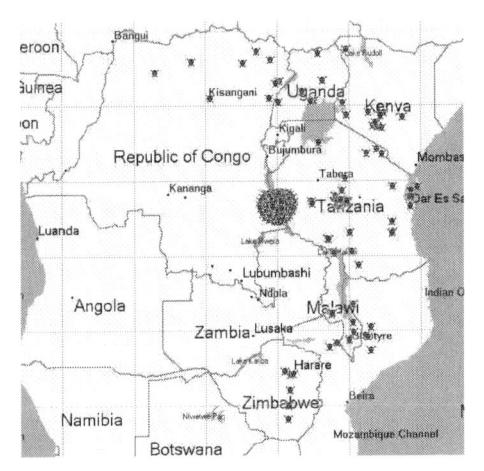

The famous map: Underground bases in Southern and Eastern Africa

We were finally charged with a minor misdemeanour because they could not otherwise have kept us any longer, not even in Zimbabwe. The charges amounted to "depositing an object in a place that is not designated to deposit such object" – littering, in other words – under an ominous-sounding "miscellaneous offences act". They told us that we should sign an admission of guilt and we would be released in no time with a minor monetary fine. We signed because it seemed senseless to deny the charges of having thrown something out of the window. Now we were no longer permitted to sleep in a tent but moved to the normal police cells.

Police detention cells in Marondera

In a way we were still privileged because we were allowed to keep all our clothes on (normally only one pair of trousers and one shirt, no underwear and no belt were all that was allowed) and to get food from our car.

We were even allowed to take our sleeping bags into the cell after some negotiation. And we had a cell to ourselves.

The more luckless "ordinary" prisoners get no food or water whatsoever, they are deprived of some of their clothes, and they sleep on the bare concrete, that is, if they sleep. They may often stay like that for several days, so that they arrive in court already in a quite dehumanised state.

The toilet in our cell

I was even able to smuggle my camera into the police cell on one occasion and took the snapshots of our luxury hotel depicted above.

Mr Tata at Marondera

During the day we were for the most part allowed to move freely in the grounds of the police station under loose supervision. As in Nyamapanda, we had soon established a good rapport with the ordinary police officers. But in hindsight I feel that some of the senior guys just played confidence tricks with us to get our friendly cooperation and make us voluntarily go to prison, giving them all the time in the world to think about what they were finally going to do with us.

Anything was possible: They could have planted explosives or drugs in our car to get us locked away for a long time, or they could have "shot us while trying to escape". The options are endless, and I believe that it was due to the wonderful support of many people on the spiritual and etheric level that none of these quite feasible possibilities materialised.

After spending three nights at Marondera police station, with high hopes that on Monday it would all be over with a slap on the wrist, worse was to come.

On the Monday we were escorted to the court to see the public prosecutor. This slick and well-dressed gentleman had no inclination to treat this as a simple case of littering, but insisted that the forensic report must be in first.

So we were checked into the labyrinth of holding cells, and all our personal belongings were now finally taken away.

After hours in those ice-cold cells with crowds of awaiting trial prisoners, we were presented in court, where a mean and lazy looking lady magistrate decided to keep us in detention. So we were to become acquainted with real prison life in Zimbabwe.

And to prison we went!

We were led back into the cold mass holding cells to await transport to prison.

By now it dawned on us that we would be well advised to seek the help of a lawyer.

But how to find one?

If you are used to scenes in American movies, where prisoners have the right to a phone call and access to a telephone book, you'd think that's surely how it's done in Zimbabwe.

In fact if you don't know a lawyer already, you are dependent on the warders who are eager to link you up with an attorney-buddy, getting a nice kickback from the learned man in due course. And what about the loyalties of a lawyer so deeply enmeshed in the court and prison system?

But we had no choice but to go that route and when we chatted to one of the nicer warders we asked him to find one for us.

But first we were to be tossed into prison for the night.

Transport was a ramshackle old bus that had to be pushed into gear by a bunch of prison warders every time it attempted to make a trip. It was filled to more than double capacity, with each of us having another prisoner on his lap, plus the grocery shopping of the warders returning from town to prison and their wives and kids.

A colourful, almost funny affair.

The bus was to finally break down completely during our detention, after which we had to cram in the back of a pickup truck with an armoured shell. That was really fun then ...

Prison was about 15 km out of town, invisible from any major road, and looked like a derelict concentration camp with the multiple perimeters of rusty barbed wire sort of holding the crumbling buildings together.

Watchtowers and armed guards completed the picture.

Here we were "declothed", meaning that we had to stuff our civilian clothes in a bag and put on a pair of thin torn khaki shorts and a similar shirt with short sleeves. (Too bad, no photos of this episode.)

Then we were tossed into separate cells in 2 adjacent but separate blocks.

Next shock:

Before entering the cell for the night (it was almost dark by then) I had to strip naked, then to enter a cell where 6 other inmates were already waiting.

Luckily initial fears proved unfounded and my fellow inmates turned out to be quite decent guys, mostly family fathers who had fallen foul of the alleged law in their desperation to obtain food for their starving families.

I soon learned that some had been sitting there for more than 3 years without ever being brought to trial, just because they could not afford a lawyer to get them out on bail or expedite their trial.

They kept their cell clean and had invented many clever mechanisms to cope with everyday prison life.

One of the many small amenities they had developed was a game of chess.

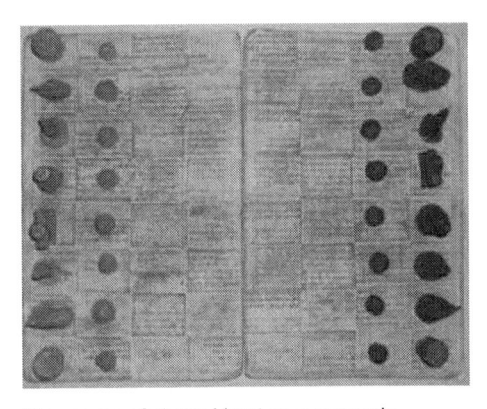

This game of chess I kept as a souvenir

The white pieces were made of dried maize porridge, the staple prison food, sometimes accompanied by baked beans.

The black pieces were made of the same porridge but were pigmented with ash from burnt newspaper.

The board was made from cut up Bibles of the type that all these American mind control churches so freely distribute in Africa, especially among the prison populations.

The next day we were ferried to court again, this time in foot shackles because we were now suddenly classified as high risk and high security prisoners (and these cut into your flesh quite deeply after you've hobbled along for a while) to sit for hours in the ice-cold holding cells. I learnt to keep myself warm by doing lots of exercises all the time. (Yoga headstand and push ups in shackles: one could introduce that to fancy urban gyms as a novelty form of yuppie exercise.)

This time we finally met our lawyer.

By the way: If you think that the privacy of conversation with your lawyer is a universal right of the accused: Not in Zimbabwe! You talk to your lawyer under the eyes and ears of a prison warder!

It turned out that we had already seen him and greeted him while lingering at the police station. He turned out to be quite all right and helpful after all and promised to move the case.

He also got us a tube of toothpaste, soap and a minuscule towel as well as some juice to brighten up our prison diet.

Thursday was now the day set for our next appearance in court.

Our lawyer also told us that the case had been complicated because of a "national security dimension" that was attached to it.

Famous at last: Article in The Herald of 20 July

The friendly older warder who had offered to contact the lawyer for us, told us that we were famous now because an article about us had appeared in the main national newspaper that normally parrots exactly whatever the current government opinion is, The Herald.

The article was highly manipulative and false in most of its facts; for example, that we had been spotted doing our "evil deed" by some villagers, while in fact they were all police agents in civilian clothing.

We spent another long day in prison, during which I played about 10 games of chess against 3 of my fellow inmates, lost some, won some, all the time thinking about what was going happen to us.

XL had decided that he would go on a hunger strike by then to show that he was sick and tired of being friendly and cooperative (and, by the way, he did not like the food anyway). That got them quite scared and they offered him meat, a rare and desirable commodity in this prison, but when he saw what it looked like, he gave it to his cellmates.

They always came back to me for reassurance and wanted me to persuade him to eat.

I told them it's his decision and they should not worry as we would be out soon. (I tried to convince myself of that.)

On the Thursday we were taken to court again (in shackles) where we had a short meeting with the lawyer.

He assured us that everything was under control.

Hours later we appeared in court and the miracle happened:

The sentence was "cautioned and discharged".

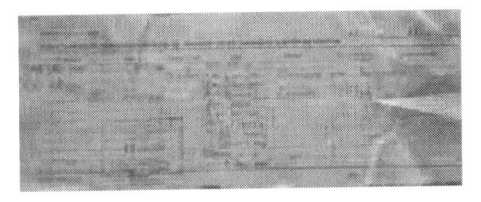

Our criminal record in Zimbabwe: "cautioned and discharged" (after 9 days)

Freedom was finally in sight! It still took hours, but discharged we were. The deputy prison director, who had certain sadistic tendencies, seemed to regret it greatly that we were to be withdrawn from his sphere of absolute power.

But he still had the audacity to ask me to keep my ears open, when free again, for some sponsors who might fund a new prison bus. This made me think that if they wanted to execute you, they would probably ask you first to buy the bullet for them ...

I still had a late night meeting with the lawyer and some of his friends.

He turned out to be quite a likeable fellow privately and so were his friends.

I asked him to have a look at the files of my cellmates and left some money to cover his expenses. I hope that we can get some of the guys out at a reasonable cost, where the case is a straightforward one and just needs a lawyer's assistance.

We headed straight back to Nyamapanda, this time to leave for good, and our extreme apprehension only left us after we were safely in Mozambique. Unfortunately our feathers were quite ruffled by then, including the loss of some 1200 USD that were stolen from the vehicle. Luckily not much else was missing.

XL felt like breaking off the trip immediately, while I was all for continuing at least as far as possible.

The compromise found was that we would at least continue to Malawi, some 600 km from the Mozambican/Zimbabwean border, to liaise with Dr Chipangula from the International Traditional Healers Council of which I am a member. From there we would decide what to do.

Either XL would fly home, leaving me to continue if I could find a suitable companion, or both of us would go home by car.

Mozambique

The border crossing into Mozambique was easy and relaxed, quite a relief after what we had been through.

Our main target on the short passage through Mozambique was Tete, according to our by now famous map, home to 2 nasty underground bases.

Tete had been a stronghold of RENAMO, the Western-sponsored rebel army, that destabilised the "revolutionary" MPLA government for about 20 years with the help of the apartheid government and of course the whole bouquet of **One World Order** involvement.

The energy in and around that town accordingly felt very nasty.

Hilltop array above Tete (Mozambique)

A hilltop array above Tete, which proved inaccessible in the limited time we had, was neutralised by putting a distant drawn out chain of TBs and one HHG. We busted the transmitters in town, of course, while urgently searching for diesel.

The bases were on the way out of town and both felt very nasty. One was near a bombed out RENAMO base with smoke-blackened remnants of concrete bunkers; the other one tellingly near a large UN base with lots of white Nissen huts with "UN" painted on them in super size letters. Another base en route to the Malawian border made its presence felt by a strange electric feeling, similar to what one sometimes feels near a giant beehive or anthill.

Tete bridge: notice the very negative energy

Malawi

Arriving late at night in Blantyre, the economic hub of Malawi, we found only the best hotel in town really inviting and crashed for a good night's sleep after a sumptuous meal.

In the morning we called Dr Chipangula and were met by his associate Dr Kazua and Chipangula's son, a brilliant kid of 14 years.

They showed us the way to Dr Chipangula's house, a modest little structure in one of the poor parts of town. Dr Chipangula is well known and respected all over the country and far beyond, and is the president of the 250 000 member strong International Traditional Healers Association of Malawi, with which I am proud to be associated.

The sky looked hazy and oppressive in the morning, but that

The body of evidence

was to change quickly after we put up a CB at Dr Chipangula's place.

The sky above Blantyre before we put up a CB

He was no novice to orgonite because TBs and HHGs had been brought to Malawi by associated healers from Johannesburg, who were also the ones who invited me to become a member because of our environmental healing work.

Together with Dr Chipangula, we found Dr Chazerezeka and other healers who were eager to meet us and a steady stream of visitors was to come and go during our stay.

We agreed to leave most of our orgonite in the capable hands of Dr Chipangula and his organisation, for distribution all over Malawi, which had recently also been hit by one of the NWO fabricated HAARP-droughts in order to create hunger and "donor dependency", as usual.

My feeling is that with the Healers' Council's grassroots network, that spreads into the last corner of Malawi, the 3 CBs, more than 1000 TBs and multiple other gifts will do magnificent work, better than we could ever have done by ourselves on a 3 day drive-through visit. We also left 10 orgone zappers with Dr Chipangula.

Dr Chipangula, his son, Dr Chazerezeka and myself with CB

What a change: the sky above Blantyre after placing the CB

This sky is really looking alive now!

This is the general lesson of this aborted trip: We cannot do it alone! In the future we will do much more to liaise with people in Africa who are already distributing orgonite, like the group of excellent busters in East Africa such as Doc Kayiwa and colleagues in Uganda, Judy Lubulwa, David Ochieng and friends in Kenya and Dean Nyalusi in Tanzania.

After all, Africa cannot be liberated from outside, however well meaning such intervention may be.

The networks of genuine traditional healers who are not yet corrupted by their various governments (most notoriously in Zimbabwe), will also play an increasing role in this "True African Renaissance".

So, in line with this new found approach we sent lots of orgonite straight to Nairobi and Dar es Salaam right after returning home. This in effect guarantees that all the gifts we were intending to distribute on our trip will find their place in the intended destinations after all. In addition, the emerging African Orgone network will be strengthened, thus achieving much more than we could ever have achieved alone.

While I was still hoping to continue the trip at least a little bit longer, XL was determined to head home.

His girlfriend had heard of our detention only through the Austrian Embassy and was frantic with worry by now and his intuition said it was not advisable to continue.

I was not at first willing to accept that decision and tried to persuade him to at least accompany me to Dar es Salaam, where I hoped to find a new companion for the rest of the trip.

However, in conversation with a friend who is not only psychic but also has some reliable links into the shady world of secret services, we learnt that it would really not be advisable to continue. Mugabe's secret police had sent messages to other African countries on our route, to detain us again and harass or disappear us in any possible way.

We also learnt that the German embassy in Harare had been involved in the plot to detain and possibly disappear us in Zimbabwe; quite frightening, considering that Friederike had put high hopes on the German Embassy to intervene on my behalf.

We probably owe our survival to the determined allies all over the world who etherically blasted the snot out of Robert Mugabe's occult power structure. (Like all NWO dictators, his power rests on deeply occult foundations of voodoo, sorcery and Masonic black magic.)

We were advised to go home as quickly as possible, via Zambia and Botswana, avoiding Mozambique (which would have been the shorter route) and certainly avoiding Zimbabwe.

So, after spending 2 nights in Malawi, during which time we had much opportunity to get to know the wonderful and gentle Dr Chipangula even better, we were given a full muti (African medicine) treatment for our protection and left Blantyre at midnight on the third night to be at the Zambian border when it opened in the morning.

Psychic attacks were still rampant on the way out. I hit the barrier of a poorly lit police roadblock at almost full speed, just 80 km before the border, a stupid situation from which we could extricate ourselves only by negotiating a juicy bribe with the 2 senior officers. (We could have landed in a prison again for that.) The dent in my bumper is an acceptable punishment for this negligence.

Home via Zambia and Botswana

We headed straight west through Zambia on a mostly bumpy and potholed road, leaving our customary trail of orgonite gifts along the way. We didn't have time to do anything in the capital Lusaka, except leave a few gifts on the way through. Lusaka would have to be left to some future visit or an as yet unknown future Zambian activist.

XL at the headwaters

We camped near Livingstone, the Zambian town near the Victoria Falls.

The falls were in fact the second of the seven wonders of Africa we originally wanted to cover on our trip, the first being the ruins of Great Zimbabwe.

We visited the falls, which were almost in full flood, in the morning. Quite an impressive sight and of course some gifts found their way into the wide and mighty Zambezi above and below the falls. It was noteworthy how many HAARP towers were concentrated especially on the Zimbabwean bank of the Zambezi. Surely an attempt to manipulate the strong positive energy of the place.

While we did everything in Livingstone, we could of course not access the ones on the Zimbabwean side, so had to be content with a large orgone pyramid on the Zambian side.

Elephants in the Zambezi river above Victoria Falls

Vic Falls – Mosia o Tunya (The smoke that thunders)

We crossed the border into Botswana with the Kazungula ferry over the Zambezi (plop, plop, plop again) and found the Botswana border post refreshingly unbureaucratic.

Botswana is the NWO's "best managed" African country. Thinly populated and relatively prosperous because of its 2 main industries, diamond digging (all in the hands of De Beers' joint venture with the Botswana government called Debswana) and the export of beef.

You may find it odd, but after so much misery and poverty it's just great to have roads with proper markings, well-lit intersections and a border where you don't have to pay an arm and a leg just to be admitted to the country.

Kazungula Ferry from Zambia to Botswana

After hectic almost non-stop driving for 2800 km, we were finally back in Johannesburg, and after XL had left, I joined my family who were spending some days at the coast with friends. We had a very nice boat trip, seeing a large pod of dolphins from very close by (of course we had tossed some orgonite) and 2 humpback whales.

Dolphins near Shelley Beach, Kwa Zulu-Natal

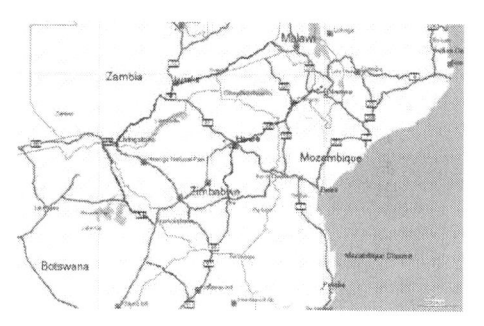

We left some traces after all (blue dots are orgonite gifts)

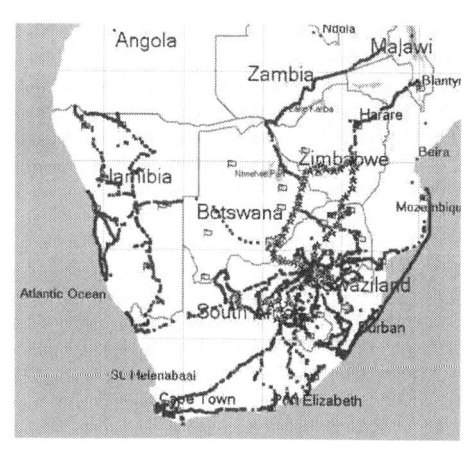

State of distribution of orgonite gifts after the trip

Afterthoughts

Surely we achieved something on this trip, but I don't know yet what it will be that comes out of it. I am still sad at having missed meeting all the wonderful people and seeing the wonderful places that were lined up on our route.

I hope, however, that the new approach of working much more closely with our orgone compadres in Africa will be fruitful and that orgonite will become a mass movement in Africa.

I will soon be going to Zanzibar to meet some of the East African activists to exchange experiences and generally get to know one another.

All the gifts that were intended to go north have been distributed, not all at the intended places, but none of the sponsorships for cloudbusters that we received was wasted.

The most gratifying part was of course the interaction with the Malawian healers and especially Dr Chipangula to whom I spoke just a few days ago. He told me how fantastically well the CB in Blantyre is working. He is really excited about it.

Dr Chipangula will soon come to Johannesburg and we will be able to strategise even further together.

Zanzibar - spice Island with a new flavour

Zanzibar, December 2006

After our aborted Orgone Safari in July 2006, continuing the spread of orgonite in East Africa has been my main priority. All the orgonite that was destined for Tanzania and Kenya was sent there to local gifters who are distributing the tools to appropriate places.

Yes, Zanzibar has those dream beaches...

So it came in handy when I saw an advertisement for a cheap holiday package Zanzibar in the newspaper.

All of us (that's Friederike, the Kids, my mother, who was visiting from Germany at the time, and I) went on a family holiday there, using our combined luggage allowance to bring in a CB, and some 150 other orgonite tools.

Zanzibar is a tropical island, off the Tanzanian coast, close to the former capital (which is still the economic hotspot of Tanzania), Dar es Salaam.

Zanzibar used to be the seat of the Sultan of Oman, who controlled the East Coast slave and ivory trade from there.

The Arab influence is still strongly visible in the buildings and decorations of Zanzibar City, also known as Stone Town. The vast majority of inhabitants are also Muslims as a result of this history.

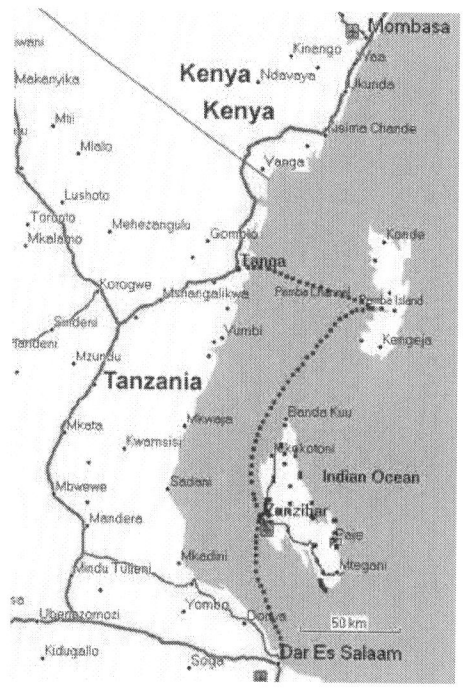

prosperity except for some very small pockets of luxury.

This map shows the Zanzibar Archipelago with the 2 Islands Unguja (often referred to as Zanzibar) and Pemba. The blue dots represent orgone gifts; the little flag symbol represents a CB. Another CB is already doing work in Dar es Salaam

Arab style carved door in Stone Town

Even though Zanzibar is an international tourist destination, westernisation has so far not gone very deep. There are no shopping malls or supermarkets on the island; all commerce is conducted out of traditional small shops. The island is quite densely populated and most of the population seems to be poor, but not desperate. After all, they live in a tropical paradise that produces food of all kinds in abundance. Despite its international fame as an architectural monument, Stone Town lacks any signs of

Sultan's palace near harbour

Is it a coincidence that the most expensive hotel on the sea front is so very close to the offices of UNICEF and the WHO?

A sanitation or storm water system seems to be largely nonexistent with the result that urban areas drown in a sea of brown mud with major rainfall. A worthy target!

Apart from its dreadful history as a centre of the slave trade that devastated East Africa for centuries, Unguja, the main island of the Zanzibar archipelago, is a renowned centre of Arabic magic as much as its sister island Pemba is a known centre of African traditional healing and witchcraft.

Having gifted these places may thus have repercussions in the etheric realm beyond our imagination.

As if additional recommendation was needed to point out the place as a worthy target for a gifting expedition, a few months ago a mysterious event led to more than 400 dead dolphins being washed ashore.

The psychics at the Etheric Warriors Chat saw a group of American submarines operating in those waters with the aim of fighting and possibly destroying as many as possible of our powerful etheric allies, the dolphins. (We blasted them good, I think).

In addition, we had information on two suspected underground bases on the island.

When we arrived at our destination on the southeastern coast of Unguja (the main island of the Zanzibar archipelago), the temperatures were extremely hot, with humidity near or over 100% and the whole atmosphere felt very oppressive and negative. Since we arrived late at night, we could only put up our CB the next morning.

And what a difference it made!

Friederike and I went on a gifting tour of the whole island in a rented 4x4, while the others relaxed on the beach. Outside of Stone Town there were only a few microwave transmitters, and I'm sure we got them all. We also put orgonite in the rivers whenever we crossed one.

Zanzibar Town had quite a few death force transmitters.

Transmitter site on the north-eastern coast

Even though it stayed hot and humid, the atmosphere changed from hazy and oppressive to a crisp and clear sky with nicely articulated cumulus clouds (initially forming a great ring around the CB) almost instantly. We also got daily rain showers for the time we spent on the island, quite in excess of what is considered normal for the season.

Those showers were short, intense and very refreshing.

East African gifters get-together

We had hoped to make this little outing a great get-together of all gifters active in East Africa. So we had hoped for Doc Kayiwa from Uganda, Judy Lubulwa, David Ochieng and others from Kenya and Dean from Dar es Salaam to come over for some exchange of ideas and recreational gifting sorties.

Of all the above, only Judy finally made it, accompanied by her 18 year old son and his friend of the same age.

Their trip had been hampered by all kinds of obstacles that seem almost too much for coincidence. The same may be true for those who did not make it.

Even though it was not to be the big get-together we had anticipated, meeting Judy in person was great, since we had been corresponding a lot. I was excited to find her a lively and resourceful "go-getter" person, just as she seemed to be in her emails and forum postings.

We spent a whole day gifting the island, including the location of a suspected underground base at the northern tip.

Judy, her son Myna, Friederike and me near the busted UG base

Taking the ferry from Dar to Zanzibar and then on to Tanga, just south of the Kenyan border via Pemba island, Judy was able to lay quite a trail of water gifts throughout the Zanzibar strait (see map at top of this report), those sensitive waters where more than 400 dolphins were killed by the US Navy in mid 2006. Great stuff! Judy was to continue her water gifting run from Mombasa a few days later.

We finally did it: swimming with the dolfriends

It's been on the cards for quite some time, so it had to happen this time. Lots of expectations and some apprehension had built up in me about this mystical encounter with our etheric comrades in arms... Zanzibar has a small, luckily much unregulated, industry of dolphin encounter boat trips, starting from the southwestern tip of the island, where the otherwise continuous coral reef has a gap, allowing for encounters in not too rough waters. So, out we went in a lovely boat, just like 4 or 5 other parties in their respective boats.

The skippers of these boats are in contact via radio or cell phone, so that after a while of lingering out there waiting (not without tossing a few marine orgone gifts of course) we got notice that a large pod of dolphins was sighted further north, coming towards us.

Unfortunately about 5 boats had heard the same call, so there was quite a feeding frenzy of tourists hopping into the water all over the place and we were in the middle of it.

So maybe it's no surprise that

nothing mystical happened to me, and yet it was a great experience to hear their strange and beautiful sounds in the water, the high frequency squealing overlaid with fancy electric clicks. In fact their sounds are audible in a very transparent way and one gets a totally different feeling for the vastness of space in the ocean.

Our Skipper

See the dolphin fin in the distance?

It's like their echo sounding gives you a full 3D rendering. It was a large pod and we encountered dolphins swimming under and beside us for quite a while. My kids came very close once or twice. They said they came up to 30cm, but hey, kids love to brag a bit, don't they?

The Kiddos on the Dolphin Tour

So what?

Zanzibar is well busted now and a stretch of some 350km of Indian ocean has been gifted in this sensitive and important area. According to Judy, Dar es Salaam also already looks quite good due to the gifts we sent to Dean some time ago.

Obviously there's lots of work still to be done in Tanzania and Kenya. Kenya has at least two CBs now and so has Tanzania, but what's lacking is a full coverage of the area with TBs. There are still lots of un-busted death force transmitters and underground bases.

Our East African associates all still lack the resources needed to do such a job quickly by car, so orgone delivery is a slow process of filtering through, passing from hand to hand and the occasional outing with buses or minibus group taxis.

Judy has put the second CB up in northern Kenya where the monstrous New World Order was busy engineering one of its famous drought emergency crises, complete with refugee camps, emaciated babies and the usual horrible footage blasted into the homes of mind controlled Westerners to enhance the view that Africa is a hopeless continent...

As we all know, a few CBs and a few hundred TBs can stop all this nonsense forever.

Wherever such a manufactured crisis shows up, it can be quickly reversed and the place turned around, creating paradise on earth in the process.

Eventually, we believe, massive orgone gifting will help Africa to awake from her centuries-old trauma induced slumber and take her rightful place among the continents of the world, in full command of her creativity, spirituality and abundance of mental and material resources.

Matatiele revisited and a mountain paradise

End of December 2006 - January 2007

Over the year's end of 2006, our friends Walter and Sandy had booked accommodation in a very special place called Sehlabatebe Nature Reserve in Lesotho.

The place is high in the Drakensberg Mountains and can be accessed through the South African town of Underberg.

Masakala – sooo green!

On the way from Underberg to Sehlabatebe one can pass through Matatiele and that's what we decided to do. A welcome opportunity to revisit this place that we had busted exactly a year earlier. (See page 203) We found the place in a totally different condition. Everything looked lush and green. Already when we called to book for the night, Nomonde, who handles the booking became very excited because she remembered us very well.

The CB still where we left it

Robert, who had accompanied me on my busting tour of the surrounding areas, was unfortunately away on a guided hiking tour with some guests. But the 2 ladies who do the cooking and cleaning at Masakala Guesthouse were very happy to see us again.

The CB was standing undisturbed exactly as we had left it a year ago. Not only had they received good rains, but the general atmosphere was also looking very good.

Finally done: UG base at Quacha's Nek

Round hut in nicely dressed stone masonry

Of course we did some detours to spread out the orgonite a bit. The maps we had were extremely inaccurate and a road we were following over the Tsoelike River actually did not exist any more, which we found out after following it for some 50 km.

Surely no damage to the objectives of our trip.

Pedestrian and vehicle bridge over the Tsoelike River

Steep and narrow gravel roads, often partly washed away

Arriving in Sehlabatebe, we found the place a bit derelict, but spacious enough to accommodate all of us.

The lodge consists of only one house made of many bedrooms and a large living room.

There is no electricity up there and all cooking, lighting and even refrigeration runs on gas.

The house was a prefab structure with metal frame and asbestos sheeting as cladding.

That was probably considered smart and modern at the time of its erection.

The house had actually been built as a guest house for the king of Lesotho.

Sky transformation in Sehlabatebe

We placed a CB in a little forest nearby. In fact those were the only trees wide and far and they were growing in a shallow depression near the pond next to which the house was built.

Immediately the sky began its transformation.

The dense fog that was present on our arrival had hidden a rippled blanket of HAARP cloud and both were now rapidly dissolving.

We noticed immediately that the fauna was much different from the intensely utilised tribal lands around. The protection from grazing cattle allowed a vast plethora of grasses and flowers to blossom and that was quite amazing to behold.

Sphinx and reptile stone formations

Much of this beauty was on a very small scale, but the vistas and stone formations up on the windswept edge of the escarpment were no less intriguing.

HAARP changing into orgonised sky

Far views

The body of evidence

And a fine and special fauna

Luckily there were some horses available so we could explore the landscape a bit further than was possible on foot. By now you should know that my kids are only satisfied on our trips, if they can get on a horse's back.

Scenic outrides

The Orgonite was doing its job and we saw a nice fresh sky with lots of cumulus clouds and even a few sylph like formations most of the time. The difference between riding and walking is of course that you can cover a lot more ground in a given period of time. And the perspective is different, you are moving more in the open space than through the thickets.

This is apart from the fun of course and the connection to those powerful friendly animals.

Sylph over the Drakensberg

An alive sky with beautiful cumulus clouds

Another sylph like structure

Herd boys' shelter under a rocky overhang

Even though cattle grazing is no longer allowed any more in the conservation area, lots of structures remind one of the harsh and simple life of the cattle herders that used to come up here to graze their beasts on these high pastures.

Alpine micro fauna

Crystal clear and dark silent pools were everywhere, with the most amazing water lilies growing in them. Some of them don't even have roots attached to the ground but just float on the water with the roots sucking up the nutrients dissolved in the water.

Loam crystallised in vortex like structures

There were many little miracles to behold and I can only show you a few examples as this is not a botanical expedition report.

But I always feel that I want to show you "my Africa" the way I experience it, because in order to heal a place you have to love it first, I think.

Shallow rock pool

Floating lilies

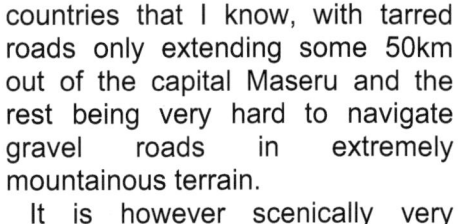

countries that I know, with tarred roads only extending some 50km out of the capital Maseru and the rest being very hard to navigate gravel roads in extremely mountainous terrain.

It is however scenically very rewarding to go there and the people are very friendly, especially the further you get out of the few towns.

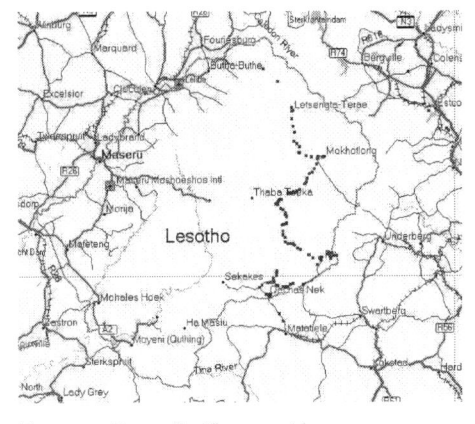

The orgonite we "lost" on our trip

The situation in Lesotho after our trip

We went home through Lesotho in order to connect our busting trail from the KwaZulu-Natal side to the western part of the country that we had done previously. Lesotho is one of the most inaccessible

We will hopefully be able to go back there soon and finish what we have started.

Cape Town – Sylphs in the sky and a nuke plant revisited

January 2007

In January 2007 my daughter Kika and I paid a short weekend visit to Cape Town. We visited some friends and did some busting in areas that we did not get around to on previous visits such as Tygerberg, Durbanville and Parow, where we had information of a suspected underground base.

Generally we found the atmosphere in Cape Town already quite good.

It's hard not to feel good there with so much scenic beauty. But I

Cape Town 2007

think that the orgonite distributed there during previous visits and a few CBs that have sprung up in the region around Cape Town had a lot to do with it.

Towers above the vineyards in Durbanville

View from Chapman's Peak drive

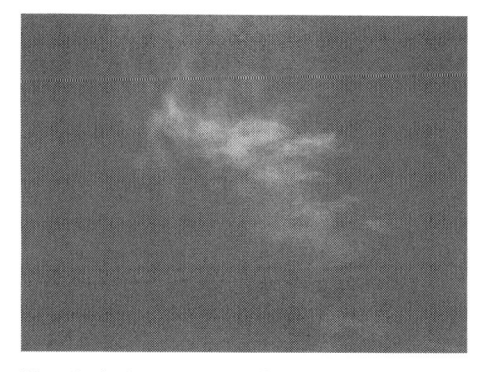

The sky looked nice over Cape Town

The sky looked vivid and we saw sylph-like cloud formations everywhere.

Only north of Bloubergstrand and the Koeberg nuclear power station did the atmosphere still look brownish, which is a good indicator of DOR.

The absolute highlight of this short visit was to be the completion of an unfinished job: Doing the Koeberg nuclear power station from the sea side.

I had tried to get some orgonite near it in the past (see page 115 ff.) but it had proven quite inaccessible.

Our friend Robert organised a boat and we planned to go out to surround it with a string of marine busters from a safe distance.

Koeberg is pretty unique in its design as it uses sea water for cooling.

Aerial photo of Koeberg power station

The intake and outlet are separated by a mole of some 500m out into the Sea to prevent the 2 water streams from mixing too early.

The last time I had only been able to approach the outlet from the beach side and threw some orgonite into the gushing stream of expelled DOR- and nuclear polluted cooling water. This time the deadly influence of this powerful DOR-emitter was to be shielded from the sea and really confined to the innermost reactor core.

Koeberg seen from the sea

The actual gifting was relatively unspectacular apart from the high swell that made it very difficult to get any straight shots with my digital camera.

We were even followed by a few dolphins!

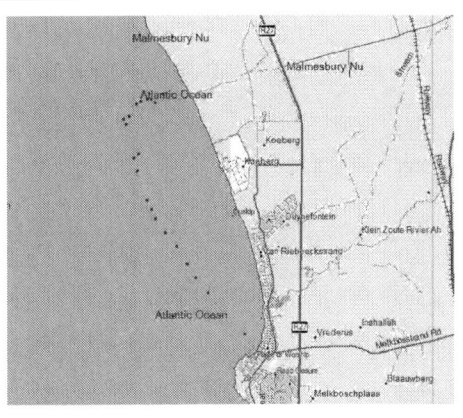

Orgonite dumped offshore of Koeberg. The main concentration is on the inlet side.

We ended with a visit to a nice restaurant where Kika bravely tried oysters and a sip of champagne for the first time.

After all, this was also intended as a father and daughter bonding experience...

The water gifting around the Cape Peninsula is of course to be continued, especially now that I have a boat and a skipper's licence.

The Vast Interior

Karoo and Kalahari, Easter 2007

One of the last white spots on my South African orgone map, the vast interior semi desert of the Great Karoo, had called to be tackled for quite a long time.

With the recent unexpected drought in parts of South Africa and neighbouring countries, we felt that closing this giant gap could be the most significant step in order to bring back normal or above normal rainfall such as we achieved in increasingly larger portions of the subcontinent in 2002-2006. In February and March the conditions were very dry which provoked a swift rescue operation to the Free State where we did some more busting in the Welkom/Virginia area where most of the mining is concentrated.

We also did much of the southern and western parts of the Free State province and left a CB near

Virginia.

But this alone was not enough and it was too late to turn the situation around. The next step to avoid a repetition of this temporary setback will have to be a much bigger expedition to Zambia, where we feel the rain that was abundant in Zambia, Malawi and northern Mozambique and Angola was blocked off along the Zambezi. We are getting ready for this one as we speak.

This is what Wikipedia has to say about the Karoo:

"The Great Karoo has an area of more than 400,000 square kilometres. A vast inland sea covered this region approximately 250 million years ago, but as the world's climate gradually changed from cold to hot the water evaporated, leaving a swamp where reptiles and amphibians prospered.

In recent history - less than two hundred years ago - large herds of antelope and zebras still roamed the Karoo's grass flats. The Hottentots and Bushmen, last of the Southern African Stone Age peoples, shared what they called the "Place of Great Dryness" (from which the name "Karoo" is derived). The two groups differed substantially in their cultures and lifestyles; the Hottentots were sheep and cattle farmers while the Bushmen were classic hunter-gatherers. With the occupation of the region by European settler stock farmers the sheep gradually replaced the game, while the grass receded due to the changed grazing and weather patterns."

The Karoo is even drier than the Kalahari which starts north of the Karoo and stretches into Botswana and Namibia, the change being gradual but noticeable.

Due to the vastness of the area and the absence (largely) of conventional targets, such as microwave transmitters, we decided to lay out a string of TBs every 5 km, with extra TBs for rivers, including dry river beds, the odd microwave transmitter along the way and special gifts at significant points. This is a similar strategy to the one we'd employed in Namibia in September 2005 with great success.

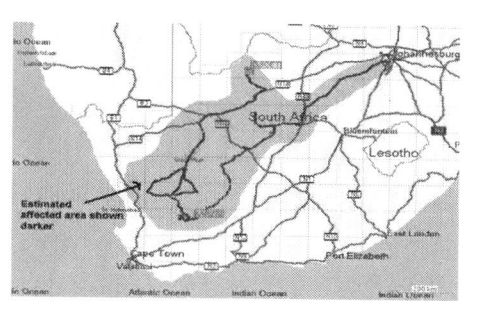

The blue dots show orgonite gifts distributed on this trip. The grey area indicates the estimated sphere of influence of this recent busting effort

We were carrying some 850 TBs, 30 or 40 HHGs and pyramids, several earth pipes, 2 full grown CBs and seven single pipe mini CBs.

We haven't used those mini CBs before, but felt that they could be a good addition to our arsenal, given how easily they can be hidden in the bush or dug in without the need to find a custodian who will assure their continued placement.

Leg 1: Jo'burg - Sutherland

On the first day we left relatively late and only made it to Kimberley which had already been gifted in previous expeditions.

The body of evidence

Interesting lenticulars (UFO clouds) on way out to Kimberley

Some hint of chemtrails - first I've seen in a long time.

becoming lovely cumulus as we went along

dissolving as we approach

After Kimberley, our first target town was Prieska. Strangely that little town had always figured big on my list of busting targets. I can't really give any good reasons for that, except that repeated dowsing with a pendulum had always shown a strong reaction for this place.

On the way back from Namibia and the Kalahari Expedition with Karin we had come close to do it, but not close enough.

This time it was definitely on the agenda.

Would you be astonished to hear that according to my information there was also an underground base near Prieska?

David Livingstone's first mission church in Campbell

Every conquest of a territory starts with the conquest of the minds of its people So, in this barren land, the churches stand out as beacons of this strategic spiritual takeover which is not much older than 150 years in most places here. The famous David Livingstone surely played his part in this scheme of things.

This may serve as an explanation why you will see more churches in this report and, be assured, they have all been gifted properly.

Lonesome Kalahari tower

The confluence of the Vaal and Orange rivers

The Vaal and Orange rivers are the largest and longest rivers in South Africa. So we felt that their confluence near Douglas would warrant a first single pipe mini CB and lots of other orgonites in the water and around the place.

Planting a single pipe mini CB

There he sits in the hole

Quite inconspicuous - that's the beauty of those minis

Prieska received plenty of gifts and another mini near the banks of the Orange River. I seem to have forgotten to take any photos there.

Wide open spaces

We drove hundreds of kilometres on such gravel roads. The vast interior of South Africa is so thinly populated that the economic activity (mostly sheep farming) does not warrant the building of tarred roads. These are the main arteries of life in this area, not just little farm tracks.

Isolated thundershowers - what a beauty

Towards the end of day we witnessed a spectacular sunset near Van Wyksvlei with those isolated streams of rain pouring out of spectacularly illuminated clouds.

Sunset mirrored in car window

Our camping spot was approximately 60 km outside Sutherland and we arrived there late at night, only to find the place occupied by droves of heavily partying youngsters. Too bad, but we managed to pitch our tents somewhere and slept to the never ending thump-thump-thump of some very "low vibration music" and the frequent laughter over ever more stupid practical jokes. Next morning we set out for some horseback riding (no holiday without horses could have any appeal whatsoever for my two girls, Isabella and Katharina).

Our new expedition vehicle in appropriate surroundings

On Easter Sunday we decided to

get away from our loud company by going on an extended off-road trail and do some Easter egg hunting on the way. Maybe we would also find a nice hiding place for our first CB which we intended leaving in this area.

Easter egg hunt in the Karoo

We found a nice picnic spot for our Easter egg hunt and from there spotted an attractive rock formation that promised to provide ample opportunities for hiding a CB.

There it is

Looking back at our CB - who can spot it?

Friederike planting CB in mountain cleft near Sutherland

The rock formation also looked like a good and powerful spot to amplify the effect of the CB. Continuing on the 4x4 trail, we saw some amazingly lonely wide open views.

The area around Sutherland is probably among the most thinly populated stretches of the Earth's surface, sheep farming being the main source of income.

The body of evidence

Looking down from Karoopunt

High pass road near Sutherland

More wide open spaces

And more of these breathtaking distant views

This frighteningly steep descent is called "Banggat" in Afrikaans which means "hole of fear"

Sutherland is of course world famous for its astronomical observatories. It was chosen as an ideal spot because of its dryness, its high altitude and sparse population, meaning minimal light emissions from human sources.

However we found that apart from environmentally harmless optical telescopes a host of other strange installations had popped up in the surroundings of Sutherland that warranted some close inspection.

The vast interior 2007

Is it HAARP or Memorex?

Is this a radio telescope or a microwave ionospheric heater beam? We can only guess, but we felt that leaving a few gifts around could do no harm.

Weather radar and other high powered transmitters on a lonesome hill near Sutherland

These installations are mostly placed in the middle of huge private farms with multiple fences and gates to cross, all complete with the usual "Private Property - Do not trespass" etc. signage. We act responsibly though and always close the farm gates.

It took us about one hour to get close to this monster and of course we ignored several "Strictly no entry" signs.

We have often trespassed on private property on our trips, feeling entitled to such liberty by our conviction that we are doing a public service. The emissions coming from such installations are violating people's vital and inalienable right to enjoy a healthy environment and be free from assaults on their life and vitality.
"Thou shalt not kill", in other words...

SALT (South African Large Telescope) is the largest telescope in the southern hemisphere

Quite impressive this line up of scientific gear on the high plateau near Sutherland. We were not allowed to be there, so we hurried

271

to leave some gifts and drove out again. They do public tours by prior appointment but none on public holidays like the day our visit fell on.

"Astronomy Alley"

Leg 2: Sutherland - Kuruman

An Oasis in barren Land - Hantam Huis in Calvinia

Another one of those beacons of conquest - church in Niewoudtsville

This one in Loeriesfontein looks like a fortress

This one is like a very aggressive rocket

Night busting near Williston

Buster's sunrise

Unholy trinity - the ruling forces in the Karoo as elsewhere

I found this set-up noteworthy. Why would one have a death force transmitter (aka "cell phone tower") an aggressive Christian cross and the town's central water supply concentrated on one spot?

I'd speculate the underlying motto is something like:
- control their food and drink
- nuke their brains
- bind their souls

Nowhere as obvious as in these barren lands where everything, including the means of oppression, gets reduced to the naked essentials.

Did Phoenicians roam this inland lake more than 2000 years ago? Now it's a dry salt pan called Groet Vloer

Credo Vuzamazulu Mutwa, the custodian of tribal history not only of the Zulu nation, tells of a group of Phoenicians who sailed up the Zambezi and founded a cruel empire based on enslaving the Bantu people in their area. This may have coincided with the destruction of Carthage by the Romans some 240 years BC. The Phoenicians were known to the Bantus as the Ma-Iti, the strange ones.

Much of the now dry interior of Southern Africa was then much more watery and large inland lakes were found where there are only dry salt pans now, in the Karoo and Kalahari.

The centre of the empire of the Ma-Iti war a town called Makarikari situated on a vast inland lake in present day Botswana, which is now a system of dry and shallow salt pans known as the

Makgadikgadi pans. The slight shift in spelling is probably due to the modern name being derived from the Tswana language, while Mutwa uses the Zulu spelling.

But the empire stretched much further into present day South Africa and even as far as present day Swaziland.

It was destroyed in a Bantu uprising after flourishing for a few hundred years. Legend has it that the first Monomotapa, the king of the civilisation that built Great Zimbabwe and other similar stone fortresses, carried off the stones of the sacked and destroyed city of Makarikari in order to incorporate them into the walls of Great Zimbabwe, possibly in a bid to assimilate the "imperial power" of the Ma-Iti into his own empire.

Colonies of social weaver birds indicate we're back in the Kalahari

Strange shiny stones - they look like cast iron

Tree aloes - a rare sight

A bit like anthills, these giant communal nests.

The vast interior 2007

Oasis on the Orange River: Keimoes

Kalahari Sunset 180 km north of Kuruman

The Orange splits into several arms here and feeds irrigated viticulture

A Landy is good for many things: Outlook...

The previously well busted stretch from Uppington to Kuruman looks verdant and the sky quite fresh

...shaving cabinet

The body of evidence

The Bush Camp near Black Rock, where we stayed for 3 nights

For my kids a holiday without horses wouldn't be a holiday at all (Bella getting mounted)

Midday rest

When taking the whole family along on my trips I always have to find a balance between my busting objectives and the entertainment needs of the rest of the family. So we have found a mode to combine the necessary and the pleasant. The wish to cover previously unorgonised areas on each new trip forces us to explore much of Southern Africa.

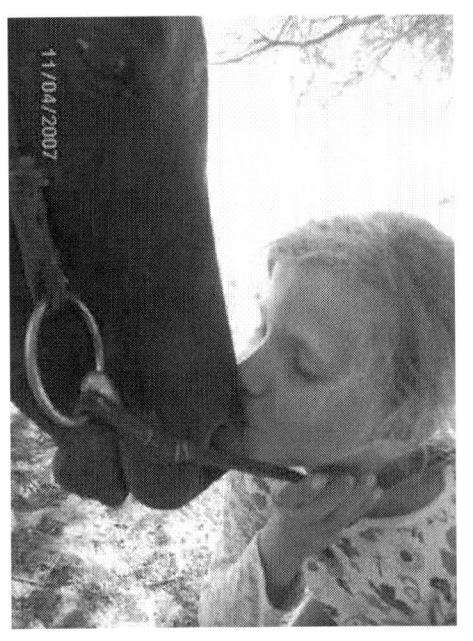

So much love...

Our host Louis H with his new CB

Our host Louis proved astonishingly open to the idea of orgone energy, being a very grounded "hands on man", involved in many business and professional activities, besides his large farm. So we were glad to leave a CB in his custody which will hopefully do some good work for the region. Louis told me that the deep mines in the area had done much to desiccate the landscape with their pumping of ground water, needed to keep the shafts free from water.

Old rivers that used to flow quite regularly now stay dry for periods of 15 years and longer.

If orgonising those mines can remedy part of that damage?

Leg 3: Kuruman - home

A strange show of lenticulars and dissolving HAARP as we move along

On our way home we paid a visit to Donald Rikiert in Kuruman who has been collecting minerals in that area for decades. He has written a substantial volume of poetry in Afrikaans and is in a way a surviving exponent of an era that seems to have passed, even in the Kalahari. We buy quartz crystals, sugelite and other minerals from him when he occasionally visits the gem shop near Magaliesburg with his age old Landcruiser.

Donald Rikiert - The poet of the Kalahari - he's our man for hand mined crystals from the area

Donald has an intuitive grasp of what orgonite does and a lot of local knowledge concerning the power points and holy mountains of the Kalahari cherished by the San and Khoikoi people.

Giant iron ore mine near Sishen - Note the towers on top of the dumps

Following our conversation with Louis, we could of course not leave the giant open cast iron mine at Sishen unattended.

A lot of towers on the mine dumps were enforcing the already gargantuan negativity of the place.

As final resting point in our itinerary we had planned a stay in a game reserve near Kimberley for 3 days.

The place itself was a bit of a disappointment as the farm was quite close to Kimberley and one could see the city lights at night.

We also felt the atmosphere there was quite negative which was reflected in the behaviour of the staff towards us.

The reserve was also not very big and was used for commercial hunting, which probably contributed to the feeling of negativity that permeated the area.

Of course we decided to make the best of it and while it rained most of the time, we did some wild offroad driving with the Landrover, getting near to the numerous giraffes and zebras.

Nice rains around Kimberley - a first reward?

Another tower of power got turned around

This one was in the middle of the game reserve where we spent our last 3 nights, near Kimberley

This is not a postcard

We had the immodest feeling that the plentiful rain was a direct result of our busting in the wider Karoo.

Had to dig him out of the mud

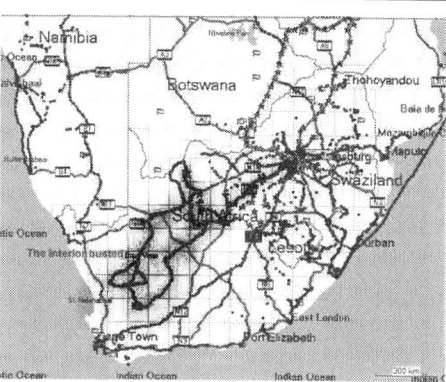

The total situation after the tour: Gaps are getting smaller

This one looks like a mighty and somewhat warlike sylph

When we got home we found it had rained there as well and it was to continue raining in unseasonal but very pleasant quantities.

The feeling of drought had disappeared completely and gave way to a wonderful freshness.

A large orgone gap is now closed on the South African map with only the West Coast remaining as a major area that needs attention.

There are of course other unbusted pockets left, but no more large areas.

The mighty Zambesi – gifted

May 2007

The Zambesi is the fourth longest river in Africa, flowing from its source near the Zambian - Angolan border through Angola, Zambia, Namibia, Zimbabwe and Mozambique. Its water masses feed two large hydroelectric dams, Lake Kariba and the Cahora Bassa Reservoir.

The idea to make gifting the Zambesi, especially Lake Kariba, an absolute priority was fed by two different lines of thought.

1. Recent drought and weather anomalies in Southern Africa

Our rainfall in Southern Africa,

south of the Zambesi had been constantly improving since we started massive large scale gifting of the region in 2002. Now suddenly, in January - March this year, an unexpected drought hit large parts of the region, while countries north of the Zambesi, especially Malawi, northern Mozambique, parts of Zambia and Angola, received more than the normal rainfall, leading to flooding in some parts. Also, the Mozambican coast was hit by a cyclone named Flavio that caused some devastation around the city of Vilanculos.

The way this happened and the orchestration of the events in the press definitely had a strong flavour of weather manipulation.

Flavio just had that "artificial look" on the satellite weather images. The crisis was much exaggerated by the media and there was no more talk of flood relief now.

Contacts in the area actually told me that the cyclone (the equivalent of a hurricane in the Indian Ocean) had already lost its power before it hit the coast, where it was downgraded to a strong storm.

Probably the fact that we had orgonised the coast up to Vilanculos on land and by sea and had stationed a CB in that town, helped to bring that about.

We often find the press "strangely out of sync" when a manufactured weather event does not unfold as planned.

They just cannot change the song sheet fast enough.

My contacts also told me that the rainfalls were strong, stronger than normal, but rather welcome in most parts. The reported flooding mostly affected wetlands that were never meant for human settlement, because they are natural overflow areas and occasionally become submerged in the natural course of events.

Most adjacent communities use them for seasonal grazing and do not find anything dramatic in abandoning these lands during the rainy season. Population pressures in Mozambique and Malawi may have persuaded some villagers now to settle permanently in the areas, which of course isn't really sustainable.

Another factor is overgrazing, resulting in the destruction of the natural wetland ecosystems, destroying their water retention capacity.

Zambia and Malawi in fact had such good harvests recently that they replaced South Africa as the biggest exporter of maize in Africa. Could that have something to do with our 1000 or so TBs and four CBs that Dr Chipangula distributed in Malawi last year?

For him at least, that connection was clear, as Malawi was also "earmarked" for drought in early 2006 but experienced wonderful rains right after the orgonite was deployed.

Another suspicious piece of information reached me by word of mouth: The United States Military was planning to increase its presence in Mozambique where there are already gigantic UN bases. What better pretext for bringing in the heavy equipment and infrastructure than a manufactured humanitarian crisis?

We can see this pattern all over Africa and when your vision is primed with some alertness and natural suspicion you can see these forces at work in every, really, every African crisis. I have enough information by now to back up this claim if ever challenged.

They are ALL manufactured, one or the other way.

The Powers That Be do not want Africa to prosper in peace for whatever obvious or unfathomable reasons. (Trying to understand the minds of compulsive predators and parasites is something I do not want to waste energy on).

The impression we got was that an artificial weather barrier had been created along the course of the mighty Zambesi River, causing all the rain to come down north of it and leaving nothing for the countries further south.

This impression was enforced by one of the EW chatblast sessions, where Carol Croft, who is known as a very accurate psychic, pointed at Lake Kariba when I asked for a strategic spot that I needed to gift in order to end the drought. The impression was confirmed by the other psychics present In that session as well.

That got me excited because it coincided with the other piece of important information pointing towards Lake Kariba from a very different direction, namely its meaning as a central and important holy place of all tribes of Africa – probably one of the cardinal power points of the continent.

2. Lake Kariba - a desecrated sanctuary

Credo Vusamazulu Mutwa dedicated a whole chapter of *Indaba my children* to the history of this place which he identified as one of the holiest places in Africa.

He speaks of an order of clairvoyant telepathic healers who chose this spot to perform their sacred healing work many hundreds of years ago. The sick and desperate from as far as the Congo River would flock to Kariba Gorge in order to find healing and spiritual enlightenment.

These healers were known as THE HOLY ONES of Kariba.

From one day to another they disappeared, without a trace.

After them "another band of thinkers and witchdoctors" (Credo's words) took their place, reviving the traditions and knowledge of the original HOLY ONES.

About 15 generations ago they were replaced by the tribes of the Ba - Tonga and Tonga Ila, who lived in Kariba Gorge and adjacent areas until the construction of the great dam in the late 1950s.

When the dam was finally built, the Ba-Tonga and Tonga Ila were forced to leave at gunpoint. Several members of the tribes who initially resisted the eviction were killed.

Mutwa sees the act of building the dam exactly in this holiest of holy places as an act of spiritual warfare and doesn't believe the government of what was then the Central African Federation (Now Zambia, Zimbabwe and Malawi) could have been unaware of the grave consequences of this destructive move.

He describes in great detail a gruesome ceremony held by 17 sangomas (witchdoctors/spiritual healers) during which a serious curse was placed on the dam. He was one of the participants in that event.

Of course these many generations of healers did not congregate at this particular place by accident.

The location must have some very special energetic properties.

"...that not only is Kariba the navel of the earth, but that also the knot of time is located there, where the past, the present and the future of the entire Universe are tied together in a knot. It is also said that somewhere in Kariba there is a cave, and that in this cave the future of the world is carved in sacred characters on a great slab of rock." (Credo Vusamazulu Mutwa *Indaba my children* p. 578)

Conquering powers have always used the deliberate desecration of their holy spots as a means of spiritually breaking the preceding culture or civilisation. How many holy oaks have been felled by zealous Christian missionaries in the forests of Germania, Gallia and Britannia for example? This is etheric power politics and it has been going on forever. Before you kill a nation, you've got to kill its soul...

In the past ancient "heathen" places of worship were often replaced by cathedrals of the new Christian faith. The 19th and 20th centuries' faith is technical progress; hence dams, mines, highway interchanges and massive groupings of death force transmitters (falsely labelled as cell phone masts) are now the beacons of etheric and spiritual conquest.

When we first approached the large artificial lake that had buried all that Credo talks about, the feeling was that of a major disappointment, the place felt dead!

Getting ready

So the idea was born to gift this vast body of water intensively, in order to turn the whole energetic situation of the region around. Don wrote to me, that he thought that intensive water gifting could disable HAARP influence in a very large area, even when not all land based microwave towers are busted.

His recent work on the HAARPicane infested coast of Florida seems to support that hypothesis and of course our trip was meant to be another experiment to verify this idea.

In order to access such a large stretch of water (the goal was to gift the Zambesi on a length of about 600km with at least 1 TB per km) I figured I needed to bring my own boat. Relying on local fisher boats or renting boats from the (few and far between) tourist lodges along the river appeared very unreliable and potentially time consuming.

So I bought a used semi rigid inflatable with a 40hp outboard motor on a trailer and that's what we towed all the way up to Zambia.

Also the Landy was fitted out with a lot of extra safari equipment, such as an expedition roof rack with holders for "jerry cans" and gas bottles, roof tent and other useful stuff. Also the boat, quite an oldie, had to be looked at and the engine serviced before undertaking such a momentous trip.

"A man is nothing without his boat"

This was only made possible by some generous support from friends to whom our thanks go out. The equipment will of course be used for **many more projects in the future**.

We took some 180l of 2-stroke mixed petrol in jerry cans and the tank of the boat because we already knew that petrol was much more expensive in Zambia, but we had no idea how much more expensive it would be.

Petrol and diesel proved to be the major cost factor on this trip with about 1000 km driven by boat on the water and almost 5000 km driven by car on land.

A boat of this type uses approximately 50l per hundred km.

So, total consumption was about 500l petrol + 25 bottles of 2-stroke-oil and 700 l of diesel. I really can't wait until some viable free energy devices come onto the market that will liberate us from this horrible need to pay toll fees to the petroleum cartel whenever we want to go anywhere.

We took approximately 800 water gifts, mostly TBs some of our special dolphin balls and lots of HHGs as well as some mini cloud busters (single pipe) and 2 full blown cloud busters that were also sponsored by supporters overseas.

I was accompanied by Robert, a friend from Stellenbosch near Cape Town, who brought rich experience in boating along as he uses boats a lot in his job as a marine surveyor. I think without his competent help I would never have managed.

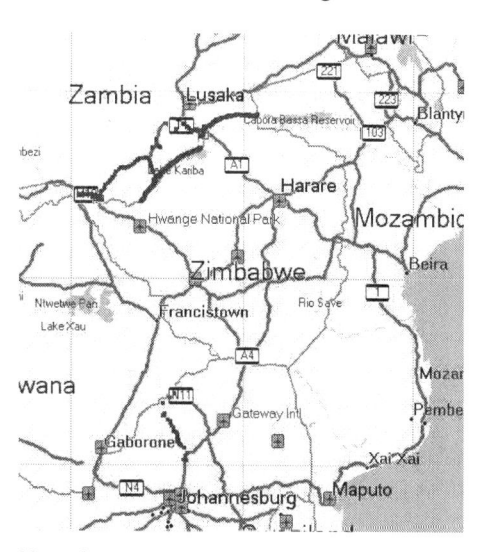

Map of the places gifted on the expedition: The blue dots are orgone gifts as usual. Because of their proximity and the scale of the map they form a continuous line here most of the time.

I am now going to show you some pictures from our trip. They are not all meant to prove a point, as water gifting rarely produces the same dramatic and immediate results in the atmosphere as, for example,

283

tower gifting in previously untreated regions or putting up a CB in totally DOR infested territory.

Most of the main roads we took had been gifted previously and we only put out additional orgonite were we felt that the energy was still bad.

But I hope that by illustrating the narrative with some pictures, showing the landscape, the people we met on our way and the wildlife, we can give you a feeling of what this work of large scale continent gifting is all about and maybe entice you to do similar work in your region or come along on one of our future Orgone Safaris and experience Africa in all its beauty and occasional ugliness, often far away from the well trodden tourist routes.

First camp stop 20 km after Francistown, Botswana

The upper Zambesi above the Victoria Falls is quite wide ad looked navigable from Livingstone, which I had never visited before. So, when we arrived, we looked for a boat ramp, which we found at the local Boat Club. A bit of a leftover from colonial times, we could say, the boat club must have seen better days...

Waiting in line at the Kazungula ferry

We only saw 3 boats there and none of them were out on the river. We were told that the river was only navigable up to 12 km from Livingstone. Well, off we went, only to find that indeed some 12 km upstream the river divided into several fast flowing channels with rocks under the surface, which can be dangerous if you hit them with your propeller at high speed.

So we went very slowly, watching the water intently.

The Zambesi upstream from Vic Falls

After a while we felt discouraged about going any further, without the help of a competent river guide. The rapids looked faster and faster and we scraped stone here and there. The idea of having to go back all this with the stream, where you have very little control, once you're in it, was a bit frightening.

Luckily we saw some boats tied to a jetty and went ashore to find out if someone could at least give us directions as to how to proceed. And here we got very lucky, as we met Mylos, a professional boatman and river guide who normally drives large tourist groups further upstream. There were no groups that day and so he agreed to come along.

He knew exactly how to jump the rapids and so we could continue our journey upstream at full speed. He even organised a life jacket for each of us, in case we toppled over. Great fun!

That way we proceeded upstream for another 30 km or so, after which distance also Mylos' knowledge of the river ended, but not the rapids.

Mylos

Elephants on the Zimbabwean river bank

We went to a village where some villagers were busy with their dugout canoes and Mylos engaged in a lively conversation with the fishermen, to find out what they could tell about the rapids further upstream.

Robert and Mylos, our river guide

Traditional Zambian village on the river bank

Villagers in discussion with Mylos about the best route on the river

Unfortunately the information was not very comprehensive and so we did not proceed much further and slowly turned back instead. In the meantime some lively energised cumulus cloud had started forming above us.

Mylos had already taken a keen interest in what we were dong with the orgonite and was quite sympathetic to the idea, so when we talked about finding a suitable place for a cloud buster, he suggested an uninhabited island that he knew.

Cumulus forming after some gifting

We had to go back to the Boat Club, where the Landrover was parked with the CBs on board and load the CB. On our way back we took a little detour, getting as close to the falls as we safely could without getting sucked in and unloaded quite a bit of extra orgonite at the headwaters of the falls.

The smoke that thunders - spray from Victoria Falls

The falls were very full and the spray mist was visible from afar as a standing cloud with brilliant rainbow light refractions. The African Name of the falls is Mosia - o Tunya or "the smoke that thunders".

Please note the phonetic analogy between "Tunya" and "Thunder" as well as "Mosia" and "Mist". Credo Mutwa has found hundreds of such words that are very similar in Bantu languages (all sub-Saharan black African people except the Nilotic people of Ethiopia, Somalia and Sudan and some other groups belong to the Bantu group of languages) and Indo-Germanic languages of Europe. Who is then still surprised that Mama is absolutely the same word in Zulu, Italian, German, English and many other languages with slight

variations.
So much about our common roots in a more ancient civilisation than the tower of Babylon...

The first hippos - we'd see millions more

We got the CB and embarked to land on the island a few km upstream again.

Apparently the only other visitors there were elephants and hippos.

We found a giant wild fig tree that was hollow inside and used it to protect the CB.

If that's not producing synergy...

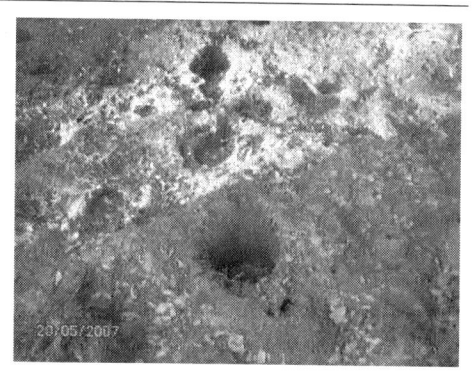

Those elephants have footprints like craters

Mylos, Robert and the CB

Puttering home after a nice day of work

The body of evidence

We went home in a very satisfied and peaceful mood and had a few drinks (the national brew in Zambia is aptly named Mosia-o-Tunya, what else) at the bar of the Zambesi Waterfront with Mylos. I hope he will read this report on the internet and stay in touch. The website URL he has.

Next morning we went down to the falls. But since we had both seen them (and I gifted them) previously we did not enter the little park. It would have taken too much time and the intense spray would just have made us wet without seeing too much.

Instead we went on the old bridge in the no-mans-land between Zambia and Zimbabwe, not without tossing a few more gifts just below the falls.

The bridge was built in the time of Cecil Rhodes (the great plunderer of Africa) time and is a major tourist attraction. At the centre point adrenalin junkies and those loath to admit their cowardice (like myself) engage in the deepest drop bungee jumping, or so they want to make you believe.
Not for me!

These trees are surely not indigenous - gotta call the Department of Forestry, I guess...

I did not feel too easy virtually entering Zimbabwe with orgonite in my pocket again, but luckily the next Zimbabwean officials were always at a safe distance. Phew!

Tossing it from the bank

The town of Livingstone has become a virtual circus for the "safari-industry" with microlight flights, booze cruises, and all kinds of stupefying herd-activities advertised on every corner.

In my mind also a way of desecrating a power spot that Mosia-o-Tunya certainly is.

But Zambia has an easy going laissez faire approach to all kind of operators in the tourism industry as long as they bring revenue and employment.

I hope they will be wise enough to preserve some tranquillity in such a great and wondrous place.

This is how far we got. Not too far, and we had felt that the stretch between Kazungula where we entered the country and Livingstone was energetically particularly bad.

So we decided to bust the parallel road very intensively on our way home much later (1 TB every 2 km between L'stone and Kazungula)

288

The mighty Zambesi 2007

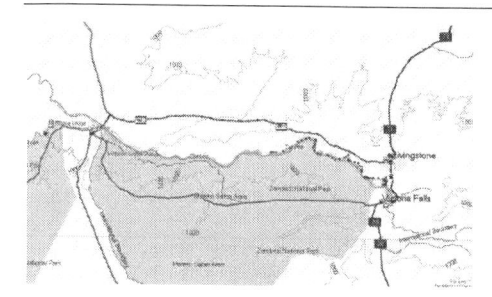

What we did upstream of Vic Falls

Lake Kariba

The road to Sinazongwe and Kariba

Next day we took off to Lake Kariba our "core destination".

The descent from the main L'stone-Lusaka road is about 80km through mountainous terrain with fascinating views.

We sensed a strange blackness in the atmosphere above the lake, long before the lake became visible.

First glimpse of the lake

The lake itself presented itself with a leaden, oppressive feel and it was very damp and hot.
Strange in wintertime!

Giant baobab in Sinazongwe

Launching the boat on Kariba

We found a place to launch the boat the next morning. The wind had picked up considerably and my experienced companion was already concerned about the waves.

289

Typical fishing pontoon on Kariba

Indeed, the wind was standing against our direction of travel and the lake was very choppy. It was extremely unpleasant and we got completely wet in the first few minutes.

It was actually very cold due to the wind chill factor and we were getting that creeping feeling of slow despair.

We tied to hug the coast as much as possible to stay out of the strong wind but that didn't work too well either, because we had to avoid those sunken forests close to the shore.

We went very slow at approximately 8-9 km/h and noticed after 2 hours that we hadn't really made much progress.

Finally I lost all my patience and decided to try a very different approach: Full speed ahead!

This meant we were hopping the waves and often landing very hard, because of the choppy uneven rhythm of those waves. I was often afraid that the boat would break and we were later to learn that this cruel treatment (of the boat and our own backs) did in fact finish the old pontoons of that boat. The old seams just didn't like that treatment.

The old lady had probably been looking forward to a comfortable retirement as a fun- and fishing boat on some small South African river and we were treating her as if she was a high strung race horse in her prime. But we got there! The goal had been to reach the inflow of the river at the far end of the lake and we would have never made that in a day and back at the previous cautious speed. Too bad about the boat...

Hiding it in a cleft

At the very end of Lake Kariba, where the river comes in, we hid a mini CB. The river looked navigable for a bit further up but unfortunately we had to consider time and our limited petrol on board. One wouldn't want to be on such unpredictable waters after nightfall, especially if one doesn't know where the hidden tree stumps and rocks are.

The skipper waiting till I'm done

Sometimes the skipper allowed me to steer the boat as well

Dead trees remind us that this was not really meant to be a lake...

For our next stretch we had to go all the way back to the main road, drive eastwards and return o the lake. A detour of 300km to get to a point 85 km further down on the lake shore where we expected to be able to launch again. We decided that Robert would move the boat to that place called Chipepo, a simple fisher village where white people are still a curious occurrence.

Tower near Gwembe, on our second approach to the lake

There was a road close to the lake shown on the map but I could not find it. After trying some overgrown and bumpy tracks, I returned to the main road and asked the driver of a small construction truck for directions. He knew the road very well but advised me not to take it, because he was part of the team that was just rebuilding the bridge there and he advised that only with

2 or more vehicles (for recovery) and some guys going ahead and chopping the thorn bushes would that road be navigable.

Traditional village on the way

We did not plan to stay at Chipepo but continued all the way to Siavonga, a little holiday resort town near the dam wall, our last stop at Lake Kariba after picking the boat up in Chipepo. That was another almost 600km drive (in order to progress some 120 km on the lake) so that we only arrived there after midnight.

Waiting for my man @ Chipepo

But we had saved a whole day that way, by moving the boat and the car in parallel. I think that's the best way to gift large water bodies.

And there he comes...

Travel with 4 people and always move the vehicle and the boat at the same time, switching the teams so that all can share in the water gifting fun.

Faintly in the background you can see the actual Kariba Gorge - That's the energy hot spot, I think

As I said earlier, over large stretches I was actually disappointed by the lake. Had I expected too much?

A lot of it felt outright boring and dead. I am not sure which part is the original Kariba Gorge. Looking back in the direction of the dam wall (see above) I felt a strong positive and peaceful emotion. Was this the original spot Credo was talking about?

Another place that felt very strongly (and got gifted massively) were these 2 islands:

Typical kapenta fishing platform

These two former mountains, now islands, also felt energetically strong

Could it be that these are identical with the two great rocks about whom Credo Mutwa said:

Getting choppy again

"And there was a place, now forever buried under water, where, if one listened carefully in a crevice between two great rocks, one heard the sound of running water. But it sounded as though it came from far below the crust of the earth.

Around this cleft, between the two rocks grew the legend that Kariba was also the gateway to the underworld..."

Picnic bay

Yo, it's a big lake

Peaceful picnic break

293

It's actually all the smoke in the air that makes the sunsets so beautiful

Market in Siavonga

We didn't go close to the wall as it's under constant camera surveillance

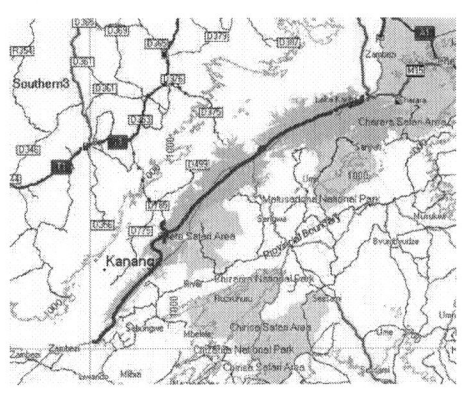

Our orgone trail through Kariba - approximately 280 gifts

Gifting Siavonga on land

Hiding a thing

The lower Zambesi

From Siavonga we proceeded on the road that leads to the main border post, Chirundu, in order to branch off on a very small dirt road, just before the Zambesi. The main road through to Chirundu is presently under reconstruction, which means it mostly consists of bumpy detours on gravel and mud, road construction African style. The branch off was blocked by trucks waiting to cross the border and it took us a while to find it.

Our first stop was at a camping site in Gwabi, just 5 km upstream on the Kafue River, a tributary of the Zambesi.

The mighty Zambesi 2007

as possible in order to continue our orgonite trail as uninterrupted as possible.

Kafue River @ Gwabi

This is the main border post bridge at Chirundu which we passed underneath

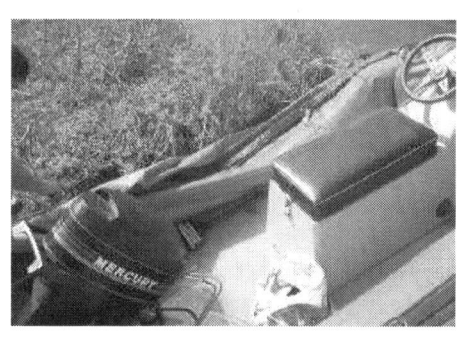

And another one of those picture postcard sunsets

And then she gave me that sinking feeling...

Some nice cumulus clouds were showing as soon as we started gifting

From here we launched the boat the next morning with the goal of getting as close to the dam wall of Kariba from the downstream side

CB on the lower Zambesi

Unfortunately after another 30km or so we noticed that one of the pontoons was losing air very rapidly. We had to make landfall and inspect the damage.

Apparently one of the seams had come lose from the intense hammering we gave her on the first day on Lake Kariba.

We decided to try and fix the leak, which would take a few hours. In the meantime I looked for a good spot to place the CB. It seemed unlikely that we would continue our journey further upstream that day.

Robert trying to patch the leak.

There it is... Thank God we had some patches and glue

After that we went back to Gwabi, avoiding pods of bathing hippos all the time. They can turn over a boat without much hassle if they feel annoyed by our intruding presence.

On the next day we split up again, this time it was me who moved the boat to our next stop, Mvuu Lodge, about 50km further downstream and close to the entry of the Lower Zambesi National Park. Robert took the car.

And then she gave me that sinking feeling again...

Unfortunately our patchwork only held up for the first 25 km. So, half the way I had to navigate with the limp pontoon held up by hand to limit the inflow of water a bit.

Arriving at Mvuu lodge I found that I was still faster on the water than Robert on the land route.

Camping with elephants

Soon after we had set up camp a

young elephant bull visited us. We heard later that he was an angry one because village kids had thrown stones at him. Obviously our camp was blocking his way to the river, where he'd been drinking before, before we arrived.

But he kept a curious distance and never made any threatening moves. We would see him again and again during our stay at that site, mostly rummaging through the close by bush and small tree vegetation.

The mighty, mighty Zambesi - It's quite a character, this river

So here we were, in the middle of pristine wilderness with a dilapidated boat and we felt somewhat subdued again. Luckily we found that the lodge had 3 fibreglass boats for hire with strong outboard motors. So we decided to leave our own boat in its sorry state, take one of theirs and afterwards try to fix ours just for the short leg back to Gwabi, where we had left the trailer.

The boat was rented "dry" but with a competent skipper and river guide to steer it. In fact, in hindsight I must say it all worked out very well, because with the 85hp outboard, we could go so much faster than we could have ever done with or own boat. As a result, we actually made it through the whole Lower Zambesi National Park and to the Mozambican border and back in one single day. Previously we had anticipated only to going two-thirds or so through the park and back, or trying to camp somewhere on the river bank.

Transversing this magnificent park was one of the most impressive wildlife tours I've ever done.

Getting ready to throw again

Chengerani was a cool and competent skipper

The place just teemed with life, birds flying over head, myriads of hippos in the water, elephants, waterbuck, buffalo, and other game on the banks and the odd crocodile basking in the sun.

Don't wanna meet him under water, do you?

The gorge on the way to Mozambique

I spoke to her first...

Two young bulls fighting it out

Cuppa tea warms nicely

Another dinosaur...

This was really most gratifying and the satisfaction of having gifted the river down to the Mozambican border was enormous. So next time, I can skip Zambia and start on the Mozambican side right away, where the Cahora Bassa Reservoir starts only a few kms downstream. That will be the theme of the next boat safari, together with Lake Malawi.

The gorge

Waterbuck, the wildlife was really stunning

They look a bit stupid on land

Buffalo

Getting home late

The next day we just lazed around, the only chore being to fix the boat again.

I got some lacquer thinner from the guys at the lodge and by washing the seam with that and sanding it very thoroughly, I hoped to get a somewhat more lasting fix and indeed one that would at least last the whole way from Mvuu to Gwabi on the next day.

On the way back, Robert took the car again and I the boat. And we met at Gwabi to put the boat on the trailer and get ready for the long journey home.

The body of evidence

River bank

The pontoon ferry over the Kafue River

Those monkeys raided our camp for food

We were to sleep over in Livingstone again and then cross the border early in the morning at the Kazungula ferry.

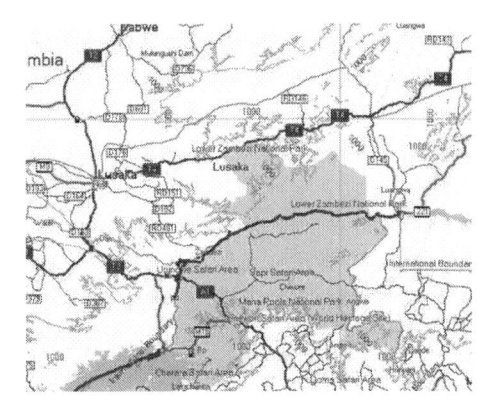

Lower Zambezi gifted

Cooking a meal

Back in Kazungula - with a bit of excitement

On the ferry a little fracas ensued when someone noticed me slipping a few extra TBs into the river. Suddenly I was surrounded by yelling people who wanted to "report me to the authorities".

"Oh my god - not Zimbabwe all over again" I thought. But somehow the whole commotion subsided when we arrived on the other bank (Botswana) and everybody left without saying a further word.

Phew...

My feeling was someone must have been planted there to create the excitement because normally I never find it difficult to explain to African people what we are doing.

But here they went on and on whether I had asked the government for permission to do this, just like the Zimbabwean police women a year ago.

Authoritarianism is deeply rooted in Africa, and the idea that you are not even allowed to sneeze if you haven't asked the king's or the chief's permission is millennia older than all the bad things we Muzungus may have done in Africa.

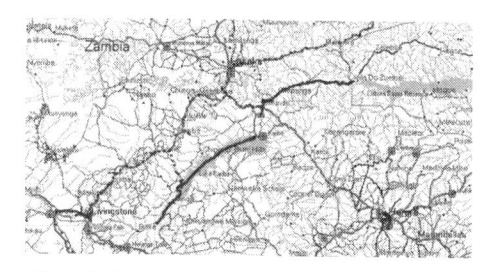

All in all about 600km of the Zambesi gifted

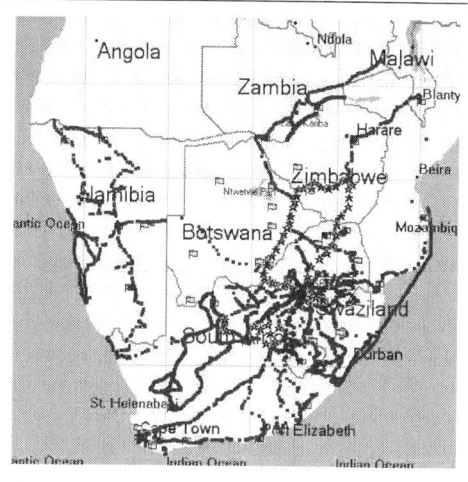

Southern Africa gifting status after the trip - The further north we go, the more new white spots we discover.

Confirmations

Right after we returned, the weather in Johannesburg was very unusual for the time of the year. There was (and still is) a lot of moisture in the air, which is unseasonal for the normally dry winter season.

Five days after we returned we got rainfall of more than 40mm in one night and the following day that was absolutely extraordinary for the season.

The Western Cape, where winter rainfall is normal, is getting a lot of rain presently. Some say it's been enough now...

The true proof of the change in the energy pattern will of course only be seen in the coming planting season in Zimbabwe and the parts of South Africa that were hit by the drought earlier this year.

Outlook and future plans

October 2007

As you may have figured out by now, this is work in progress. In the meantime, I have overhauled my boat and done a skipper's certificate which allows me to take the boat out to sea. Subsequently we have completed some more water gifting on the Vaal River in South Africa and a stretch of coastline at the south coast of Kwa-Zulu-Natal.

I am planning to do the southern leg of the intended ocean gifting with my own boat, piece by piece. Following the course of the Zambesi down to it's delta at the Indian Ocean is on the agenda.

Of course the completion of the gifting project for Kenya, Tanzania Uganda, Rwanda and Burundi is very close to my heart.

Since I have noticed that things always turn out differently than anticipated, I am not speculating about dates any more.

By the time you possibly read this book, all such plans would be obsolete.

I have never been to West Africa. However, of course, if an Invitation or contact comes up, I would love to go to Ghana, Togo, Mali, Nigeria and Senegal.

I think for now the Sahara is the natural boundary of the territory I wish to treat intensely, but who knows?

It is all a question of opportunity and funding.

A grid of CBs in the Sahara every 50km would probably reconvert this fast growing desert into the grain basket of Africa that it was up until Roman times.

As our network grows, more and more people are entering the picture who commands greater financial resources.

If you feel that you would like to contribute to this endeavour by participating in one of our upcoming expeditions or by material contributions to this work, please do not hesitate to contact me through our website www.orgonise-africa.net.

AND IS IT WORTH THE EFFORT?

How much happiness can you stand?
Don Croft

Of course that's the most important question to answer here, and I wholeheartedly answer it with yes!

So many things have changed since we started this work. There are no more any chemtrails worth mentioning over the whole of Southern Africa. They seem to have given it up. The whole atmosphere in South Africa has changed on the perceptible and intangible level.

Even though there are still a lot of problems, such as rampant and often violent crime, the general spirit is one of optimism.

It is a wonderful country to live in and so can our whole planet be, if we only want it. Of course, orgonite is no automatic fix-all; there is still work to do for each and every one of us.

But creating a more alive energy matrix with the help of orgone devices such as those described here definitely sets the right conditions for people to come up with more constructive ideas for the further development of our global society.

It will even help those clinging to their illicit power and hidden control to let go and become part of the productive mainstream of humankind.

Just imagine how nice the world could be!

III. YOU CAN DO IT TOO!

CREATING PARADISE: THE SIMPLE ART OF GIFTING

People have different talents and preferences

People develop their personal styles in gifting. What you have read in Part III is my style of doing it. Your style will most definitely different. However, there are a few things that we all should do.

Firstly: All so-called cell phone towers must be gifted, wherever accessible. If you have a cloudbuster and feel it is not working properly, most likely you have not done enough gifting in your wider area.

Sometimes a place of very bad energy even a hundred kilometres away can bog down a CB as we experienced with the one at Eddie von Maltitz's place. (See page 56)

Many people have special sensitivities, like Laozu who specialises on opening vortices so that the life energy can flow heavenward in an unobstructed manner.

Others are sensitive to etheric influences on a different level and I can just feel which place needs more gifting.

An experienced dowser, who specialises on earth pathological stresses, will first try out what orgonite does one a clearly identified negative water vein.

If you live in a densely populated area in one of the highly developed "first world countries" where most likely many other gifters are already active, your situation will be different from mine. You will tend to pay more attention to detail and really make your town or country into paradise on earth before you venture out further. Before you do that you will probably seek contact and exchange with other gifters in the area to avoid duplicating their work.

Sort out your own life first

We all start out by improving our immediate environment first and there's nothing wrong with that.

Basic protection for a house is as follows:

Put at least one TB at every corner of the plot.

Put one TB on every window sill.

One TB gets into the electrical main distribution box, one is taped onto the main water pipe where it enters the house.

Sources of radiation such as TV sets, computer monitors etc. should also have a TB nearby.

I would put at least one HHG in the bedroom, near or under the bed. (four TBs at the corners of the

bed are also great0.
Maybe put a CB in the garden. Nevertheless, that is not necessarily the next step.

A HHG or two in the garden will do to begin with.

It is more important to neutralise the cell phone towers at least within your immediate radius of 5km first.

That's to neutralise the direct mind control influence they're having on you.

Then of course you will think of your workplace, the school of the children and other places you visit frequently.

It is logical to start expanding this "circle of wellbeing" in concentric rings around where you live.

Gifting FAQ

Q: How many tower busters do I need for a normal cellphone mast?

A: One TB is normally enough. Believe me, you do not need more. It can be up to 500m away in order to still neutralise the DOR output. The closer the better for the protection of those in immediate vicinity of the death force transmitter.

The only reason to use two or more is if the number of panels seems excessively large, or if you feel that the TB might be found and removed and you won't pass by that place any time soon.

Also, large groupings of towers, so-called arrays, need more than one. We often place a HHG and surround the area with anything from 4-12 TBs. This is a matter of intuition if you're not able to see the energy changes directly.

We often use a pendulum to determine the exact number in such cases.

Q: How do I place the TBs

A: This really depends on the local conditions.

Generally the TBs can be buried or hidden in bushes or shrubs, hollow trees or any place where you feel they will not be removed. In the open landscape, where dense vegetation will swallow, them we have often just thrown them out of the window of the car. We make our field pieces in camouflage colours like olive green, ochre or brown, so they don't visually litter the landscape and are not so easy to detect.

It is more difficult to bust dense urban areas where there is little greenery and most surfaces are sealed with concrete or tar.

Here you have to become ingenious.

People have made magnetic TBs that can be attached to sign posts, by casting a strong neodymium magnet. This is of course relatively expensive. Another ingenious invention is the signpost inlay.

Here a small piece of orgonite is cast in a cylindrical mould, to be slid into the inside of signposts, street name signs et cetera. Sometime you have to remove the plastic caps and replace them.

I have thrown TBs on low flat roofs where they will lie undisturbed for a long time.

Another approach is to slide TBs into the storm water drainage gullies at regular intervals in inner city areas.

In some places, this may be the only inconspicuous hiding place; even if a lot of them will get washed out of the area, some always remain and create a sort of orgonite grid. Even those that are washed out to wherever the storm water is discharged will still work as water gifts and be connected to the city by the orgone conductive water borne network of drainage pipes.

Every city has its specific gifting opportunities. And I'm sure you will develop your own style and array of solutions soon. Be creative!

Q: What if a tower or array of towers cannot be reached

A: Vicinity can be substituted with number, probably in some exponential relation. We often find situations where towers are on distant mountains on private farms, protected by fences and locked gates. Rather than spend the whole day to get up there, we have now resorted to the alternative method of laying out strings of 10 or more TBs at intervals of 500m along the road. If possible it is even better to create an L-shaped figure, if any roads branch off in the direction of the mountaintop array, so that the array will end up being flanked by a row of TBs at least on two sides.

Also here, the number and intervals needed can only be determined intuitively, but the results will be perceptible on a normal 5 sense level.

A similar strategy can be adopted when travelling on a highway at high speed and not wanting to make detours of 50 km and more that are often needed to get close to distant towers or arrays.

Q: How can I treat negative fault lines or water veins (geopathic stress)?

A: A circle of six TBs with a diameter of 60-90cm seems to be the ideal configuration to transform any negative energy line into a positive one. Look at Laozu's report about the work done near the Matopos Hills in Zimbabwe (see page 219 ff)

Q: Do CBs have to be grounded?

A: No, absolutely not. This is a widespread misconception, stemming from the original Wilhelm Reich cloud busters. Those, in absence of orgonite were just bundles of pipes that had to be connected to a large water body in order to discharge the negative energy that was drawn from the sky in a sweeping movement. Orgonite cloudbusters do not need to be physically connected to soil or water.

Q: Why do you use aluminium?

A: Aluminium has proven its worth in orgonite applications beyond any doubt. Often people's scepticism about the use of aluminium is based on some remarks that Wilhelm Reich made some decades ago. As we cannot repeat enough, Wilhelm Reich's experiments were of a totally different nature than what we do with orgonite and his experimental findings cannot be taken out of context. There is absolutely no evidence to discredit aluminium as a powerful ingredient of orgonite.

Aluminium filings have several advantages: They are easy to obtain; they are normally quite fine, which allows more alternating layers in the orgonite matrix and hence makes the effect stronger.

They do not rust. They do not make the orgonite as heavy as iron filings. They develop crystalline structures at the shearing edges in the process of shaving off, which seems to enhance their potential for energy transformation.

So, treat anyone who tells you that there's something wrong with aluminium with extreme suspicion. He or she probably belongs to the disinformation brigade.

Other metals can be used and may give off a "softer" vibration, which may be welcome for personal orgone healing devices. But aluminium is unsurpassed when it comes to sheer neutralising energy transformation tasks as needed in large scale environmental healing.

Q: Is beeswax a substitute for the polyester resin?
A: No, it is not. Beeswax does not form the same kind of matrix that polyester resin does. The long chain molecules seem to play a role in the energetic effects we observe. Opposition to polyester resin is mostly ecological in nature as people would love to work with natural materials.

However, this opposition is not based on experience or experimental verification.

Some other resins may work as well but are usually a lot more expensive. Cured polyester resin does not emit any measurable quantities of solvent after a while.

We even find that the finished pieces start smelling delicious, as if perfumed with fine etheric oils after a while. This is probably due to a heightened olfactory perception of positive energy.

Make sure you only work with resin outside or in very well ventilated rooms and if doing it frequently, use professional breathing protection (mask for organic solvents).

Q: Do CBs need to have added ingredients like coils, magnets et cetera?
A: None of this is really needed. Some of it may even be counterproductive. We always put in a sprinkling of additional healing stones such as amethyst, pyrite or black tourmaline. If you are experienced in the application of healing stones beyond the required quartz crystals, you can experiment with adding some different ones.

Generally speaking, healing stones will display their already known characteristics, only in an amplified manner. A good and empirically well-founded encyclopaedia of healing stones and their applications can be found in the books by Michael Gienger.[35]

I recommend that you build your first experimental orgone generators as simply and straight forwardly as possible, so you always have a reference for future refinements.

Even greater caution is advised when it comes to the use of any occult or esoteric symbols. As I explained earlier, all esoteric teachings circulated on the general New Age Marketplace are infiltrated by the dark side. You do not know what deeper intentions and beings you are connecting your orgonite with, if you use esoteric symbols. This includes the widely known Reiki symbols as well. (See also page 12)

Q: What targets should I bust?
A: The absolute obvious ones are all microwave transmitters of whatever description. This includes all "cell phone masts", radar installations, military installations and any large transmitting sites such as TV or radio stations. If you are not sure, place some orgonite. I use the adaptation of a Latin proverb, "In dubio busto" in all cases of uncertainty. It can do no harm.

Once you have done that in your area, you may focus on targets of a subtler nature: All places where negative emotional or mental energy or mind manipulation is generated on whatever level:

Masonic Lodges, places of worship of any organised religion[VI], government buildings, secret services(if location known) political party offices, police stations, prisons, large corporation headquarters, places of past and present human suffering such as concentration camps, battle sites, places known for human sacrifice or occult(satanic) ceremonies, crack houses, places of high incidence of violent crime, residences of known proponents of the New World Order, the list is endless and open to your own intuitive evaluation and preferences. However, the priority is to get all the transmitters neutralised first.

Q: Which role does water gifting play in this context
A: I think it is good practice to toss some orgonite into every river that you cross on a busting tour. Water seems to conduct orgone energy very well and also carries a lot of the negativity. So by gifting rivers and creeks as well as the ocean we help to distribute the positive charge over a wide area.

If you live in a town with navigable waterways, where you can embark on some kind of fun cruises (it does not have to be Venice, many cities have these) take one of those rides and drop orgonite at regular intervals. Massive water gifting is a bit cost intensive but seems to yield profound long-term results. We are only at the beginning of collecting empirical data about it. It also seems that the oceans are as full of underwater transmitter sites as the land and that ocean gifting is the next frontier after the land is sufficiently covered.

[VI] *This does of course not constitute judgement of any religion. If they promote genuine spirituality, the orgonite will only promote that even further.*

DIY – MAKE YOUR OWN ORGONITE

Making orgonite is easy!

This is the most important thing I have to tell you in this section.

Many people on the internet and elsewhere are spending a lot of time and money to make you believe it is otherwise.

Orgonite always works, even if you think you have it all wrong. Also the designs of the basic orgonite tools are very error tolerant. When you read about the mix having to be 50/50, that just means that you pour a bucket full of resin into a bucket full of aluminium filings. People have asked me the weirdest questions about how to determine the exact volume of the filings since they come in this woolly state and….

It's much easier than that!

Making beautiful orgonite takes practice and is not that easy, but as much as we all love to make things beautiful, a rough and dirty TB will neutralise a cell phone tower (death force transmitter) just as well as a high gloss one with neatly arranged gemstone inlays. At first you will need to source resin. Most of us work with simple polyester resin. This comes in different qualities. Preferably use the "clear casting" quality that is also used to embed butterflies and dried flowers into nice clear blocks, often used as key rings or for other decorative purposes. We buy this from industrial wholesalers who cater for the boat building and swimming pool manufacturers. If you have no idea where to get resin in your town, phone the guys who work with fibreglass and ask them where they buy their stuff. Polyester resin stinks a bit when it is curing because of the chemical reaction and release of solvents, so you should always work outside or in a very well ventilated room.

If you plan to do this regularly, get yourself a protective mask (against organic fumes as with spray painters) or build a fan into your room that guarantees at least a 40 x per hour air change.

The resin needs to be mixed with a catalyst that will bring about the chemical reaction that makes the resin cure into a crystalline clear substance. Please follow the instructions of the manufacturer regarding percentage of catalyst to be used etc.

Many people have tried other substances as a matrix in which to suspend the metal filings in, such as beeswax, sugar, tree resins and epoxy resins.

The epoxy and tree resins (when they are treated in a way that they can be cured to a non-sticky crystalline matrix) seem to work OK, but we have not tried it. We have learned to handle the polyester well and find it works so fantastically that we need not look for alternatives. Even sugar seems to work but is of course not exactly weatherproof for outside application.

Beeswax has been a great disappointment even though it is

still periodically brought up by people who do not like the notion of using a "chemical" material to restore the natural energy balance.

See it in a different way: Isn't it fun, that we can defeat the plans for global control by the self-proclaimed elite, using exactly the addictive substances that are most pivotal in their global enslavement policies: mineral oil (resin) and sugar.

Next you will need lots of aluminium shavings (some call them filings). You can get these at machine shops that work with aluminium a lot such as window manufacturers sign makers etc...

A lot of people who have read Wilhelm Reich's works are very prejudiced against aluminium because of some observations that Reich made in connection with his orgone accumulators. He spoke out strongly against aluminium use in accumulators, but nobody in our network has so far found any evidence that this would hold true for orgonite.

Don has also built many classical Reich-style accumulators with aluminium and found no adverse effects. Could it be that another factor, as yet unknown, created the negative results, Reich was reporting?

Last but not least you will need crystals. Clear quartz crystals, that is. But they can also be milky or otherwise of "inferior quality".

We have even used white and completely opaque quartz chips we found on a mountain near the track we were driving on, to add into some improvised TBs that we had to make when we ran out of ammo in Namibia in September 2004.

They worked well.

For TBs, any small crumbs of crystal breakage will suffice. For HHGs use single terminated crystals, that is, crystals with one naturally formed tip.

For CBs one should preferably use double terminated crystals, which means they have a natural tip in both directions. Even when multiple small tips point all in one direction we still speak of single terminated.

The easiest to start with: making TBs

TBs or Tower Busters are the easiest to make. That's why I strongly recommend you start with them. You will get a feeling for working with resin that way which will come in handy when you start making the more sophisticated pieces. We make our TBs in standard muffin moulds, but you can use anything that will hold approximately 100-150 ml (3-5 oz.) of resin and shavings. Plastic or paper cups are also popular.

If you want to re-use the mould, we strongly recommend that you wax it before pouring. We use "silicone release wax" which we get from the place that sells the resin and catalyst. Baking fat will work as well.

We use aluminium filings (or sometimes they're also called shavings). Other metals work as well.

Making orgonite is easy

We get best results when the shavings are not too big or too small and sufficiently loose so that the resin can run in between them.

Waxing the form

Shavings the way we like them

Apart from the shavings and resin, the mandatory ingredient is quartz.

You don't have to use A-grade tips. Any quartz breakage even of a milky or opaque quality will do. We used white quartz pebbles collected from the road with great success on our Namibia expidition when we ran out of TBs.

We like to add some low-grade amethyst because we get it cheaply and it makes the TBs nicer. Also we like to add a few crumbs of black tourmaline. If available, powdered pyrite makes any orgonite much stronger in sheer power.

But again: simplicity is the rule. You do not need any crystals other than quartz in order to achieve stunning results.

Typical ingredients the way we make our TBs

The best resin for orgonite is polyester resin of the so-called "clear casting" quality. It's the same that is used to cast insects or leaves into decorative key ring pendants and the like. Make sure you go to the industrial suppliers.

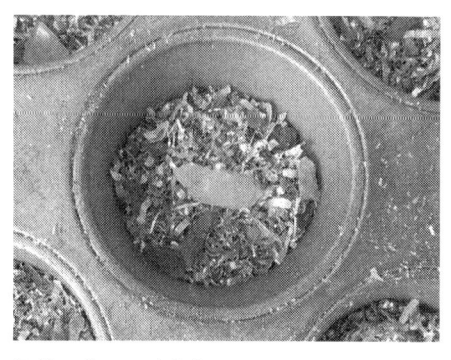

Putting the crystals in

Otherwise you will pay a fortune for small quantities.

If you don't know where to find those suppliers, talk to the guys who work with fibreglass. (Swimming pool and boat builders for example) They will know.

We start with a thin layer of filings and place the crystals on top of this little nest. That way they will end up being approximately at the centre of the finished TB.

Top layer

We top up to just under the rim. If you want to add some crushed pyrite or tourmaline, you can sprinkle it over the top layer in the end.

Now we can start the pouring procedure. We need the resin, and a suitable quantity of catalyst. The resin suppliers normally sell special measuring bottles for the catalyst and we recommend that you get one if it is not supplied for free.

We also recommend that you use industrial strength rubber gloves for the larger works while surgical latex gloves are good for finer work. If you plan to do this often you should get yourself a mask with a filter against organic solvent vapours. You do not really need that if you can work outside.

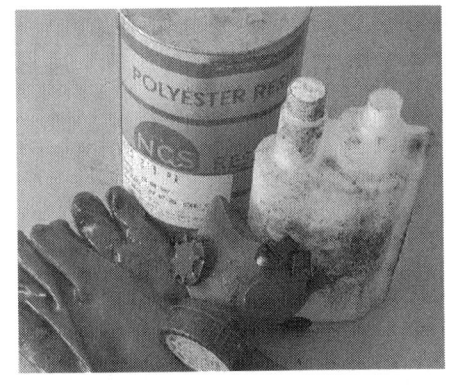

What you need for pouring

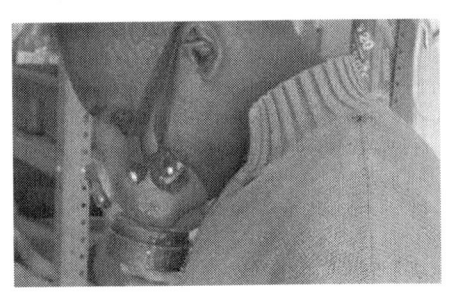

Wear a mask if you frequently do this inside. Make sure rooms are well ventilated.

Use bucket with measurements

Pour a sufficient quantity of resin into a bucket with measurements.

For one standard muffin tray, we use approximately 1.1-1.2 litres.

Making orgonite is easy

Measure the needed quantity of catalyst

With most makes of resin the standard mix is 2% catalyst at 20°C. But beware: temperature and size of the piece you want to pour influence the need for catalyst. The hotter it gets or the bigger the piece, the least catalyst you need. Refer to resin manufacturer's manual for exact quantities.

Add pigments if you want colour

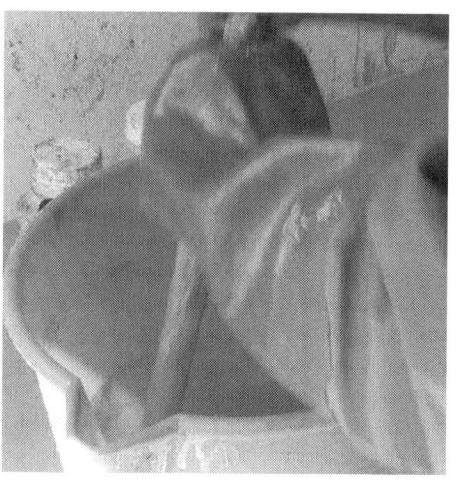

Stir thoroughly!

Pour catalyst into resin

Pour into small jug with spout for easier pouring

You can do it too!

And start pouring

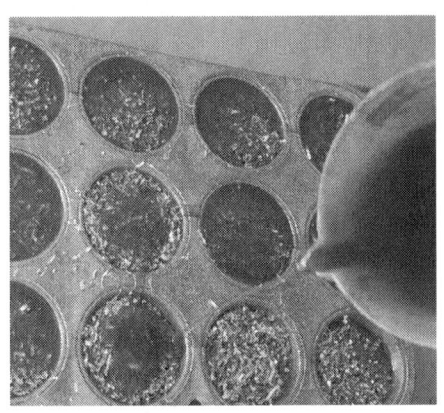

Continue until muffin pan is filled to the rim

Since the resin takes a while to sink in you will have to pour in several passes. It is always good to have a few more objects prepared on the side that can take any surplus resin in case you have miscalculated the quantity.

You have (depending on the make of the resin and room temperature etc.) 15-25 minutes to do this. That is normally not a problem. If you feel that the resin is becoming jelly-like before you are finished, quickly mix the remaining resin with metal filings to make at least some kind of usable orgonite. Keeping your bucket and jugs clean helps to avoid premature gelling.

When the process is finished, you have to wait a while. The resin will now start its chemical reaction during which it will get quite hot. If you have used the right amount of catalyst, the TBs should be easily removed after curing by just turning the pan upside down. A few gentle taps with a rubber hammer are sometimes needed.

If the mix has not cured properly (too cold or not enough catalyst) it can be put in direct sunlight to give it some after-curing.

The next step: making HHGs

For making HHGs you want a conical mould. We use ordinary household funnels because the ones we have found have a nice proportion with the base as well as the height being 100mm. But many other forms have been successfully tried: from conical paper party hats to cocktail glasses.

You have to close the nozzle in some elegant way. We used to do that with window putty which could be shaped any way we wanted but now we make a small cone of masking tape that we insert with the sticky side facing outwards.

Apart from the filings you need 5 single terminated crystals 30-40mm in length. Additional healing stones are optional. We use crushed black tourmaline and a few of our low grade amethyst pebbles to beautify the energy emanating from the HHG.

Making orgonite is easy

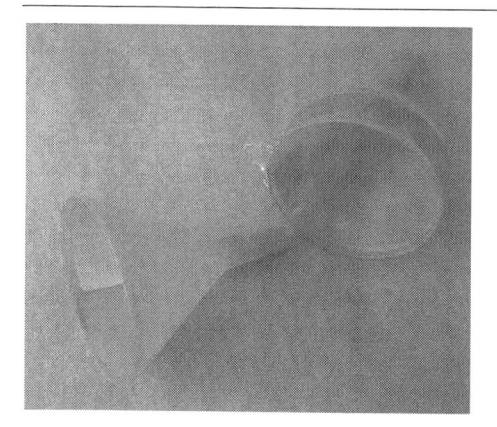

Household funnels

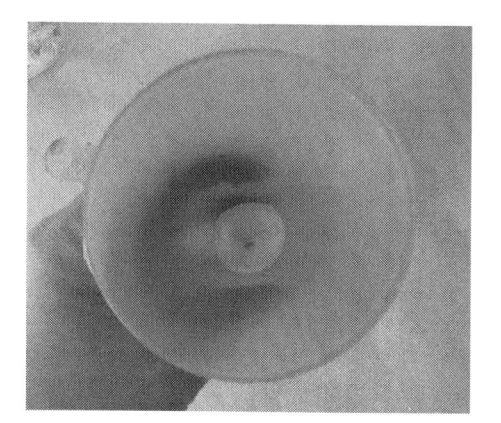

Nozzle closed with masking tape

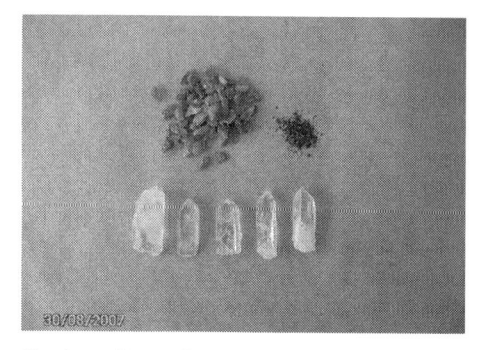

Our ingredients: 5 mandatory crystals, optional amethyst and tourmaline.

We start by putting a few filings into the top in order to make a nest for the top crystal. We want all the crystals to be embedded in the orgonite. See the following picture sequence for the further procedure.

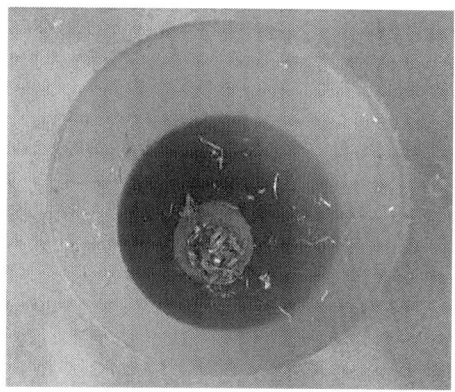

Make a nest for the top crystal

Place top crystal into nest with tip facing downwards (up in finished HHG)

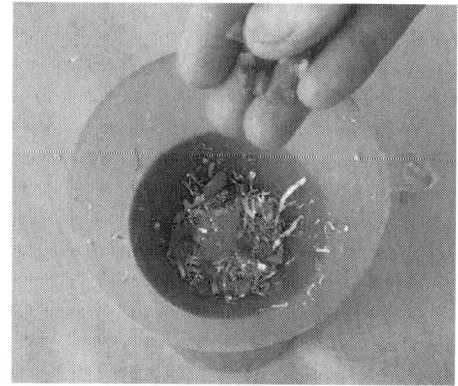

Add more filings and some of the optional additional stones, if you wish

315

You can do it too!

Add more stones as you build up in layers (optional)

Until they are invisible

Place the bottom crystals in a cross formation. Leave enough space for the crystals to be covered with a thin layer of filings

Start pouring

Cover crystals

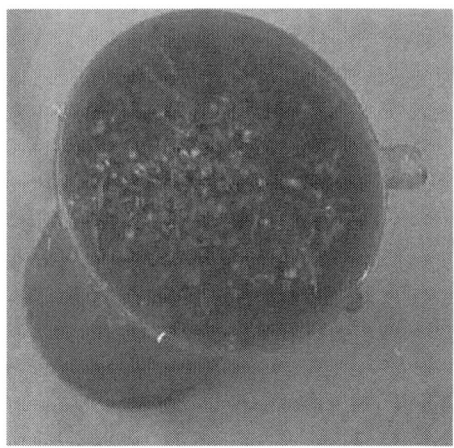

Repeat several times until no more air bubbles come up and funnel is filled to the rim.

Making orgonite is easy

Now you only need to break the rough edge with a file (or a sanding disk) and sand it until smooth. That's only if you want to make it into a nice piece of art, of course. The full power is there without the cosmetics. Of course any other conical mould will do the job. Cocktail glasses, party hats – anything will do.

There are other variations to the theme such as the ones that Don makes nowadays. They only have a crystal in the tip and a clockwise spiral (from the bottom up) is replacing the four bottom crystals.

This is how the finished product comes out of the mould.

Finally: Build your own CB

Again, this is only one way to make a functioning orgonite CB. Following these instructions will give you enough of a feel for the matter to deviate from the procedure wherever you feel it would lead to better results.

The standard pipe length according to the inventor of this device is 6' or approximately 1800mm.

The recommended pipe diameter for a standard CB is 28mm that is almost but not quite the same as the US 1-1/4".

The crystals may already be fitted inside the short pipe ends. We mostly insert them afterwards and fix them with a bit of resin.

In Don's original instruction they are wrapped into a short piece of garden hose and glued into the bottom end of the pipe.

That's what goes into the bucket

The short pipe ends should be closed with a stop fitting (standard from plumbing suppliers) or a copper plate soldered on (see picture below). It is intended that the pipes form a resonant cavity, so the bottom should not be open. One could use thin foils to close it.

317

You can do it too!

Short pipe ends with bottom plates and connectors soldered on

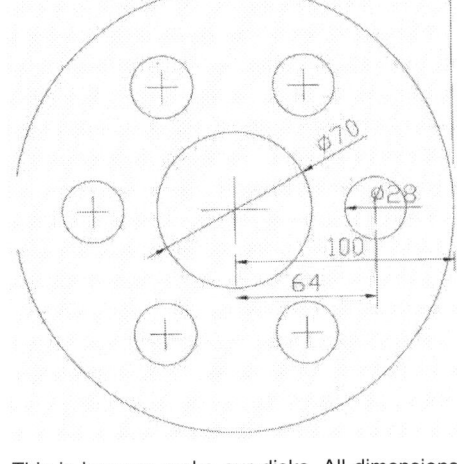

This is how we make our disks. All dimensions are in mm.

We use 3 of our standard spacer disks to connect the long pipe ends to a stable rig. We have found that better than inserting special spacers into the bucket as in Don's original instruction.

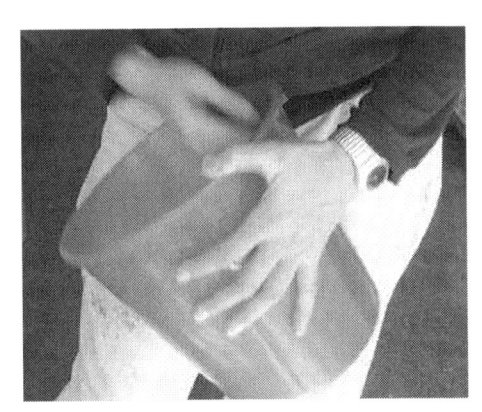

Wax bucket with silicone release agent.

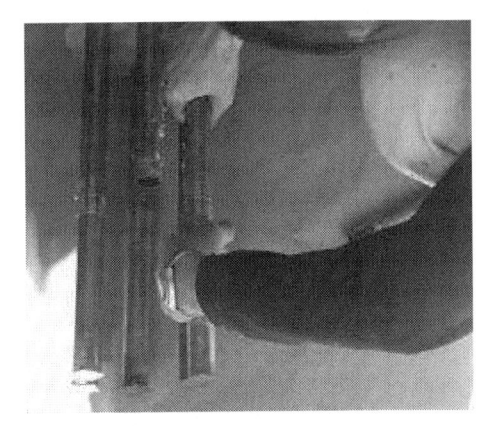

Long pipe ends forming a stable rig

Stick short pipe ends onto the rig

Making orgonite is easy

Insert into bucket

You may have noticed that we have already prepared a bottom plate in a previous pouring session. We don't want the pipes to go through to the very bottom but rather want them embedded in orgonite. We make that plate approximately 20mm thick.

Apply some preliminary bracing

We always put it up next to a table. After applying some bracing, we start to make sure that it's really standing upright and the distance to the border of the bucket is equal on all sides. It helps when the floor is level, of course. Otherwise you should use a piece of wood levelled with some wedges as floor. By looking at the pipes from various directions with one squinted eye, you can also ensure that they are parallel and not "drilled".

Laozu's vortex buster is something else. There you want the pipes "drilled" in a spiralling motion. So don't be afraid if you don't get them totally straight. Your CB will work nevertheless.

It is amazing how error tolerant these designs are. As long as you end up with six copper tubes with some sort of crystal in the closed bottom, sticking in a bucketful of

Place the rig upright

resin-metal mix in a halfway circular arrangement, you will have a powerful working cloud buster at hand.

Make sure the pipes are level

Now you can start filling up with filings

We fill up to about 2/3 of the intended height. This allows us to pour a substantial amount of resin in one go which will be pushed into the filings by its own gravity. We put in some "misfired" TBs or other orgonite that hasn't passed the quality test. That way we can prevent cracks even when pouring in one go. Some people still advise pouring in layers. We don't really like it because it takes very long and resin always runs behind the finished parts, resulting in an uneven and messy surface.

Pouring

It is advisable to pour only from one side so that air can still escape on the other side. It helps to have a translucent bucket because then you can see how far the resin has penetrated.

Depending on the texture of your metal filings, you may also premix the orgonite and pour the mix of filings and liquid resin. That way you can prevent air bubbles more easily, but it is also more messy.

Making orgonite is easy

Resin almost down to the bottom

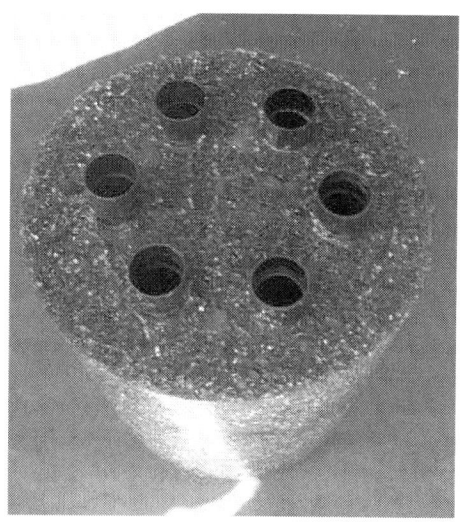

This is how the raw CB base will look like

Fill up and pour to centre of connectors

In most cases you will find that the surface of the raw base might need a final "glazing" coat for aesthetic purposes.

The easiest way to do this is by just taping a rim with masking tape. Small irregularities in the tape will be filed and sanded away afterwards when you break the sharp edge.

Once the resin has saturated all the filings, we fill up with filings to 1cm under desired height which is in the middle of the connectors. We do that quickly, so we can still use the same resin "wet in wet".

It is important to do this in one session with the same resin. Otherwise you'll have to wait about 2 hours and get the problems described previously when pouring in layers.

Pouring a smooth top coating with tape

321

This is how our finished cloudbusters look.

one. In Uganda we built one with the only copper tubing we could get and that was 22 mm on a roll. We had to straighten it by hand on a concrete floor, so it was never straight and we had no end caps, only chocolate paper to seal the pipes at the bottom.

We also had no pure quartz crystals but only amethyst with some quartz veins. Despite its irregular shape its influence was perceptible for hundreds of kilometres around its location in Kampala.

Yours may look slightly different.
It is very difficult to build a "bad"

SP-Crystals and Mobius coils

Text based on Ryan McGinty's article on www.ethericwarriors.com with permission of the author.

Photos courtesy of Ryan Mc Ginty

The items you will need:

One cordless drill. 1 spool of 30 gauge aluminium wire from Radioshack, comes in red, blue and white in 50ft. Do not get the magnet wire that is copper. The copper is very stiff while wrapping, also the enamel insulator easily scrapes off causing minute shortages.

First select a length of wire that will be appropriate for the size of crystal. Very small crystals will need only three feet of wire, larger ones with a diameter of 1 inch or larger will need 20-25 feet or more, the whole spool for giant crystals.

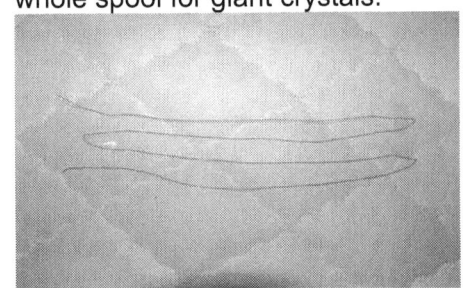

Fold the wire in half, and then fold that in half again. You are basically folding the wire into quarters.

Now take the end where both ends are bent, place them into the locking chuck of your cordless drill. The easiest way to keep them together evenly in the drill is by starting a small twist to hold them together.

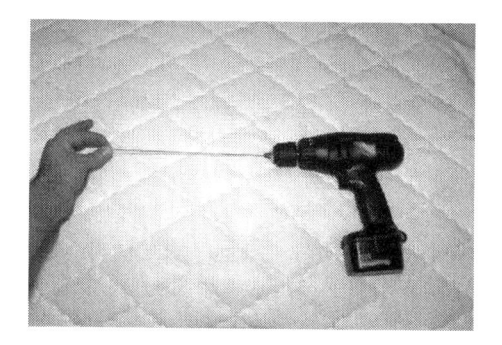

Set the drill direction so that it will remove a screw (lefty loosie). With your other hand, hold onto the end with the two leads. Make sure you keep good tension while the drill is rotating. This will minimise irregularities. If the wire is longer than your arm span, have someone help hold it or clamp it to a sturdy stand.

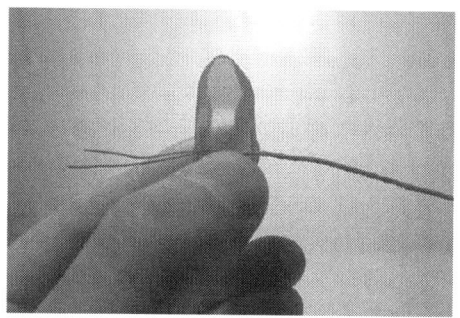

Hold your crystal and wire like so. You will be doing a counter clockwise wrap that works upwards.

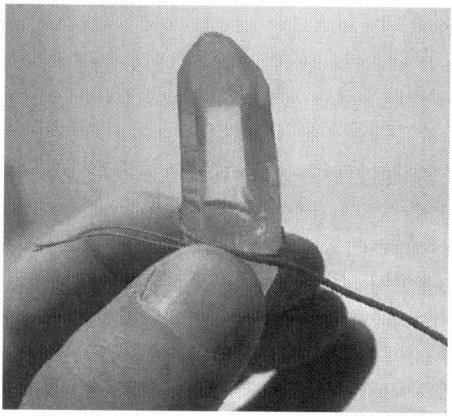

Here is how you start your first knot.

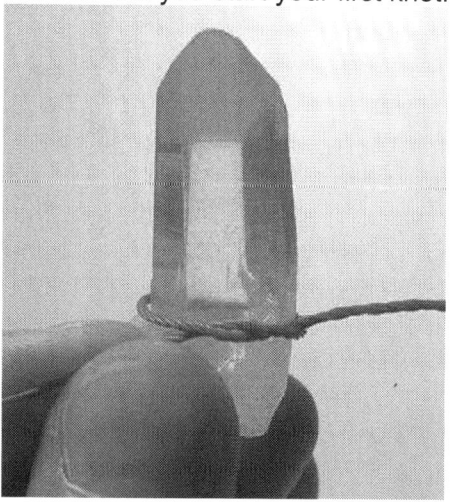

You will know the wire is correctly wound when the thread angles are at 45 degrees.

You can do it too!

Notice that the knot goes over, down, up-around. It is basically a square knot. Keep this knot a little loose because you will need the space for the remaining knots.

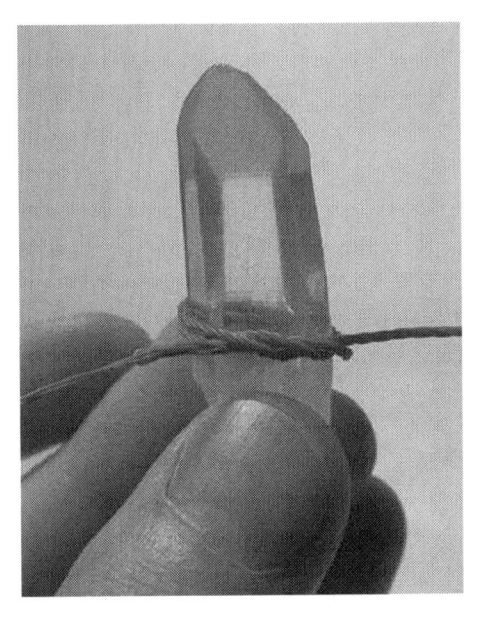

Now repeat the process. You will notice the wire working upwards while the knot keeps getting larger. Start pulling the wire tight.

This is what it looks like going around a third time. Each time you start a new knot you start just before the last one. Remember to keep the wraps tight. This will ensure you do not have any wires overlapping on the back.

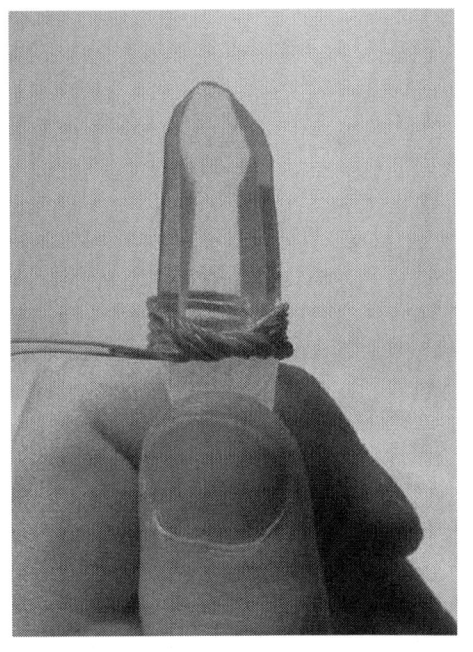

Here is the finished result. You will notice that the knots start right after the previous one begun. Use glue to hold wires in place, a hot glue gun or goop works great. Strip the ends and you got your self an SP!

If you notice the knots are getting too difficult to overlap then start another row the same way as the first. Pull the excess just a little above the first Mobius wrap, wrap the wire around CCW then make the knot and keep repeating as many times as needed. It's basically a simple pattern that is repeated.

IV. FURTHER READING

The following books and websites can help to understand the perspective from which this book is written and further the depth of your enquiry into some subjects marginally touched here. This does not mean that the author identifies with or endorses all particular views expressed in these sources.

Books

By Dr. Wilhelm Reich:
Character analysis
Mass psychology of fascism
The function of the orgasm
The discovery of the orgone
The cancer biopathy
Ether, god and devil
Cosmic superimposition
Contact with outer space

About Dr. Wilhelm Reich:
Wilhelm Reich – the evolution of his work - David A. Boadella
Der Traumvater - Peter Reich

Orgone and related:
The Life Etheric with Carol Croft – Don Croft
Die Wiederentdeckung des Lebendigen – Prof. Bernd Senf

Science and secret technology
The Tao of physics – Fritjof Capra
PSI – Ostrander, Schroeder
The world weather guide – Pearce, Smith, 1993
Lost science – Gerry Vassilatos
Scalar waves - Prof. Konstantin Meyl
Wholeness and the implicate order – David Bohm
The holographic universe _ Michael Talbot
The self aware Universe – Amit Goswami Ph.D.
The coming Energy revolution, by Jeanne Manning

HAARP the ultimate weapon of the conspiracy – Jerry E. Smith
Angels don't play this HAARP – Nick Begich
Underwater and underground bases – Richard Sauder Ph. D.
Death in the air – Dr. Leonard G. Horowitz
Reich of the Black Sun (Nazi secret weapons) – Joseph P Farell
Fire from Ice (cold fusion) – Eugene F. Mallove

Natural power lines and power spots
Points of cosmic energy – Blanche Merz
The new view over Atlantis – John Michell

Mythology and the origins of mankind
Indaba my children – Credo Mutwa
The 12th Planet – Zecharia Sitchin

Alternative history:
Rule by Secrecy – Jim Marrs
None dare call it conspiracy – Gary Allen
And the truth shall set you free – David Icke
The biggest secret – David Icke
Secrets of the Federal Reserve – Eustace Mullins
Liquid conspiracy – George Piccard
Wall Street and the rise of Hitler – Jeremy F. Sutton
Die CIA und der 11 September – Andreas von Bülow
The conspirators – Secrets of an Iran Contra insider – Al Martin

Medicine
Inventing the AIDS virus – Peter H. Duesberg
Emerging viruses – AIDS and Ebola – Dr. Leonard G Horowitz
The cure for all diseases – Hulda R. Clark

Websites (URLs were accurate at time of writing)

On Orgonite and related issues:

www.ethericwarriors.com
www.orgonise-africa.net
www.cb-forum.com
www.worldwithoutparasites.com

Conspiracy research and suppressed news:
(Read with discernment)

www.educate-yourself.org
www.whatreallyhappened.com
www.prisonplanet.com
www.chemtrailcentral.com

Text References

[1] David Boadella, "Wilhelm Reich. The Evolution of his Work"
[2] Dr. Wilhelm Reich, *Character Analysis*
[3] Dr. Wilhelm Reich, The Function of the Orgasm
[4] See for example Jim Marrs, "Rule by Secrecy" or Gary Allen, "None dare call it Conspiracy" or David Icke, "And the Truth shall set you free"
[5] A good book about these rearguard tactics is "The Liquid Conspiracy" by George Piccard, Adventures Unlimited Press
[6] Zacharia Sitchin, "The 12ths Planet" and other books from his "Earth Chronicles" cycle.
[7] The Bible, authorised King James Version, World Bible Publishers, Iowa, USA
[8] Read some of the popular conspiracy primers like Jim Marrs, "Rule by Secrecy", David Icke, "And the truth shall set you free" and others for the structure and history of the secret society network and its pervasive influence on our society past and present.
[9] See James E. Ewart, "MONEY", Principia Publishing, Seattle 1998
[10] G. Edward Griffin, "The Creature from Jekyll Island – A Second Look at the Federal Reserve"
[11] Eustace Mullins, "The Secrets of the Federal Reserve" (Out of print)
[12] Check www.thematrix.com or go to the next video store to get the movie. The sequels Matrix II and III don't have that quality of being "hidden documentaries" of what's really going on. They rather distract from the message of the original movie.
[13] See "Wall Street and the Rise of Hitler" by Jeremy Sutton, Buccaneer books, New York 1976
[14] See Herman and Chomsky "Manufacturing Consent" for a scholarly analysis of the mechanisms used to manipulate "open societies".
[15] See Cathy O'Brien with Mark Phillips "Tranceformation of America" for a compelling account of a surviving Government Mind Control Victim.
[16] See www.centerpointe.com for more details
[17] See http://www.whale.to/a/electrical_h.html for more links to resources on electronic mind control.
[18] See Dr. Leonard G. Horowitz, "Death in the Air", Tetrahedron Publishing Group 2001
[19] See for example www.carnicom.com for a knowledgeable presentation of the chemtrail programme yet with a fear inducing debilitating twist to it. This is typical for the way in which the Illuminati run their damage control operations once certain aspects of the conspiracy become obvious to a large number of people.
[20] Legend also has it that large parts of the black order that constituted the occult inner core of the 3rd Reich and its technical elite were evacuated to a large base on Antarctica and several secret bases in South America and high polar regions of Canada, Alaska and Greenland, where they allegedly continue to operate.
[21] Gerry Vassilatos "Lost Science", Adventure Unlimited Press
[22] S.D. Kirlian and V. Kirlian, "Photography and Visual Observation by Means of High-Frequency Currents, *(Russian) Journal of Scientific and Applied Photography,* Vol. 6 No. 6.
[23] Sheila Ostrander and Lynn Schroeder, *Psychic Discoveries Behind the Iron Curtain* (Englewood Cliffs, New Jersey, Prentice-Hall, 1970)
[24] www.ethericwarriors.com is the most authentic website for orgonite application and etheric warfare against the New World Order with many onward links and the more than 90 episodes of "The Adventures of Don and Carol Croft". The site features a forum with invited members who are

all active gifters.
[25] See www.donebydooney.com
[26] See www.ethericwarriors.com or www.cb-forum.com (in German)
[27] "Indaba, My Children" by Credo Vuzamazulu Mutwa, Payback Press, Great Britain 1998, first published 1964 in South Africa by Blue Crane Books
[28] "Song of The Stars, the Lore of a Zulu Shaman" by Credo Vuzamazulu Mutwa 1996, Station Hill Openings, Barrytown Ltd.
[29] "Profiles Of Healing – Vuzamazulu Credo Mutwa: Zulu High Zanusi", Texts by Credo V. Mutwa, edited by Bradford Keeney, Ringing Rocks Press 2001
[30] "The Reptilian Agenda", Credo Mutwa interviewed by David Icke, published by Bridge of Love Foundation and available through www.davidicke.com
[31] See page 274, "The Social System of the Zulus" by Eileen Jensen Krige, Shuter & Shooter, Pietermaritzburg 1950, first published in 1936
[32] See "Hearing Visions – Seeing Voices" by Mmatshilo Motsei, Cape Town 2004
[33] See http://www.geocities.com/saufor/
[34] Völkermord an den Herero?:Widerlegung einer Lüge by Claus Nordbruch, Grabert Verlag, Tübingen, Germany 2004
[35] See for example: Michael Gienger "Healing Crystals: The A-Z guide to 430 Gemstones" or "Crystal Power, Crystal Healing: The complete Handbook"

Made in the USA
Middletown, DE
05 December 2023

43351450R00190